Coups and Earthquakes

Coups and Earthquakes

Reporting the World
for America

Mort
Rosenblum

HARPER & ROW, PUBLISHERS

New York, Hagerstown, San Francisco, London, Sydney

Distributed in Great Britain by Harper & Row Limited, 28 Tavistock Street, London
WC2E 7PN and in Australia and New Zealand by Harper & Row (Australasia) Pty.
Limited, P.O. Box 226, Artarmon, New South Wales, 2064.

FIRST EDITION

Designer: Stephanie Winkler

Library of Congress Cataloging in Publication Data

Rosenblum, Mort.
  Coups and earthquakes.
  1. Foreign news—United States. I. Title.
PN4888.F69R6   070.4'3   79-1680
ISBN 0-06-013654-5

79 80 81 82 83 10 9 8 7 6 5 4 3 2 1

To my mother, who never knew where in the world
her kid was;
And to the memory of my father, who, like his wife,
could never stop giving.

Contents

Preface

This book was begun in Singapore as an insider's look at foreign reporting—a simple spilling of the beans. The idea was to share with readers some of the unsettling elements behind what they see in dispatches from abroad. In Argentina, frustration broadened the project. Whatever we correspondents did to explain significant and tragic events, they were unnoticed—or misunderstood—back home. I tried to find out why. And then a fellowship at the Council on Foreign Relations in New York gave me a chance to study foreign reporting from the receiving end. I toured the country talking to editors and executives and readers and viewers.

The result is still a spilling of the beans. I have included the anecdotes about my colleagues and me and have exposed some things we do wrong. And I have explained some of the things we do right. This is in some ways a consumer's guide to foreign news for people who want a realistic view of what is happening in their world. But I have tried to make it more than that, presenting a case for a better system of international reporting. The way our world has grown, this is no longer a luxury. It may well be essential for our survival.

So many thanks are in order that to offer any specific acknowledgments would be to leave out others. Correspondents, editors, executives, scholars, social scientists, "average readers" and friends have been generous and helpfully critical. But thanks must be given to Elisabeth Jakab, my editor, who patiently guided me through the discovery that correspondents are not necessarily immediately authors. And to Randi Slaughter, Paul Chutkow, Karen E. Wenig and Nancy Pitt, for various important reasons. Some of the mistakes and feats described are my own, committed and performed during a dozen years of reporting on seven continents. Some are my friends'. A few are part of correspondents' folklore, and attempts have been made to weed out the apocryphal. Names have been named only when a specific purpose is served. In a profession like ours, anyone who doesn't make a few embarrassing slips is not active enough to earn a salary.

Finally, an important clarification: I reported abroad for the Associated Press from 1967 to 1979, and I completed the manuscript while I was chief of the AP's Paris bureau. My employers were exceedingly considerate in allowing me time to write this book, and they have been understanding enough not to object to its frankness. Many of my anecdotes involve AP people because, obviously enough, I know them best. But I have not attempted to portray the AP—or any other organization—in any particular light. I am now editor of the *International Herald Tribune* to which this disclaimer equally applies. This work is my own, and my reflections engage no one but myself.

M. R.

Paris, 1979

1

The System

"Whenever you find hundreds of thousands of sane people trying to get out of a place and a little bunch of madmen struggling to get in," wrote the classic American foreign correspondent H. R. Knickerbocker, "you know the latter are newspapermen."

Foreign correspondents do often seem to be mad as loons, waiting on some source for hours in the rain so they can write a dispatch which might well end up blotting spilled coffee on an editorial desk back home. Editors seem madder still, suffering hypertension over whether their own man reached some obscure capital in time to duplicate stories available to them by other means. And their combined effort, when it reaches breakfast tables and living rooms across the United States, often appears to be superficial, supercilious and sloppy.

But Knickerbocker's madmen are in fact a surprisingly stable and talented bunch. The madness is in the system. Each person involved in presenting foreign news to Americans is part of a process which is riddled with failings, beset by obstacles and tailored largely to wheedle attention from a public assumed to be apathetic and only mildly literate. This system is geared as much to amuse and divert as it is to inform, and it responds inadequately when suddenly called upon to explain something so complex and menacing as a dollar collapse—or a war in Asia. Yet it is the American citizen's only alternative to ignorance about the world.

Because of the system—and in spite of it—most Americans are out of touch with events which directly affect their lives. When crisis impends, they are not warned. When it strikes, they are not prepared.

They know little about decisions taken on their behalf which lessen their earnings, restrict their freedoms and threaten their security. In their blissful unawareness, they give up their chance to have a hand in events and leave themselves vulnerable in an increasingly competitive world.

As nations grow more interdependent, this unawareness becomes progressively worse. More Americans are overwhelmed by it all, and they simply tune out. Correspondents and editors who might do a better job are reinforced in their misguided rule of thumb: "All anyone cares about is coups and earthquakes."

But interested readers and viewers can make the system work for them, and they can make it better. It is not nearly as difficult as it might seem. Keeping up with the world does not require following every flare-up and famine in 170 countries; it takes only knowing what to look for and how to find it. There is no monolithic and untouchable "The Press." Each news organization is essentially a cottage industry made up of individuals who are susceptible to criticism and open to change.

The pages which follow explore the components of the system to help readers and viewers allow for shortcomings and blind spots. They describe the people who cover and relay foreign news; they outline the problems newspeople face and the procedures they use; and they discuss the news itself. This is an insider's viewpoint from a correspondent who has bumbled along in the system and has talked over ways of improving it with colleagues and consumers at all levels.

The first step toward understanding news from abroad is realizing how vital it all is. If Americans needed to be shown how closely foreign events touch their lives, the oil boycott of 1973 and 1974 did the job with painful clarity. As even the rich and privileged sat for hours in their Lincolns, radiators bubbling over as they inched toward the Exxon pump which might run dry two cars ahead of them, it was suddenly clear that even small desert states with strange names affected world currents. Oil had always been there, like cheap coffee and allies in Europe. Middle East politics were just too Byzantine to follow. But when heat was lowered in the children's bedroom and weekend trips to the lake were canceled, foreign news was no longer solely the province of cocktail party bores.

The embargo reminded Americans who had forgotten World Wars I and II just how vulnerable they are to international pressures, however isolated they may want to be. Countless events abroad have an impact on Americans, whether immediate or delayed. A revolution in Bolivia alters tin prices, and a drought in North Africa affects the grain market. A centrist victory in the French National Assembly means a stronger franc, raising the price of wine and cheese. An invasion of Zaire's Shaba Province triggers a chain reaction which endangers détente with the Soviet Union and rattles sabers all over the world.

There was another lesson in the oil crisis: people who had seldom given a thought to foreign reporting suddenly realized that they could not depend upon getting accurate, complete information when they needed it. The embargo had sneaked up on them, and the explanations offered for it were vague and confusing. There were plenty of colorful dispatches about robed sheiks cascading chips onto the tables of Monte Carlo but few analyses about what was behind Arab strategy —and what might happen next. In fact, those who knew where to look had found warnings tucked in unlikely corners of newspapers and back in the business pages of newsmagazines. Later, more informed readers followed the crisis by probing far beyond the large black headlines. The oil boycott was only one example. Very little in our system of foreign news presentation can be taken solely at face value. The system can be believed—but only if it is understood.

On the surface, America's newsgathering apparatus appears sophisticated and all-encompassing. The carrier pigeons have been transistorized, and the battered trench coats have given way to drip-dry safari suits. Television anchormen, exuding believability and thoroughness, can produce a hair-styled news analyst in color to explain from Beirut what happened only hours before. Correspondents finish school now, sometimes amassing an alphabet soup of specialized degrees. They can skirt warfronts in jet-powered helicopters and make direct-dial telex calls from darkest Africa. But for all the changes, there has been little real improvement.

At one time, the main problem of the system was that there were not enough words. Now, it is that there are too many. The new technology makes possible such a flood of dispatches, broadcasts, tapes, films and photographs from abroad that only the initiated can tell which are important and which accurately reflect the situation they portray. And the editors and news executives who determine what eventually reaches the public are not always among the initiated.

Some important developments are not reported at all—or are reported so briefly that they are lost in the tide of words.

Today, readers and viewers must learn to separate the substance from the razzle-dazzle of packaging. And they must take into account the distorting elements of the system. Illogical factors often determine what correspondents cover in the first place. Dispatches pass through so many hands en route to the reader that sometimes a reporter cannot recognize his own work in print. Governments refuse visas and send death squads to terrorize reporters. Sun spots and censors bedevil communications. Delayed planes and new strains of dysentery make their own editorial contributions. If an important story manages to survive the gauntlet and land on a newspaper copy desk, a moon shot or a last-minute supermarket ad might crowd it out. Bold displays and television time are reserved for crises which have already erupted; an impending crisis is not considered much of a story while it is still impending.

Even the most avid news junkies read and hear only a small fraction of what correspondents report home from abroad. Many average-sized American newspapers publish less than 1000 words a day of foreign news, throwing away more than 100,000 words provided daily by news agencies, feature syndicates and freelance writers. Some days, fewer than 200 words are printed in papers serving cities of more than one million. Often the few dispatches which are printed must be trimmed sharply, leaving out vital background elements. For television, producers of the main news shows use an even smaller percentage of material available; they must frequently ignore crucial political and economic stories which cannot be simplified. In 1977, one network reported at length how Communists and Socialists might win a government majority in French elections. But when a coalition member walked out, and the "Red Menace" story was essentially over, nothing was said about it on the main news programs. The correspondent in Paris explained why:

"Very simple. New York [the headquarters editors] said to me, 'Let's see, this guy Fabre of the Leftist Radical Party walked out. Now, is he a radical or what?' And I explained that in France a Radical is not really very radical—he is fairly moderate, normally —it is a different political term. And then New York decided that it would take me twenty seconds to explain the background, making the overall piece a couple of minutes long, and that's just too much time. So they said to forget the whole thing."

Because of this competition for space, correspondents tend to squeeze the last drop out of stories they cover. This leads to a malpractice known as hyping. Few exaggerate purposely, and almost none ever lies outright. But reporters often are tempted to reach for dramatic conclusions or wide generalizations to make their stories more attractive to editors. Occasionally quotes are "cleaned up" slightly to sound catchier. In borderline cases, stronger words are usually preferred: "riot" rather than "demonstration," "massacre" instead of "killings."

These factors aggravate the average person's natural tendency to see more than is really there. As a result, readers and viewers must also protect themselves from themselves. They must pause to realize that two political murders in Italy do not mean Rome is ablaze in gunfire any more than a bar shoot-out in the South Bronx makes New York State a war zone.

. Few of the failings of the system are intentional; there is no conspiracy by mysterious press lords. Irresponsible journalists are shunned by their colleagues; and liars, if discovered, are summarily dismissed. But the system allows certain flexibilities which can be ludicrous. A few papers, for example, liven up stories with dramatic emphasis on their correspondent's Act of Arrival. One now-retired British reporter was a master at satisfying his London daily paper's penchant for the hard sell. Once, rushing into Pakistan during a crisis, he arrived only moments before his deadline. There was not even time to interview colleagues, as newsmen often do in such straits. But he was not about to disappoint his editors. He hurried to his hotel and sent his story: "I arrived in this war-torn capital tonight. Pick up agencies." His "account," splashed the next morning in his paper, was simply a rehash of the same news agency reports used by every other paper without its own man on the spot. Readers were not misinformed, but they were not getting the incisive analysis he was capable of providing when time allowed—and which they thought they were getting.

One serious endemic problem has been built in over the years, largely through lack of imagination. The entire system depends heavily on shorthand catchwords and labels which reporters and editors use almost without thinking. The aim is to save space and to simplify, but the result is often more confusion than elucidation. Once a correspondent in Argentina reporting an armed raid wanted to differentiate the attackers from terrorists of the extreme left and right. His story began: "Moderate gunmen killed eight . . ." Whatever the attackers' beliefs, killing eight hardly bespeaks moderation. Often correspondents dismiss with a label like "pro-Peking" or "Marxist" a political movement with its own fifty-page ideology. A communist is a "communist" whether he is a wealthy French businessman running for the National Assembly or a hard-line Russian commander ordering tanks into Czechoslovakia. Single words like "left" and "right" mean little by themselves in international terms, but they are sprinkled liberally throughout dispatches and narrations. Anyone who tried to follow the Lebanon civil war by watching "left-wing Moslems" and "right-wing Christians" was trying to tell the players without a program. There were also left-wing Christians, right-wing Moslems and non-affiliated atheists in a conflict that went far beyond those simple factors.

The language of international reporting can trigger false images in other ways. "Former colonial villa" evokes a rambling mansion with marble staircases and gardens of bougainvillaea. In fact, in many former colonies, it is any dwelling of more than a few rooms which is not made of slats and straw. A "private army" might be a few sleepy Palestinians on someone's front porch. "Swiss bank accounts" can be overdrawn just like a checking account at Irving Trust.

People who understand the problems of the system often apply a sort of suspended belief. They know that a good reporter can tell them more about a country in 700 words than they could learn for themselves in a week on the spot; but they don't always know who is a good reporter. With this in mind, they accept provisionally whatever seems to be reliable, and then they compare it to as many other reports as they can find. And they depend upon the full range of media. Television can take them directly to a story and show them how it unfolds. It lets them hear Anwar Sadat tell Israelis, in their own parliament, that he wants peace, and it provides an unedited picture of the atmosphere. But television does not show what is not on camera, and it often cannot tell viewers why what they are seeing is important to them. It is an excellent transmitter of experience but a poor transmitter of facts. Newspapers are a filter between the reader and the events, but they can explain overall patterns, with background and analytical comment. They can bring in information from other places and other sources to complement reporting of the situation at hand. Newsmagazines can deal only with a handful of subjects each week,

but they have room for essential color and detail, with related interviews and stories.

Still, unless the system is improved, even the most resourceful
reader and viewer must accept critical gaps in his understanding of
world affairs. Basic practical and philosophical considerations prevent
complete coverage of all the news. One of the most important of these
is that no one can really define what news is.

In a general sense, news is the exceptional, something out of the
ordinary which threatens, benefits, outrages, enlightens or titillates. It
might be a speech, an accident, a price increase, a scientific break-
through, a revolution or a man chomping on the leg of his Samoyed
dog. And there is also what one analyst calls "news in the air"—not
specific events but rather trends and patterns which amount to
change. If we are told something new which in some way takes us a
step further in any direction, it is news.

Foreign news must be defined even more vaguely than local or
national news. News and truth are not the same thing. No group of
people can take a slice of reality, with all of its nuances, and relay it
from hand to hand without some distortion. With local events, an
American is aware of what is new and important because he is nearby;
he can add his own context. He has aunts in San Diego and he travels
each summer to New York, so he at least has a frame of reference for
evaluating national news. Within the United States, heavy competition among news organizations and conversations with friends provide an automatic system of checks against incomplete and inaccurate
domestic reporting. But when cultural barriers are crossed, and reporting is from faraway places which stir no familiar responses, any
piece of information is new—and possibly news.

With such sweeping definitions, obviously the "news value" of a
particular story is highly subjective. Whether a piece of information
reaches the public often depends less on its actual importance on any
fixed scale than on the tastes and values of those making the selection.
Correspondents play an important part in selection by determining
what to cover in the first place. But most of the process is in the hands
of editors at different stages. These are the gatekeepers. Each medium
and each type of correspondent operates in a different fashion, but the
principle is the same. A correspondent's dispatch first goes to one
gatekeeper and then what emerges—if anything—goes on to others.
All along the way, the original dispatch may be shortened, length-

ened, rewritten or thrown away entirely. This series of editors determines what is to be eventually shared with the public; and they decide what the American people may never know.

Most of these gatekeepers tend to feel that what readers and viewers want is not necessarily what they should know to be well informed. A responsible minority is more concerned with a story's significance than its possible interest to large groups of readers. "If we think a story is important, and two per cent of our audience will be interested in it, we'll run it," said one ranking New York *Times* editor. The theory here is that audiences accept what they get, in the long run, and they should be conditioned to a serious treatment of news from abroad. Many of the others play to the masses, arguing that if people don't get what they want, they will buy different papers and switch channels. Gatekeepers in this category sometimes throw in dull but important stories because they feel they must, but they generally follow what they think is the average taste of their market. This means, to most, a bare minimum of foreign news. An old saw at the long-defunct Brooklyn *Eagle* set the tone for this approach: "A dogfight in Brooklyn is bigger than a revolution in China."

There is growing evidence that a great many readers realize that a few sparring spaniels down the road will not start World War III; whether editors know it or not, they want to follow revolutions in China. The Louis Harris organization reported after a special nationwide survey in 1978 on public attitudes toward news, "Those who work in the media (editors, news directors and reporters) feel that only 5 per cent of the public are greatly interested in international news. A much higher 41 per cent of the public express deep interest in world affairs being covered in the news media."

Daniel Yankelovich surveyed readers for the Washington *Post,* asking a test group to check categories they found "interesting and important." The highest number, 66 per cent, listed foreign news. United States news scored 65 per cent and news from the White House 60 per cent, in a long list of categories.

About the same time, a large group of newspapers organized a national readership study. They asked a cross-section of 3000 adults —eighteen and older—to choose between a newspaper made up entirely of hard news and one with a news summary and entertaining features. Fifty-nine per cent preferred the all-news format, and a majority expressed more interest in foreign and national news than in "the average local story." Continuing surveys by the newspapers' researchers find similar results.

But readership surveys are difficult to conduct and are often inconclusive; many news executives guide themselves as much by their own instincts—and prejudices—as by poll results. Whatever audiences might really want, news organizations have put increasingly diminishing emphasis on foreign coverage over the past decade. The number of correspondents abroad has been dropping, sharply and steadily. Editors are relying more and more on substitute means of coverage which add new forms of distortion to the system. The most responsible of gatekeepers cannot pass important news on to readers and viewers if it has not been covered.

At the heyday of correspondents, just after World War II, there were somewhere near 2500 Americans abroad reporting home on a regular basis. By 1969, the total was about 565. In the mid-1970s, with far more independent states to cover and with growing world interdependence, there were an estimated 430. This includes not only regular correspondents who report daily news events but also magazine writers, specialized correspondents and a number of semi-retired reporters who keep full-time accreditation to live comfortably abroad.*

It costs between $80,000 and $140,000 to keep a single American abroad, not counting communications expenses, and the downward trend is not likely to be reversed without a basic change in the system.

The decline in the correspondent corps is more serious than it appears to be on the surface. A total of 430 does not mean that 430 reporters divide up the world and share coverage. Most compete hotly with one another, and often huge numbers of them are all in the same place at once, reporting the same story. Since most of them are based in major news centers, more than half of the world's nations have no permanent American correspondent in residence. When last counted, 72 per cent of all U.S. correspondents were based in ten capitals: London, Paris, Tokyo, Hong Kong, Bonn, Rome, Moscow, Beirut, Ottawa and Tel Aviv/Jerusalem.

*These figures were compiled by Ralph E. Kliesch and John R. Wilhelm of Ohio University, Athens, in a report for the Overseas Press Club in New York. They are not exact because of difficulties in categorizing newsmen and collecting data. But they are close.

And the quality of reporting varies widely from place to place. In the major Western countries most familiar to Americans, reporting is often by comfortably ensconced specialists with time to dig and to ruminate. Assignments to these places are frequently rewards for service in the jungle or a result of special training. But from the Third World, where Americans' childhood stereotypes and Hollywood's distortions make careful backgrounding essential, reporting is left mainly to fast-moving young correspondents who must spend more time hustling visas, finding telephones and avoiding censors than collecting information and composing dispatches.

For day-to-day reporting from most developing nations and the smaller industrial countries, news organizations rely on part-time local correspondents called stringers. Some are highly competent and dedicated professionals. But others are untrained in Western press traditions and unwilling to risk unemployment, jail terms or worse for the sake of a few dollars paid by some faceless editor in New York. Local authorities often pressure them to report what the government wants. Even if there is no pressure, many are reluctant to reveal hard truths about their own cultures and societies. One stringer in Nigeria reported nothing about a coup d'état, ignoring urgent cables from his news agency editors. Days later, he apologized, saying he had had the flu. The motivations for selective reporting can be more direct. An American agency correspondent traveling with Queen Elizabeth to an island colony—soon to be independent—was greeted effusively by the chief minister. When the reporter asked the chief executive if he knew who his agency's stringer was on the island, the man replied, with a broad grin, "Me."

Sometimes news organizations hire nationals as full-time staff reporters to cover their own countries. Since they speak the language and have wide local contacts, they are often of great help. But few handle English with native fluency, and many know little about their American audiences. In Japan, local reporters kept dispatching stories about the "Anti-Communist" Party until someone figured out the reporters called it that because it was so far to the left that it considered the Communists to be right-wingers.

In a number of developing and socialist countries, news organizations have no representatives at all. They monitor official news agencies, seldom more than government propaganda services.

To counter these imbalances, there is a growing trend to what some call parachute journalism. Special reporters working at home or in large foreign bureaus will rush off to major stories wherever they break. The good ones can quickly find sources and produce reasonably accurate accounts of complicated events. Sometimes, with fresh eyes, they see stories which might have sneaked up unnoticed on a reporter based there and gone unreported. Since they do not stay around to deal with the consequences, they can often report more forthrightly than if they were residents. But, in general, this compromise solution is a poor substitute for more resident correspondents spread around the world. As the basic idea is to save money, there are never enough parachute journalists available. It takes time to get to the stories; in many crises, borders are sealed immediately and it may be weeks before new reporters can get in. Often these correspondents end up in places they have never seen before, with no knowledge of the language, the customs or the background to the story they are covering.

However good, visiting correspondents misinterpret some stories because they do not have time to develop a solid "feel" for them. The case of Iran is a dramatic example. In the 1970s, until late in 1978, almost no regular American correspondents were based in Teheran. News organizations relied on locally hired nationals and stringers who stuck closely to bare facts. Roving staff reporters were seldom able to sense the depth of political discontent, and few of them understood the power of the religious opposition. When the tide began turning against Shah Mohammed Reza Pahlavi, few took the early signs seriously. And most Americans—even those who had followed Iran closely—were amazed at how quickly and effectively the shah's opponents forced him to leave the country in January, 1979.

Like firemen, parachute journalists are mainly reactive; they are dispatched after the alarm sounds. By relying on that sort of coverage, Americans miss a great deal. In 1978, few people had even heard of the Reverend Jim Jones's mysterious cult settlement in the Guyana jungle. Americans' first word came when Congressman Leo J. Ryan and four others were massacred trying to leave the place, and more than 900 men, women and children of the settlement committed mass suicide.

Parachute journalism reinforces a pack mentality which has always plagued foreign reporting. Correspondents who hurry off to a new place tend to stick together, interviewing friends who arrived earlier and competing to find the most dramatic angle of the story. Wherever there are few resident correspondents, a Parkinson's Law of Journalism holds that news increases in direct proportion to the number of visiting reporters in town. For example, the 1976 riots in Jamaica may have gone unnoticed except that they coincided with a major International Monetary Fund meeting. Scores of correspondents, taking a welcome break from analyzing sheets of figures, had a Caribbean-isle-in-flames story to cover. If any had been based in Jamaica, they may have judged the outbreaks to be less significant than they appeared at first glance. But, seen in isolation, they were a big story.

Under the air-travel-card style of reporting, news goes unreported for long periods and then erupts suddenly for reasons which often have little to do with events. In the late 1960s, a long-simmering conflict in Chad became serious for many Americans because the New York *Times*'s R. W. Apple, Jr., fresh from a triumphant tour in Vietnam, added the landlocked nation to the itinerary of a roving African assignment. He returned to his base in Nigeria and told colleagues, "I discovered a war." The rebellion had assumed few new proportions beyond what had been reported by news agencies and European papers earlier. Editors had been used to discounting Chad as a place which was not important, and previous dispatches had made little impact. But when the story was legitimatized by the *Times*, it immediately became news, and other correspondents flew in to "catch up."

Obviously, these imbalances cause serious systematic distortions. The uninitiated, presented with a series of stories all packaged in the same authoritative manner, cannot tell what was reported by a well-prepared veteran and what was scraped together at long distance from questionable sources. There are ways of correcting for this, as will be discussed in later chapters, but they require careful attention—and they are hardly foolproof. Another problem is that the uneven spread of qualified correspondents makes it difficult for editors to keep track of major trends which cross borders. If a news agency produces a round-up on food in the world, the final story is more likely to reflect the comparative abilities of its reporters and the availability of raw data than the realities of the food situation.

In recent years, the imbalances have provoked a new problem which has placed heavy burdens on the entire newsgathering system. A number of leaders in developing countries interpret our scattershot system of reporting as a direct threat to them. The more moderate call it benign neglect which damages their international image. Others say it is willful hostility designed to weaken their stability. Leaders often charge that what we call the exigencies of good reporting are simply cheap shots at their expense. Ministers expecting glowing accounts of new housing projects are appalled when reporters concentrate instead on amusing details of court etiquette. Authorities in many countries consider rampant corruption just a way of life, and they are dismayed to find it warrants space in the Chicago *Tribune.*

Many editors, sensitized by the confrontation, have decided to take a more positive approach toward developing countries. Reporters are cautioned to avoid gratuitous sidelights which might be taken as slurs and to seek balancing "good points" when reporting on development setbacks. And they are asked to try to see things from the viewpoint of the society they are covering. But a deep-seated conflict remains, not only over how stories should be written but also over what subjects should be broached at all. Western newsmen contend that slight improvement over status quo is not news; violent change is. Coups, upheavals and economic failures, therefore, must be reported fully. Stories on peaceful development must take their place with other world stories in the selection process. Third World leaders argue that for them violent change has been status quo; their slight improvement is news. By harping on discord, they say, reporters are failing to note their hard-won progress.

Whether justified or not, frustrated governments have imposed a dazzling array of restrictive measures to hinder reporting. Border after border was closed to Western newsmen in the 1970s, and there have been expulsions of some type in almost every part of the Third World. Censorship has been developed to a high art. As a result, correspondents have no access at all to many countries, and in others they can gather news only with great difficulty.

Occasionally, government measures are vicious and irrational. In the Central African Empire, Michael Goldsmith of the Associated Press sent a story by telex to the AP Johannesburg bureau, the easiest relay point. Because of machine trouble, a return message was garbled, and authorities charged the unreadable words were a secret code from an enemy nation. Goldsmith was taken before Emperor Bokassa who, without a word, knocked him unconscious with a heavy cane. He was imprisoned for thirty days, part of the time in irons that were purposely adjusted so tightly his wrists were cut and swollen. The wound on his forehead from Bokassa's cane was left to fester, forming a permanent scar. Appeals for his release were answered with diatribes against the Western press. Finally, after more moderate African leaders intervened, Goldsmith was released.

Restrictions on reporting combine with general failings of the system to make information particularly unreliable and incomplete from huge areas of the world. Lasting misconceptions blacken the image of some progressive governments and allow some despotic regimes to commit mass murder undetected. If correspondents cannot report directly on a country in which there is little interest—according to the system's values—they just ignore it until something dramatic happens. If they are barred from someplace newsworthy, they depend heavily on refugees and political dissidents who can hardly be expected to give a balanced picture. Alternative sources in closed countries are often U.S. diplomats and State Department officials. And that poses another problem.

When reporters are forced to rely on official American dispatches, they are no longer watchdogs. Diplomats frequently depict events in a particular way, either to push a political line or to cover up their mistakes. Sometimes they are simply misinformed, and they make errors in judgment. Usually correspondents abroad can temper diplomatic reporting with other sources. But official information collected in Washington is often relayed uncritically. Washington reporters have little contact with their counterparts overseas and sometimes trust their government sources more than their own colleagues on the spot—if their colleagues are on the spot at all. Few have the background to challenge official interpretations of news from remote countries, and they cannot always provide a larger context for the reader.

All of these difficulties in reporting from abroad can cause needless —and dangerous—alarm. Events in Uganda during February 1977 showed to what lengths this can go.

Americans considered President Idi Amin Dada of Uganda a murderous tyrant and a buffoon and felt he was capable of any atrocity for no reason at all. This impression had been formed largely from secondhand accounts, and there was little fresh reporting to confirm or deny it. Those few reporters who could get visas were not enthusiastic to go to Uganda. Amin's soldiers had murdered one American freelance reporter, and they had left a news agency stringer for dead in the woods, shot three times in the chest. Although the stringer survived, he fled the country, and his successor sent only official pronouncements. Uganda was covered from Nairobi, in neighboring Kenya, by government radio, refugees and occasional telephone calls.

In mid-February, a group of Christian troops in the army mutinied at an outpost barracks, and the president hurled fury at suspected enemies. The Ugandan Anglican bishop, critical of the government, was killed under mysterious circumstances. Thousands of tribesmen were clubbed to death or shot in retaliatory purges after the uprising.

Most Americans saw only sketchy and disjointed accounts of these events. Although correspondents sent dispatches from Nairobi, little of their contents passed by the gatekeepers. There was no obvious American connection, and it was all too confusing for crisp, brief explanation. One television network ignored the massacres entirely. Another gave them fifteen seconds at the end of an evening newscast, after a twenty-eight-second account of the poverty of Winston Churchill's widow.

Suddenly, on February 25, Uganda became a story. On one network, a well-known anchorman came on the screen to say, "Good evening. Uganda's erratic president, Idi Amin, today placed two hundred and fifty Americans, most of them missionaries, under what amounts to house arrest." He said the Americans were ordered to stay in the country for three days under "virtual imprisonment" until a meeting with Amin in the capital. Several Washington correspondents followed on camera with tension-charged reports. It happened to be Jimmy Carter's first foreign crisis as president, and reporters dwelt on how the White House was crackling with concern. Carter's aides were quoted liberally. Pentagon correspondents explained with charts and maps how U.S. ships and aircraft might attack if an armed raid was necessary. On one network, the anchorman and a Washington correspondent agreed that Amin was "crazy" and therefore no rational explanation could be sought. Up to a third of the evening newscast time was spent on various aspects of the crisis. Voices were strained, expressing deep concern, and Ugandan assurances that there was no danger were treated with irony.

The general impression was reinforced the next morning in most newspapers. The New York *Daily News,* with the largest circulation in the country, carried a screaming headline: "Idi Amin Detains 250 Yanks in Uganda." Its main story concentrated on the possibility of invasion. Amin's statement that he only wanted to thank the Americans for their "excellent work" was in the body of a secondary story down the page.

Most Americans, unprepared for the sudden development, remembered the last major story on Uganda. Amin had refused to allow hostages from a hijacked airliner to leave the country, and they had to be rescued by a daring and bloody Israeli commando assault. An elderly woman left behind in the hospital was murdered.

It was certainly a significant story, and Amin was clearly a dangerous and unpredictable despot. But, at that point, there was no cause for panic. And yet only a relatively small number of Americans were provided the calm appraisal which was offered by the Los Angeles Times: ". . . despite what appeared on the surface to be ominous warning to the Americans, observers here [in Kenya] pointed out that Amin had used similar diversionary tactics before. On these occasions Amin had tried to take the focus off his own problems by creating other incidents in unrelated areas. Just last month he summoned the 400-member British community for a mysterious meeting and ended up reaffirming his fondness for the British."

The Times explained that the Americans were not hostages who were suddenly seized and held but rather mostly missionaries who had lived in Uganda for long periods and were given time to come to the capital for the meeting. Later, when the meeting was canceled and the story died, the Times was able to report that the Americans decided to stay: "Julien Schon, managing director of the Caltex oil marketing operation in Uganda, was perhaps typical of other Americans when he said in a telephone interview: 'Relieved? No, I wouldn't really say I was relieved, because I was never worried. I'm staying; in fact, I don't know of any Americans who are leaving.' "

As to Amin's craziness, the Los Angeles Times consulted an African scholar who delivered an opinion shared by many who knew Uganda well: however Amin might appear to Americans, his actions were cunningly deliberate. He was playing the international news-gathering apparatus like a virtuoso, using his antics as a means of confounding his enemies and rallying support at home. The scholar's analysis began this way:

> "The army . . . first arrested the Bishop. They tied him up and put him into a wretched hovel. . . . The Bishop implored them

not to spear him, but to shoot him with his own rifle. They did, and afterwards cut off his head and his feet. . . .

"Nearly all our best friends [were] arrested suddenly, and murdered almost before our very eyes. Yes [he said], he would put us all in stocks . . . and he would challenge England and all Europe to come and rescue us. What could white men do to him?"

Are these reports the latest news from Uganda? They bear most of the tragic hallmarks of Idi Amin's "New Uganda," yet they came out of Uganda not this week, nor last week, nor the year before. They were all written 90 years ago.

His point, well made, was that Amin's seemingly unexplained actions were part of a historical and traditional pattern.

Since Amin's dreaded meeting was postponed several times before it was canceled, the story trickled off, and most readers and viewers did not even notice its passing. For the most part, they retained their original image that Amin was certifiably insane, with no method to his madness, and some extended that judgment to cover other African leaders as well. Amin himself was hardly affected by the episode. It served its purpose by taking attention off the unrest in his army and his brutal way of putting it down. As in each past crisis, he consolidated his position and then ceased his antics, allowing reporters to go on to something else.

The Uganda incident showed clearly how the system goes wrong. Most Americans who glanced at headlines and kept one eye on the television screen considered themselves to be informed. They were alarmed and angered, and they felt they knew exactly why. The confusing events in an unfamiliar country were deceptively clear to them because they had been given what seemed to be ample explanation. If, by some strange set of circumstances, their government decided upon a military rescue operation, most would have applauded it. But those few who understood the system—and looked carefully at the story—saw a completely different picture.

Many editors and correspondents, conscious of the system's failings, have experimented with new ways of presenting a more realistic view of such stories. "We must build a bridge between the news event and the readers," one editor expressed it. "We have to help people to see why it is important for them to look closely, and then we must give them an accurate, complete account when they do look closely."

These new ways include not only different approaches toward general news but also entire new genres of reporting in specialized fields. For economic affairs, specialists are evolving styles and vocabularies to translate complicated abstractions into dollars-and-cents terms. Development and human rights reporting are new fields, responding to growing concerns of many readers.

Although the new approaches are helping the system keep pace with changing times, they each pose their own problems. For the reader and viewer, little has changed fundamentally since Knickerbocker's madmen first began to gather news abroad. An American citizen can follow what is happening beyond his borders, but only if he works at it. And if he does not understand the system, it most likely will leave him more confused than informed.

2

The West Malaria Rebellion

Correspondents are the basis of the system, the first link in the flawed chain, and it is vital for any serious reader or viewer to know how they work. They are a bizarre lot, however, with an even more bizarre set of working conditions. The best way to understand them is to watch them in action. Although the other chapters in this book deal with real people and events, this brief flight into hyperbole follows Rodney Permapress on his first foreign assignment—a rebellion in West Malaria. The account has been conjured up by a mildly jaundiced correspondent. But it is not so exaggerated.*

Rodney has arrived late because the Air Malaria flight was diverted to Paris to take on chocolate éclairs for a presidential reception. The first thing he learns is that all sixty-one newsmen in town are staying at the nineteen-room Malarial Arms, which at the time of the rebellion was already filled to capacity for an ornithologists' convention. Actually a sixty-second newsman, the military writer for the London

*Inspiration for this is from Evelyn Waugh's Scoop, a preposterous but real novel published in 1938 based on Waugh's experiences in Ethiopia. Some correspondents still study Scoop regularly as a handbook for such skills as wastebasket rifling, expense account padding and myth weaving. Like Waugh, I have concentrated here on the more colorful types of reporters, passing lightly over those with a minimum of eccentricities who receive their due elsewhere in these pages. My apologies to those of my colleagues who don't see themselves in West Malaria.

Daily Excess, is one of three guests at the larger, newer, more comfortable and cheaper Mosquito Palace. Why? It's all very simple. The first reporter to arrive was a twenty-two-year veteran who had not been in West Malaria for twenty-one years, and he headed straight for the Arms. Naturally, everyone else followed. Hunting wolves are hermits compared to most correspondents. The titled British specialist, who would sooner call an M-16 a BB gun than be confused with the rabble, then settled in splendid seclusion at the empty new luxury hotel.

Rodney finds the Arms' crumbling lobby shoulder high in odd-shaped silver boxes marked "TV Française" and "NBC News." The only sleeping space left is between the rafters on the second floor. He considers taking a suite at the Palace, but then the inevitable thought process of paranoid correspondents begins: Ah, but what if everyone says they're going up the road at eight and I spend the night agonizing whether they will really leave at seven and I rush over at six-thirty to find they all left ten minutes earlier. He strikes a compromise, staying in the rafters at the Arms and putting a Palace suite on his expense account.

His next priority is finding wheels. The last functioning vehicle in town joined the CBS fleet an hour before he arrived, but the Chicago *Daily Schlock* correspondent offers to share his wheezing Peugeot pickup with Rodney to keep an eye on him. That done, Rodney sizes up his competition. There is time, since a dusk-to-dawn curfew has confined everyone to the hotel.

The most obvious reporter is an Associated Press man from Beirut, a towering Norwegian American wearing camouflage socks he brought from Vietnam. He is staring fixedly at the UPI correspondent, a stuttering New Yorker based in Rome. Both are being coyly but assiduously observed by a South Londoner with rosy cheeks and a slight sniff who works for Reuters. An agitated Frenchman, posted regularly to West Malaria for Agence France-Presse, pops in every fifteen minutes, clutching his curfew pass, to see if any of them have moved.

A mixed group of Americans are scattered about, each doing his best to look like a professional pianist who happened to be in town and is only coincidentally interested in the furor over who sits in the presidential chair. Most are good reporters but of the school that says one must not look like a good reporter, however that is. Rodney heads for the American with the shortest epaulets on his bush jacket and asks for that wonderful labor-saving device, the fill-in. The reporter cheerfully brings Rodney up to date. He is generous because of the brotherly bond which links all poor bastards chasing news overseas for unappreciative masses back home. Beyond that, he fears no competition, because he knows no one can do a better job than he can, given the same elements. He does not tell Rodney that the president's secretary has promised him an exclusive interview with the head of state the next afternoon. Since the secretary promised the same thing to half the people in the room, with no intention of delivering to anyone, it makes little difference.

In the corner, a half-dozen jovial Britons are drinking beer and roaring at one-liners which make no sense in any language. Everyone has known everyone for years, rushed by their London dailies from crisis to crisis and driven by such cables as "OPPOSITION FRONTPAGE SAYS THEIR MAN PUMMELED KICKED VIOLATED BY ANGRY MOBS STOP FAIL TO UNDERSTAND WHY YOU NOT TREATED SIMILARLY STOP TRY FOR MATCHER SOONEST."

Across the room, French correspondents are drafting a protest note about the anti-French attitude of the government, the rebels and the English press corps. A couple of Japanese are drawing notes in thick books and distributing calling cards to the assortment of Swedes, Italians and Yugoslavs who cover for various newspapers, magazines, broadcast outlets and intelligence agencies around the world.

The AP and UPI men are developing pronounced twitches around the mouth despite efforts to look amusedly nonchalant. Both are thinking the same thing: The government has cut all three telegraph and two telephone lines, so why is that son of a bitch looking so cool? Has he found a way to file? Each has film in his pocket and is casually looking over the bird-watching conventioneers for a pigeon. A pigeon, to correspondents, is someone who can carry film and dispatches out of the country. But since the airport is closed, it is an idle thought anyway.

Some of the sixty-one newspeople at the Arms are not concerned with the communications blackout, since they aren't even sure where they would send a story if they had one. They are freelancers-cum-tourists who flock in when disaster strikes in hopes of being the last man out of the flaming city or the first one to be captured (and subsequently released, with gripping quotes and details) by the rebels. Two of the group are women. One is an emaciated but interesting-looking French blonde who has very little difficulty cadging a ride or a bit of information. Most of the Americans and all of the Brits are sure they will be in her pants the following night, but their chances are better of interviewing the president. The other woman has long since proven that women can be good correspondents, and if anyone reaches to pay for her drink she will break his hand off at the wrist. (No one ever does, by the way; they all remember ol' George, still in traction, who once suggested she had used feminine wiles to get in to see a general.)

All sixty-one, including the women, are wearing dirty low-cut buckskin-laced boots. A practiced eye can spot the big-timers, however. Their laces are tied.

The next morning, Rodney hurries off to spend two and a half hours finding the press office. Someone told him to follow the signs but neglected to mention that the signs say "Ministry of Crop Failure, Spotted Blight Division." West Malaria had had little need for a press office before the rebellion, and space is at a premium around Capital Swamp. The chief press officer just stepped out for a ten-minute tea break, the secretary says, and Rodney sits down to wait. He leafs through the six-month-old Australian cheesecake magazines left around so newsmen can stay up to date with the world. At 3:15, after Rodney has worked his way through the 1964 report of the Bulgarian fisheries industry, the press officer returns and then starts to dash out the door again. Rodney stops him and they chat amiably:

"May I see your passport?"

"Yes, sir. Here it is."

"But you have a tourist visa. If you want press accreditation you must leave the country and get a business visa at our nearest embassy, which, I believe, is in London."

"How long does that take?"

"Oh, no time at all. About four to six months once you have submitted an application with a police clearance from all the places you have lived in the past fifteen years, a letter from four references in West Malaria and certified copies of your birth certificate and those of your parents and grandparents."

"But that's impossible."

"Of course it's not. West Malaria is most interested in foreign investment, and we have streamlined our visa procedure considerably. It used to be difficult. Without a business visa, we cannot issue you a press card, and you will not be allowed to send stories, to travel to the interior or to attend press conferences. But, of course, you may visit the native art museum, the crocodile pond, and you may purchase all the souvenirs you wish. Welcome to West Malaria."

Rodney is so shattered that he hardly hears the sharp "Pssst" from the clerk outside. After five minutes of artful fencing, it is determined that the clerk would be delighted to assist in securing a press card and at the same time would be thrilled to accept Rodney's contribution of $75 toward his grandmother's hysterectomy operation.

Back at the Malarial Arms for sundowners, Rodney chucks down gins and tonic with the self-satisfied air of a man who has cleared an unjumpable hurdle. Expansively, he passes the clerk's name on to a colleague who does not have a press card.

"Him?" the man snorts. "He thinks we're schmucks enough to pay twenty-five bucks for a card that he can't even deliver. Who the fuck needs a press card if there is no way to send copy, if there are roadblocks at every exit to town and if there are no press conferences anyway? The only guy in town who has a press card is that weirdo Russian, and he has five secret police following him to the goddamned bathroom at night." The only reporter to get through the roadblocks, he added, used a New York City library card.

There is worse news for Rodney. He discovers, like others who did not dispatch stories before outgoing communications were cut, that incoming messages arrive without difficulty. Rockets—those dreaded missives from home—rain down in a steady barrage. Rodney's rocket reads:

PERMAPRESS KNOW YOU JUST ARRIVED BUT NEED FULLEST FASTEST MATCHER OPPOSITION INCLUDING NEW ANGLES BACK-GROUND QUOTES ECONOMIC SITUATION COLOR DESCRIPTION REBELS ATMOSPHERE IN CAPITAL ETC STOP WHAT ABOUT REPORT RUSSIANS SENDING ADVISERS DISGUISED AS ORNITHOLOGISTS QUERY NEED FOR EARLY EDITION AS OPPOSITION KILLING US STONESTEIN FOREIGN EDITOR.

Rodney walks over to a friendly television reporter talking to himself by the fish pond. Instead of commiseration, he gets a sharp "Piss off, f'Christ's sake." The man is actually talking to his millions of viewers, doing a stand-up narration in the junglelike hotel garden in case a miracle happens and there is a way to get it back to his network.

The correspondent, scrupulously honest, does not say that he is standing in the bush by the front lines. But then he doesn't say that he isn't, either.

Taking his own protective measures, Rodney goes off in search of news. At the press office, he finds a four-inch stack of communiqués. They are all the same: in seven lines they dispatch two rebel platoons in a nonexistent battle, describe the use of new weapons which haven't been delivered and report on the success of a huge pacification program. After an exhausting round of embassies, ministries and trading companies, Rodney finds the best-informed source in town is a gay art dealer in self-exile from Lithuania. On the way home he stops at the American embassy to get the day's rumors—duly synthesized and hyped, presented in colorful language—which can be attributed to "Western diplomatic sources."

And that's how it goes. In the most difficult West Malaria–type circumstances, the Rodneys and their colleagues always manage to get some solid copy back to their editors. But you would hardly know that from watching them work.

3

Correspondents and Contacts

When King Farouk was deposed in 1952, the Cairo correspondent for a large American newspaper was relaxing on a beach in Lebanon with a blonde he had met aboard an airplane. He had not, unfortunately, advised his foreign desk he would be out of the country. When his editor finally found him, he received a cable reading "OPPOSITION REPORTING FAROUK RESIGNED. WHAT ARE YOUR PLANS?"

The reporter's mistake was that he was caught being human. He was not around for a sudden story, even though there had been no sign that it was about to break. And he had not covered himself before going. It is not enough for foreign correspondents to be machinelike people; they must be peoplelike machines. This is partly because editors like to think they have a team of supermen overseas. But it is also because there is no room for a correspondent to make mistakes. A single slip by a sloppy reporter can cause alarm in millions of Americans and push nations toward hostilities. On the biggest of stories, a correspondent for the Associated Press or United Press International can misinform more than one billion people around the world if he makes a mistake which is not quickly corrected. It is tricky work, and it takes a certain type of person to do it.

Although there is no mold for American correspondents, many have similar backgrounds and motivations. Most read avidly as children and took frequent trips as they were growing up. They are educated enough to be curious about the world but not so much that they want to hang around ivy-covered colleges studying it endlessly. Most are upwardly mobile but still poor enough to want to travel on someone else's money. Although few are accomplished linguists, nearly all study the language of their base country and perhaps a few others; some can brokenly upbraid a telegraph operator in a half dozen assorted tongues. Correspondents are independent but not enough to keep them from working day and night, weekends and holidays included, for bosses whose necks they would gladly deliver up to the Boston Strangler. They often speak of home—their piece of land in Oregon or their ranch in Montana—but they can dump a bag on any hotel-room bed in the world and feel as if they had been reared there. A huge majority are white males, despite recent efforts to assign more women and minority-group reporters to foreign posts. They tend to be younger rather than older, though there is, of course, Phil Whitcomb of the *Christian Science Monitor.* In 1978, based in Paris in his sixty-fourth year as a correspondent, he described himself as "a withered leaf still clinging to the tree." At eighty-seven, he was still putting in a good day's work.

Correspondents take their jobs seriously; they have little choice. But because of the psychological pressures they face, few sit around idly pondering their responsibilities. Together, around a bar or a hotel swimming pool, talk is seldom of grave events of the day. They gossip and exchange exaggerated folk tales of their craft. When they discuss news, they are often concerned more with how a particular reporter handled a story than the story itself.

During major news breaks, correspondents can work for days at a time without sleeping. Even in normal times, they seldom work fewer than sixty hours a week. Each finds ways to unwind during rare leisure hours, and few spend that time poring over national trade figures. In Vietnam, one important skirmish went uncovered because it broke out after the entire press corps at an outpost headquarters had voted itself a rest and was watching *Bonnie and Clyde.* Two correspondents in Asia competed for years over who could come up with the most bizarre sexual experience.

Despite occasional release, the pressure takes a toll. Correspondents, as a group, have a dazzling array of tics, quirks and twitchy habits. One television reporter absentmindedly tears up bits of paper and chews them. Once he had to plead and bribe his way aboard an overbooked flight, swearing it was life and death. He finally got a seat, but the plane was late, and he paced back and forth waiting for it. When it was time to board, he reached for his ticket and couldn't find it. He had eaten it.

Whatever illusions reporters may have about their own capabilities, the pressures of their work sometimes show up in their dispatches. In Israel, one agency reporter, benumbed by sending cable after cable about a bloody terrorist raid, wrote at one point, "THE HOWL OF AMBULANCE SIRENS MINGLED WITH THE GROANS OF THE DEAD." Occasionally more than a simple slip may be involved. A British journalist observed after covering the fall of Biafra, "During that long day under the hot sun, we rode, worked and squabbled, foodless. . . . How many of those purple passages in the popular press—'the awful truth,' 'silent genocide'—which appeared during the following days had their genesis in sour, empty bellies?"

The way a correspondent works depends on his medium. Reporters for news agencies, the packhorses of the profession, are by far the most harried. They are responsible for all news from their area, around the clock, seven days a week, and they are expected to report it faster than their competition. Virtually every daily newspaper, broadcast station, network and newsmagazine in the United States receives full-time news wires of the Associated Press, United Press International, or both. Most have no other source of foreign news. Those that do can always use AP or UPI when they wish. The news agency reporters are squeezed from all sides. First, their time is eaten up by routine chores: selling their service to local newspapers; covering football matches for subscribers in Bolivia; writing economic trivia for their special financial services; sending weather reports; dispatching voice broadcasts to their radio divisions; fixing teleprinters; entertaining publishers on tour. When a major story breaks, they must cover every aspect of it.

It is the agency man who determines that the coup at hand is the thirteenth since the Revolution of the Honey Bees. He is the one to call every Red Cross post at the disaster scene and then compare the collected casualty figures to the Great Tremor of 1894. He clips the local news service wires, separating the provincial lottery results from the revealing remarks of the interior minister. Because he is writing for newspapers around the world, there is no specific deadline. He must write a new story—or at least a new beginning—with every development.

Since other types of correspondents have access to agency material, they can spend their time tracking down the junta leader or interviewing the guy who saved the triplets. Few of these correspondents share their best material with agency reporters, because that might mean giving it to their own competition. So, after all the spadework is done, agency reporters must then scramble to catch up with their colleagues' exclusives.

Newspaper correspondents, known generally as "specials," select the major story of the day in the country they are covering and leave the rest to the agencies. When their deadline approaches, they send one complete, well-constructed account. At the most, they might send a second or third "new top" for later editions. But their work is hardly easy. Their jobs depend on their ability to find new angles—to deal more deeply with the subject than the agency reporters. Editors assume their own man is better per se than any handful of agency reporters; and their man has to try to prove it. Specials must look for stories and details which interest their specific audience. Although the AP and UPI correspondents have more work to do, they are often helped by local staff people, with well-established contacts. Frequently specials do not see what the agencies report—even if it is going to their desks back home—and they have to do their own basic groundwork.

Newsmagazine reporters work in a more leisurely fashion, or in a mad frenzy, depending upon the day of the week. Under ideal circumstances, a magazine correspondent sends a "file" of several thousand words to his desk before Wednesday, allowing time for questions, contributions from other bureaus and a polished rewrite job in New York. But the closer the news breaks to the Friday night deadline (for *Time* and *Newsweek*), the faster the pace. Major news can be pushed into an edition on Saturday, but that creates havoc among editors, correspondents and accountants.

Television crews zero in on a single story and devote their energies to getting it on film and off to New York. For them, finding out what happened is just a simple first step. If their report is worth a satellite circuit, they must develop the film and edit it. If not, they have to find airplane connections and get their material through customs. They spend far less time reporting than other types of correspondents, but their hours often end up to be the longest.

Writers for general magazines, who can relax and ramble, have it best. They sip pernod with graying rubber planters and cashiered generals, waiting until the ulcer corps of regular correspondents makes its various errors. Then, as one *Reader's Digest* writer once put it while rifling the AP files and interviewing correspondents, they can report "what really happened." When they finally sit down to write, however, they have to produce something that will stand up weeks or months later. Events have a way of embarrassing reporters who are forced to forecast the future.

As the total number of American correspondents diminishes, the role of the agency reporter is becoming more important. Some newspapers which once kept at least a few people overseas now depend totally on AP and UPI. Others have trimmed their staffs and are using more agency dispatches than before. But the economic factors which affect the newspapers apply also to the news agencies. For the past decade, the AP has kept to about eighty its total of regular foreign service correspondents—reporters and bureau chiefs paid from New York who might be moved from country to country. UPI has consistently had between sixty-five and seventy in the same category. These regular staff correspondents are mostly Americans, though their number includes a wide range of other nationalities. Each agency also has several hundred full-time "locals," usually nationals of the countries they cover, hired at local wage scales. Sometimes locals are responsible for covering major countries, such as Iran (until 1978), Indonesia and Turkey. More often, they work in major bureaus assisting the regular correspondents.

News agencies rely heavily on various types of stringers, since they must cover every country in the world, in one way or another. Each has hundreds of names in various yellowing files around the world for use in rare emergencies, and a number of stringers contribute regularly to agency reports. Most countries of the Middle East and Africa, Central America and much of Asia are covered exclusively by stringers, with occasional visits by correspondents.

American newspapers also make wide use of syndicated dispatches from correspondents of the New York *Times,* the Washington *Post,* the Los Angeles *Times* and several other big papers. These special news services do not cover the range of stories the agencies do, but they frequently report on the major stories in greater depth.

The New York *Times* in 1978 had thirty-four correspondents based abroad. It had the largest staff of specials, but the total was just under half what the paper had in the 1950s, even though it now syndicates to 250 important dailies across the country.

The Los Angeles *Times,* with eighteen correspondents permanently abroad, and the Washington *Post,* with thirteen, have defied the general trend, since they have built up their foreign staffs only in recent years. The *Wall Street Journal* has kept more than a dozen reporters overseas, along with a large staff in Canada; and the *Christian Science Monitor* remains steady with eight. The Baltimore *Sun* still had a half dozen staff correspondents out of the country in 1979. But papers elsewhere have cut back drastically. In the 1940s, the Chicago *Daily News* had scores of correspondents, one of the finest collections of newsmen ever assembled. By 1976, the last of them had come home. In 1978, the paper folded entirely. The Chicago *Tribune* was down to its last few correspondents in 1979, after a steady decline from the days when Colonel McCormick watched the world for the Midwest. Several papers with two and three foreign bureaus during the 1950s and 1960s have gone out of the correspondent business entirely.

The television networks, the prime source of news for most Americans, each cover the world with fourteen to twenty staff correspondents. The newsmagazine staffs are in the same range.

Like the news agencies, all of these organizations use stringers, and overall figures can be misleading. Some stringers are full-time reporters who, for administrative reasons, have not been formally added to the staff. Many are casual contributors who are asked for help on stories a few times a year. The San Francisco *Chronicle* has an entire "foreign service" built around a handful of irregulars who sell background and feature stories one at a time. Other papers buy stories at random, occasionally from people they don't know who submit material by mail.

A stringer is usually expected to work for one competing news organization at a time, allowing him to cover an agency, a newsmagazine and several newspapers with different circulation areas. But sometimes a stringer can corner the market. For years, one enterprising local reporter supplied news from a small Asian enclave to the AP, UPI, Reuters, Agence France-Presse, *Time, Newsweek,* the British Broadcasting Corporation and an assortment of others. He simply used a lot of carbon paper and, several employers suspected, handed his dispatches in at the cable office one at a time according to whose checks arrived on time.

Considering the system's other problems, the number of correspondents abroad is even more inadequate than the totals suggest. By comparison, the AP and UPI each have as many reporters in their Washington bureaus alone as they have based overseas. The New York *Times* covers its home town with a hundred reporters, three times as many as it has overseas. But, because of distances, official meddling and other obstacles, it can take three times as many reporters to cover the same sort of story overseas as it does in the United States.

For example, when Moscow's 5500-room Rossiya Hotel caught fire in March 1977, AP reporters only heard about it by chance from witnesses they happened to meet. There was no radio report. Tass said nothing. Moscow fire trucks and ambulances have no sirens, and police do not discuss their affairs on CB radios. One reporter called the police, who said only the ambulance service could give casualty figures. The ambulance people referred him to the city health officials. They told him to call the hotel, which passed him to Intourist, the state tour agency, which directed him back to the police. When he called the fire department, the dispatcher slammed the phone down in his ear. (These calls, of course, were all in Russian, a language which Soviet authorities make sure not many accredited correspondents can speak. The process is slower—and far less productive—through an interpreter.) A second reporter went to the scene but was roughly handled by police and troops guarding the hotel. He got to a hotel restaurant phone, but authorities yanked it out of his hand and ejected him. Eyewitness accounts were contradictory.

And that wasn't as bad as covering a hotel fire five months earlier. A reporter standing in the charred corridor asked the manager when the fire started. The manager looked him in the eye and said, "What fire? There's been no fire here." In the United States, a reporter at a fire seldom worries about spokesmen, witnesses or access; one of his greatest problems is avoiding the flying elbows and tangled cables of mobile TV and radio crews.

Obviously, this reduced band of correspondents, even with their ragtag army of helpers, cannot do much more than sample the news of the world. They have little time to nose around looking for stories which require investigative techniques to cover. Most of their energy is spent dealing with top news events—or catching up with stories someone else has broken. Often they can sandwich in background pieces and light features, but they habitually sleep with a transistor radio by their pillows and their bags half packed.

Because they are so few, correspondents move about with precision timing, goaded by foreign editors who try to make their small bands look like armies. It makes no difference if a correspondent is expected to cover twenty-three countries at a time, eight of them on the brink of hostilities and half lying along an unstable earth fault. He must be in the right place at least a day before the right time.

Editors don't always understand the strain involved, and most reporters make it a point of honor never to say no. When reporters need a break, they sometimes resort to cunning. One television man had a handy trick. He would apply for an interview with the chief of state and then message his editor that he expected an answer soon. Kings and presidents seldom reply quickly. This backfired on him once when a reigning prince granted him an immediate audience, and he had no cameraman. He found a friend to film the interview who could only guess at what to do. As the leader was building up to a dramatic point, the correspondent heard an ominous grinding sound from the camera behind him. All of a sudden he was engulfed in coils of celluloid which cascaded over his shoulders, and he heard his friend murmur, "Stall him."

The editors who do understand the pressure forgive an occasional broken line between two points. One well-loved correspondent planned to sneak in a stop in Cairo to see an old friend there on his way home from Saigon. His boss heard about the stopover and messaged, "Fail to understand why you going to Cairo." He got the message just before leaving Saigon but decided to pretend it missed him. In Cairo, though, after several bourbons, he returned to the office and messaged, "Fail to understand why I in Cairo." His editor, more amused than miffed, stuck the message under the glass on his desk.

Whenever there is time, reporters check first with their desks before moving from place to place. But even with clearance, they climb onto airplanes with trepidation. A reporter caught off base with the consent of his desk when big news breaks might keep his job but seldom his self-esteem. He passes swiftly into the rich folk-lore of correspondentry and is saved from permanent embarrassment only by the vast company which shares his misfortune. A pair of South American coups d'état illustrates not only how distressing this can be for reporters but, more importantly, also how seriously news coverage is affected by the thin spread of correspondents. When military officers in Chile overthrew the Marxist government of Salvador Allende Gossens in September 1973, it was one of the most dramatic Latin-American coups of the century. For months, some had eagerly anticipated it and others had feared it, but all knew it was coming. The problem was that no one could say how long the armed forces would wait before moving. Veteran Latin-American correspondents hung around Santiago for weeks on end writing background stories and probing for hints of imminent action. But when troops finally marched, and Allende died in mysterious circumstances, almost no one was on hand.

Two of the best American reporters in Latin America had left a short time before after many weeks of waiting. One, a roving correspondent for a news agency, was aboard a flight to Miami for a long-delayed holiday when the coup began. (When paged at the airport in Florida, he recalled later, "I knew it was either a death in the family or a coup in Chile. I got right back on the next plane south." Unfortunately, he could only get to neighboring Argentina.) The other, a newspaper reporter, had returned to his base in Buenos Aires to meet a girlfriend visiting him from the United States. A third American reporter, who had recently arrived in South America, had gone back to Buenos Aires to finish moving into a new apartment. Most of the rest of the Latin-American press corps was in Argentina or Brazil awaiting clearer signs from Chile. Even the regular UPI bureau chief was on vacation, although he had been replaced for that period by another UPI man. Apart from the agency reporters resident in Santiago, the only American correspondents in place were a magazine reporter who was expecting to interview Allende that morning and a roving newspaper correspondent. As soon as the military moved, the borders were sealed, and they stayed closed for nearly two weeks. Daily, legions of correspondents in Buenos Aires haunted the airport and pleaded by telephone and cable with the new Chilean authorities to allow in a special charter flight of newsmen. Across Argentina in the Andes, a persistent convoy left the city of Mendoza every morning at daybreak for four hours of winding and twisting up to the freezing mountaintop border point. They did their best at begging and badgering officials to let them through. Then, late each afternoon, they would head back down the mountain in defeat to glean what tidbits they could in Mendoza. As the days dragged on, parachute crews of reporters arrived from New York, Miami, Atlanta, London, Paris and points beyond. No one got into Chile. There was only an erratic telephone link over the Andes from Santiago. The government radio broadcast communiqués and official news reports. Fleeing refugees had some information, but much of it was questionable. Correspondents were forced to report the Chilean coup through the looking glass, and that was hardly adequate.

After that experience, Latin-American correspondents were not about to make the same mistake in Argentina. Word circulated in mid-1975 that the armed forces would soon dump President Isabel Perón; by late November, it was an established fact. The question, of course, was how soon. Each "reliable military source" gave a different date. Plans were leaked continually, always followed by word of postponement. The correspondents remained on permanent red alert. Economic development was ignored in Venezuela. A shift to the right by the Peruvian military went virtually unrecorded. Trips to Chile were delayed by those few reporters who were still allowed in by the press-wary junta. Reporters would not even venture across the river to investigate human rights abuses in Uruguay for fear the border would close overnight in their absence, sentencing them to watch the coup from a Montevideo hotel, chewing fingernails and antacid tablets.

The wait went on month after month, and foreign editors grew apoplectic. "My boss just ordered me out of town," lamented one newsmagazine man after putting off a trip to Brazil for the fourth time because of strong indications that the coup was finally near. "He thinks he has the village idiot down here, and I don't blame him. But if I'm up the Amazon when Isabel goes, it's my ass, not his." A news agency bureau chief, after postponing his home leave departure three times, was ordered to start his vacation without fail three days before the date he was certain was finally the right one. He sent his wife on alone with instructions to tell his desk that he was spending the first days of his vacation in Argentina. The army moved, as expected, and he was not charged for the time.*

---

*Some correspondents were remembering Vietnam as well as Chile. Neil Sheehan, UPI's outstanding Saigon correspondent, was forced to go on vacation to Tokyo in November 1963, even though he was sure that President Ngo Dinh Diem was about to be overthrown. He went and might even

When the tanks finally rolled in Argentina, the roving press corps hardly waited for the engines to cool before rushing off to catch up on stories they had been forced to neglect. Stories on the coup's aftermath—on what it really meant—would have to wait. Since most reporters left town at the same time and would be gone for weeks, few worried about being beaten by their competition on major Argentina stories. The news agencies would provide the usual standard coverage, which would be available to all editors at the same time. Suddenly, Ecuador and Colombia appeared in the newspapers, although nothing particularly new was going on in those countries. To recount major news events of the past months, correspondents simply selected relatively minor incidents—like a political speech or an isolated strike—for what is known as a "peg" or a "nose." They used that as a starting point for going backward.

For a correspondent, getting to where he should be is just a first step. He still has to gather information. The task of reporting abroad is so complex that any correspondent asked the standard cocktail party question "Where do you get your news?" invariably turns slightly greenish and edges toward the bar. It is like asking a waiter to recite a twelve-page dinner menu.

A reporter supplements his own observations by consulting an infinite combination of officials, papers, documents, diplomats, businessmen, slum dwellers, intellectuals, dissidents, secret reports, Eric Ambler–type seedy characters, wall posters and other newsmen. He can seldom trust only his own eyes. One agency reporter hurried into a Central American republic after an earthquake and found people eating guinea pigs, a local delicacy in the best of times. He wrote that the stricken victims were reduced to eating rats. One unkind colleague, forgetting how easily such mistakes are made, dubbed him the "Rat Man." The colleague's turn will come. Surface appearances can easily deceive a freshly arrived reporter. One, for example, asked an old hand near him in Tokyo why he was unmoved by what seemed to be an uncontrolled student demonstration. The veteran glanced at

have returned in time except that when a colleague sent him a prearranged tip-off message—asking him to buy a doll—the Japanese hotel clerk did not deem it important enough to relay. Sheehan's absence during the coup probably cost him a share in the Pulitzer Prize awarded to Malcolm Browne of the AP and David Halberstam of the New York *Times.*)

his watch and said, "It'll be over in ten minutes." It was. That was when the last trains left for the suburbs.

The kinds of sources used depend on the story. For covering upheaval, disaster and outbreaks of violence, the best sources are participants and victims. During the Lebanon civil war, reporters found the only way they could find out what was happening was to ignore the gunfire and ask the people who were shooting. Sometimes reporters go to ludicrous extremes for firsthand sources. In 1964, Belgian paratroopers dropped on Stanleyville in the Congo to rescue hostages held for months by rebels. A British reporter, meeting the evacuation flights, walked through the airport shouting, "Are there any nuns here who speak English and have been raped?"

A principal source of foreign news is the good old press conference where someone presents his views on a subject and then answers questions. These are not always held in classic fashion. One morning in Buenos Aires, I received a furtive invitation to a guerrillas' news conference with instructions to wait the next morning on a busy corner in a fashionable section of town. The guerrillas, known as the People's Revolutionary Army (ERP), had been killing and kidnapping foreign businessmen, officials and police for years; and security forces were hot on their tails. Three colleagues and I were to spend the day with the ERP's top commanders, and we were hoping it would not be the day the army moved in behind a barrage of automatic gunfire.

The day was like a late-show screenplay. Our escort, in an Italian-cut suit with a pebble-grain briefcase, hopped in our car and promptly got lost in traffic. We finally got to a rented tour bus—complete with an unsuspecting guide named Frosty who thought she was to shepherd a group of potential investors on a sightseeing outing. Our gaily painted bus stopped every four blocks for the escort to telephone for orders; for security reasons he had no advance word on where we were going. Once we had to ask a policeman for directions. Frosty began to wonder why her jokes weren't going over and why our tough-looking companions, unconvincing as Ohio stocking salesmen, insisted on touring outlying workers' neighborhoods instead of the Plaza de Mayo. Finally we stopped at a social hall, rented on the pretext of a bachelor party, and were herded upstairs. Frosty took one look at a table creaking under the weight of submachine guns and hand grenades and began shrieking about her children, her disinterest

in politics and her two o'clock hair appointment. A woman revolutionary took her aside to ply her with white wine and ideology, and
we sat down for a four-hour press conference. Guerrillas denounced
U.S. commercial imperialism and served us Coca-Cola. At one point,
a high-pitched police whistle sounded outside the window, and the
guards clutched their weapons. It was a peanut vendor.

When it was over, the leaders left first; we were ordered to stay put
until they reported safely from their hiding place. We paced back and
forth, certain that security forces had heard about the news conference and were preparing an assault. When we were finally let out, we
discovered the real danger to be our bus driver, who was falling-down
drunk from the guerrillas' wine. The whole experience took ten
hours.*

In most cases, the search for news is calmer and far more complex.
Serious correspondents begin each day going over local newspapers
and magazines, scanning national news and agency wires—if they are
available—and listening to the radio. The local press is essential even
when it is tightly controlled by the government. At the very least,
officially controlled papers give the government's side of events. If a
correspondent is working on a Watergate or a My Lai which he has
to himself, the local press may be of little direct use. If he is covering
a story he can see on his own—a civil war, riots or a disaster—the
national press is useful mainly if it is accurate and sophisticated. But
if he is trying to make sense out of a chaotic political or economic
situation, or is writing a general piece about national trends, he relies
on it heavily. Resident newsmen who report from a country on a
day-to-day basis can spend hours daily looking for hidden nuances or
probing for leads to news in the personal columns, in the financial
sections and in the full texts of boring speeches. News agency bureaus

---

*There is a sequel. At the news conference, the guerrillas announced they
were forming a common front with extremists from other countries to widen
their terrorist war. Since I was the sole agency reporter there, I was confident of an exclusive, well worth the effort. But, across town, UPI's Bob
Sullivan was proving that a good reporter need not always be on the spot.
He had heard about the secret news conference before it was over, and he
was waiting for one of the local reporters who attended. Because he was not
there, he was not bound by the elaborate camouflage we had agreed upon
because of Argentine laws about consorting with subversive elements. His
story was more detailed than mine.

almost always have a radio murmuring in the background, and the shift editor keeps an ear slightly cocked for martial music or a brief announcement that a DC-10 just missed the end of a runway. Official radio reports are handy, but they are hardly gospel. The March 1977 coup attempt in Thailand was mostly just words on the radio. The rebels seized the official transmitting station and announced the government had been overthrown. The government held the television station and said those reports were just wishful thinking. Loyal troops cut off the electricity, ending the radio broadcasts—and the rebellion. During the Biafra war, official broadcasts from each side claimed simultaneous victories over towns which neither army controlled. Occasionally, false radio reports end up in headlines, and the correct version tags along the next day—if then.

Correspondents have enough trouble verifying questionable information in sloppily prepared local papers. And they must carefully sort out what might be paid propaganda in the guise of news stories. But in many countries they can barely make out what the papers say. In Moscow, most foreign newsmen depend on government-approved translators. They often must pick among the Cyrillic characters and ask for translations of specific articles if the headlines look interesting. If their rudimentary Russian does not include such phrases as "SALT talks . . ." or "War on China within a week," they may miss a major story. Even when no breaking news is overlooked, a correspondent who cannot leisurely peruse papers and magazines has a limited feel for the country he is covering. There is no simple solution. Once in Singapore a correspondent befriended the editor of the island's biggest Chinese-language daily in hopes of making up for his ignorance of Chinese. Over drinks, the English-educated editor remarked, "I'm told we had a great editorial this morning. Unfortunately, I don't read Chinese."

The language problem far transcends the inability to read the local press. If a correspondent cannot speak the language of the country he is in, his sources are mainly fellow Americans or a small elite who have learned English for a particular reason. These sources are likely to give him an atypical point of view and a distorted idea of the society. Even the easier languages can cause problems. During a peaceful but raucous presidential inauguration in Venezuela, an American television reporter rushed into the press room to alert colleagues to a story he was filming. "It's almost a riot out there," he announced. "Thousands of kids screaming protests and waving their arms." A few dubious veterans went out to find a rally for the president; youths were chanting party slogans and giving victory signs.

Interpreters and translators, never quite good enough, can be awful. I once came across an old woman in a Vietnamese hamlet which had just been raided by the Viet Cong. Her house had burned down, with all of her belongings in it. For five minutes she gestured wildly and poured out words. Her voice rose to a wail, and then she paused to weep softly. She made sounds like gunfire and grenades. When I asked a Vietnamese reporter to translate, he replied, "She says she is unhappy."

Not only languages but also traditions and custom can hamper a correspondent's work. In Japan, local reporters have developed elaborate systems to shield some news from foreign correspondents. Special press clubs cover different sectors of the government, and they control who attends briefings. Even Japanese working for foreign news organizations are often banned. Authorities support the system because it sometimes protects them from embarrassment. If local reporters decide that a piece of news might besmirch the national image, they can agree to squelch it.

And there is a reverse problem. In a number of countries, correspondents can read the local press perfectly, and they pay too much attention to it. Agency reporters especially are sometimes so busy they barely have time for a quick phone call to check out a story. Often the phones don't work anyway. At times these reporters gamble on a story's accuracy, and it is a risky practice. In Peru, where the government controls the newspapers, three Lima dailies got the president's age wrong on his fifty-fifth birthday. In Italy, newspapers sometimes put out widely varying accounts of the same public speech. The problem is worse with news from provincial areas where only a personal visit can assure accuracy. In 1976, as Luis Echeverria was leaving the Mexican presidency, news agencies reported serious peasant revolts in the north. But American reporters who hurried to the area found the story had been exaggerated by local newspapers controlled by landowners. These papers supplied the basic material for stories written in Mexico City. In this case, the region was easily reached from the United States. But when similar situations occur in places like Thailand or Bolivia, they often remain undebunked.

Although the local press is an essential basic tool, it is only the starting point. In any country, correspondents quickly develop responsible government sources. Almost all governments have information departments and press spokesmen, but these are often among the last to know about major news. Correspondents try to find ranking insiders, preferably with titles that sound impressive in a dispatch. Interviews with heads of state usually delight editors, but talks with cabinet ministers, legislative leaders and top-level civil servants often reveal more. Government sources can be very hard to reach. In some Third World countries, an appointment with a junior minister is as treasured as a Washington reporter's exclusive session with the president. And in Washington the reporter can be fairly sure the president won't back out at the last minute with no excuse. During the civil war in Nigeria, even the low-ranking federal director of information would refuse to see correspondents. At one point, a reporter went to the information office with an urgent question and had this conversation with the director's secretary:

"Can I see the director, please?"

"Do you have an appointment?"

"No, I couldn't get through on the phone."

"Ah, then you can't see him."

"Can I make an appointment?"

"The director makes his own appointments."

"Well, can I see him to make an appointment?"

"No, I've told you, no one can see him without an appointment."

Generally, the more confident the government, the easier the access is to officials. Attitudes in a country can change rapidly. In Uganda, under President Milton Obote, the foreign minister owned a night club just outside the capital. Any reporter wanting to interview him only had to find a dance partner, ask questions of the minister while grinding to an African high-life beat on the crowded floor and then write off the evening on an expense account. After Idi Amin Dada took power, an American reporter was murdered, apparently for asking too many questions.

Middle-level officials like chiefs of police, directors of immigration and economic advisers can be harder to reach than cabinet ministers. This comes as a jolt to American newsmen switching for the first time from domestic to foreign reporting. At home, almost any civil servant will say at least something to the press when cornered, not only because he feels it is his duty but also because he knows that a "no comment" in print might be more damaging than any statement he might make. But in most foreign countries it is radically different. Officials are seldom bound by tradition to speak even to the local press. In all but a few dozen countries the newspapers are so tightly controlled that officials need not fear embarrassment from a probing reporter. A foreign correspondent, however, is an unknown and potentially dangerous quantity. A civil servant gains little from publicity abroad; in fact, jealousy and fear of rivalry could hurt him badly. If he is blamed for revealing sensitive information or seeking power, he could lose his job—or worse. Correspondents often must spend a great deal of time persuading these officials to trust them.

In communist countries, lack of accessibility is a matter of policy. A well-defined philosophy outlines the role of the foreign press in those societies, and only authorized spokesmen impart the word to correspondents. "It is incredibly tight," observed an American correspondent after frustrating years in Moscow. "The idea of ringing up the army or the foreign ministry for comment on a story is unheard of. If you do, you're told to read the papers." Even in Yugoslavia, a communist nation which separates itself from the Soviet bloc, a rigid control applies. "We can talk to officials, but we are told what the leadership wants us to know," said one veteran reporter there. "Stories are not leaked, they are planted."

Getting to a government figure is no guarantee of candor. Yugoslavia's Marshal Tito remarked to Prince Bernhard of Holland, in private talks, that the colonels' coup in Greece was good because it prevented a communist takeover. But, the prince asked, wasn't Tito a communist? "Ach," Tito replied, "I was young then." Just afterward, talking with reporters, Tito denounced the coup. When a Dutch officer asked a worldly member of the prince's retinue about the contradiction, he was told, "A statesman like Marshal Tito has the right to express a private opinion and the duty to express a public one."

And even heads of government can be wrong. Thai Premier Kukrit Pramoj told reporters Phnom Penh had fallen to the Khmer Rouge long before it had. One agency carried the story and stuck with it for hours. The premier, it turned out, was simply misinformed.

Correspondents regularly cultivate opposition leaders, as well. Political opponents are not only newsworthy in their own right, they also are up to date on government failings. And often correspondents suddenly find their old contacts, after years on the outside, are running new governments.

For political and economic stories, correspondents balance official information with assessments of diplomats, international experts, bankers, businessmen or scholars. The problem is determining how reliable and objective each new source is—and under what circumstances. Reporters build up a basic handful of sources in every country they cover regularly. They check with each periodically, and when a new source comes up with something startling, they bounce it off their regulars for reaction.

The best correspondents systematically tap smaller diplomatic missions with reputations for astute observation. The Canadians are usually excellent. Israelis are good in countries where they have no direct interest—and Israeli intelligence can be helpful in countries where they do. The Swiss are either very informative or very tight-lipped. Obviously it depends mostly on individuals rather than nationalities. International organizations like the World Bank and United Nations agencies can be gold mines for correspondents who protect their sources.

There is a strong tendency for American reporters to spend too much time at U.S. embassies. Some contact is necessary, since a number of stories about Americans come from embassy sources. And U.S. diplomats and military attachés are often well informed. But a reporter must always be able to separate information from the official line, and he must be in a position to write things his embassy friends may not like.

The lure of the embassy is strong. In many countries, it is the most effective cure for culture shock. If an embassy does not always have American movies and hamburgers, it at least has Americans. That means a lot to a freshly arrived correspondent surrounded by hostile authorities and up to his ears in bureaucracy. Embassy officers tend to see foreign situations in the same uncluttered—and often oversimplistic—way as many correspondents do. They are articulate and available, and they speak English. Because of this, some reporters depend more on U.S. embassies for political news than on the local officials and politicians who can give it to them firsthand.

This factor of familiarity underlies many of the widely discussed contacts between American correspondents and the Central Intelligence Agency. Although the CIA has admitted to recruiting and paying some American newsmen abroad, most of these relationships have been casual and informal. At the most basic level, newsmen and intelligence officers are collecting information. Often they know one another socially, particularly in Third World countries where there are few Western residents. In past decades, it was accepted practice for reporters and agents to share some information which neither considered to be overly sensitive. Correspondents, as a rule, would pass along anything they might include in a dispatch for publication. Agents shared information on the basis of how good a friend the correspondent was. Occasionally, agents would try to feed misleading reports. Although there is still a limited degree of sharing, both sides are now extremely wary of any contact at all. After a flurry of condemnations and disclosures in the mid-1970s, reporters and agents decided that whatever they might learn from one another was not worth the risk of public charges of collaboration.

CIA policies have placed an unfair burden on American correspondents, since no reporter is free from a possible taint. In hearings before a Senate select committee in 1976, CIA officials said that about fifty American journalists or foreigners working for U.S. news organizations were being paid by the agency. These ranged from several full-time staff members planted by the agency to itinerant freelancers and stringers who received occasional "gifts and reimbursements." After the subsequent publicity, the CIA announced, "Effective immediately, CIA will not enter into any paid or contractual relationship with any full-time or part-time news correspondent accredited by any U.S. news service, newspaper, periodical, radio or television network or station."

But, the Senate committee reported, fewer than half of the fifty were to be terminated under the new policy, because of casual stringer and freelance arrangements which do not always amount to accreditation. News organizations try to screen their occasional contributors carefully, and some have been assured by the CIA that none of their people are on covert payrolls. Those most familiar with CIA operations say that it is unlikely that any full-time American correspondent is now linked with the agency. One expert put it: "Since foreign governments automatically assume that correspondents work for the CIA, it would make little sense to use so obvious a cover." Still, the agency provides no roster, and it has often been far less than candid.

From time to time, the CIA is the secret source of false stories planted abroad which are relayed home. This is called "domestic fall-out." A former agent told the Senate committee, "If you plant an article in some paper overseas, or a revelation, there is no way of guaranteeing that it is not going to be picked up and published by the Associated Press in this country." This is not common. Correspondents always double-check suspicious "revelations," and they seldom report them if they're not satisfied with the sources. But it happens. False reports from the Indochina countries, Thailand and Chile, among others, have been inadvertently carried in the United States.

Despite the problems, correspondents still use some American and foreign intelligence sources, especially when battlefronts and closed borders block normal channels of information. These sources can provide valuable background material, though they must be considered at least slightly suspect. Just before Saigon fell to the North Vietnamese in 1975, CIA officers in the besieged capital briefed hand-picked correspondents on what was expected to happen. They said that advancing armies in the north had massacred civilians, and they predicted widespread terror for Saigon. Even some of the most seasoned correspondents wrote about imminent danger before hastily preparing their own evacuation. Other old hands, with their own confirmed reports that the occupying armies were respectful of civilians, discounted the briefing as a deliberate attempt to stiffen resistance by scaring the Americans. As it turned out, they were right.

In some instances, reporters can find a way to use official sources which are meant to be secret. In Cambodia, UPI's Sylvana Foa kept a radio on her desk tuned to military air frequencies, and she could hear conversations of American pilots whom the U.S. government denied were involved in the fighting.

Since correspondents write about virtually anything, it is impossible to catalogue the wide range of specialized sources they use. No correspondent can be an expert on every field he covers; instead, he must be an expert on experts. He has to know how to find the right person to give him a general background—and then to find other specialists who can poke holes in his first source's observations. This compromise approach is often not enough. A handful of correspondents have written dispatches announcing the end of smallpox in the world, all of them quoting an acknowledged expert given to jumping the gun.

Occasionally reporters run into special problems with sources. "What do you do if your source has never seen the moon?" asked John

Nance in the AP's house magazine. Nance was among the first few outsiders to make contact with Stone Age tribesmen, the Tasaday, who had lived isolated in a canopied jungle in the Philippines. He could understand some of the Tasaday's basic words, using a team of interpreters going through three languages, but it took several visits to get a sense of their feelings about time, distance and life in general.

One of the most common private sources of all correspondents is other correspondents. Self-respecting reporters repudiate the idea of this, but newsmen trade and share information in dozens of ways. There is the basic "fill-in"—a briefing to bring a newly arrived correspondent up to date quickly so he can meet his deadline. Sometimes friends who trust one another will share quotes and facts on sensitive issues, dispensing with the point of ethics which requires reporters to gather such material personally. Correspondents who return from troubled areas are normally willing to pass along their observations, even to direct competitors, if they feel they will be repaid in kind sometime later on. One news agency correspondent in Cambodia went so far as to send cables to a rival agency to cover for his friend who was too drunk to find the telegraph office. He stopped when, after sending similar cables to both agencies, he got a message from his own advising him that he had been beaten by the other agency. The cable to his own desk had gotten lost, but the one to the rival went through without delay.

Among correspondents, messages reading "Others have . . . need ours soonest," are called "rockets," and they are dreaded as much as their more lethal namesakes. They mean that a correspondent was beaten, and that his desk knows about it. But rockets are a common, if indirect, means of "sharing" news. If one news agency puts out a major story, the others know about it in minutes. If they don't see it in one of the places where they sneakily monitor the others' wires, they will hear about it from subscribers who want confirmation. Once alerted, trailing correspondents can usually find enough sources to back up the story, and they can catch up within the hour.

It doesn't always work that way. James Pringle, then with the British agency Reuters, located Eldridge Cleaver in Havana after the black leader had disappeared without a trace. The exclusive story came just as Reuters was making a major effort to sign up major U.S. newspapers as subscribers. It was a dramatic beat, splashed on the front page of the New York *Times* and featured on the network newscasts. The only clue in Pringle's dispatch was that Cleaver was in a high-rise apartment building in downtown Havana, and the AP man spent the entire next day knocking on doors, without success, asking if anyone had seen a tall American black man.

Obviously correspondents debrief not only fellow correspondents but also local reporters and stringers. The results are not always precise. One news agency man talked with a Cambodian stringer back from "up the road." Neither spoke the other's language, and the session went like this:

Correspondent: "Any ratatatatata tat tat?"

Stringer: Shakes head no.

"Any boom, boom, boom?"

Negative.

"Any screee, screee, screee?"

Negative.

"Any whoop, whoop, whoop?"

Wide grin and energetic affirmative gesture.

The correspondent, thus briefed, sat down and wrote, "Cambodian troops, backed by American helicopters, battled Khmer Rouge . . ."

When correspondents relay their sources' information to readers and viewers, a whole new problem arises. The readers and viewers, to evaluate what is presented, must have some idea of the sources. At the same time, reporters often must protect their informants from even vague hints which might identify them. To get around this, the system uses a series of code words and qualifiers which are far more important than many people realize. Unfortunately, each reporter has a slightly different way of dispensing clues, and code words can vary. But there are general guidelines which can be followed.

If a story carries no attribution at all—no code words—it generally means that the reporter observed the events personally or is sure enough of his information to stake his reputation on it. Unattributed stories are rare, because many editors feel uncomfortable trusting their own people. In 1977, for example, reporters were certain that Israel was aiding Christian Falangists in southern Lebanon. At one point, an experienced reporter asked a local commander the fastest way to get to one of his outposts. The commander hedged, but a young recruit, who didn't know the reporter spoke Arabic, piped up: "Why doesn't he go through Israel like we do?" And that was just a confirmation of what the reporter already knew. In spite of the evidence, his desk insisted that he attribute his information to sources rather than simply stating the facts. There are two major reasons for this caution. If a story somehow turns out to be wrong, and it is sourced, then the source made the mistake, not the news organization. Also, editors say they note a growing tendency among readers to be skeptical of news reports. An editor might know his own correspondent, but few readers have that advantage.

Readers should beware of unattributed stories with such easily overlooked terms as "reportedly" and "believed to be." They do not mean the information is incorrect; they only mean that the writer is not really sure that it is accurate. Such qualifiers are often necessary, since a great number of details worth reporting cannot be pinned down sufficiently to be used without a hedge.

When attribution is necessary, correspondents always try to cite a name and title: "Ian McBombdefuser, the official Scotland Yard spokesman, said . . ." or "Nicaraguan information minister Juan Carlos . . ." The reader knows exactly where he stands, and there is someone to answer for the information if it is not true. But this can get tricky in some countries. In the United States, the assumption is that if a story is pinned on a specific person it is reliable; anonymous sources are suspect. But in authoritarian countries, if someone puts his name behind a piece of information, there is a strong chance that it is a propagandized version of the facts. If the information is attributed to unnamed but solid-sounding sources, it may well be a truer account which the reporter pieced together on his own from friendly authorities who agreed to speak frankly if promised anonymity.

Direct attributions like "the government said" or "authorities said" —without the word "sources"—signal a straight presentation of the official position. The information might not be true, but it is what the government has to say on the subject. In all stories concerning governments, correspondents routinely seek official comment. If there is none, they ask for a confirmation or a denial of specific details. When stories say, "Authorities refused to confirm or deny . . ." the chances are better than even that the information is accurate. But not everyone plays by the rules. In 1978, during a rebel invasion of Zaire, a French radio station reported that Foreign Legion paratroopers had left Corsica to rescue European hostages. The report was true—the paratroopers were halfway to Zaire—but the French Defense Ministry issued a flat denial. (At least one veteran correspondent was not misled. He pressed the ministry spokesman and was finally told, "Nothing prevents you from relaying the radio report." That, in the system's convoluted code, was a denial of the denial.)

The term "sources," however qualified, is difficult to evaluate. Unnamed sources amount to a blank check for the reporter. If the source is not identified, the story cannot be effectively challenged—or substantiated. Officials might deny the substance of a story, but who is to say that the reporter's informant did not actually use the words attributed to him? The only way around this, under the system, is the careful use of descriptive modifiers. Such weak versions as "informed sources" and "reliable sources" are banned on some desks. They give away nothing and sound too mysterious. An informed source may be the president himself or some low-level bureaucrat taking a stab in the dark. When a correspondent can offer more concrete clues—"federal police sources," "sources in the foreign ministry"—it usually means he is more sure of his ground.

Attributions like "unimpeachable sources" or "authoritative sources" are usually reserved for information from the mouth of some highly placed horse. But they are still anonymous. Sometimes the code words have specific meaning. When Secretary of State Henry Kissinger traveled abroad, reporters on his aircraft always quoted "a senior government official." That was, of course, Kissinger himself, and it was the worst kept secret in government. In most cases, "Western diplomats" translates to U.S. embassy officials. When writing about multinational companies, correspondents must protect their sources. But "a source close to the company" is nearly always a ranking executive.

Phrases such as "Observers said," "It is generally accepted," and "Most Indonesians believed" mean the correspondent is giving his own view but must defer to custom by adding some attribution. "Observer" in this sense is normally a synonym for the reporter himself or at least the one at the next typewriter. This is technically legitimate because the correspondent is indeed an observer, and he is saying only what he believes to be true. It is an unavoidable ruse within a system that does not allow the correspondent to speak for himself directly when writing analyses.

Sometimes correspondents also express a guarded view with terms like "claimed" or "alleged." If a reporter feels obliged to include someone's viewpoint but thinks the speaker is lying, he may write, "he claimed," instead of the standard, "he said." The word "allegedly" is a hedge designed to relieve the writer from having to make a questionable assertion on his own. But it has become so loaded that it is often a purposeful tip-off that something is fishy. If a correspondent writes, "the alleged peace accord," the reader should not expect to see any permanent settlement soon.

There is no fixed rule. Even the most waffling of code words—"generally reliable sources"—can refer to an ironclad statement by the person closest to the situation.

One rule of thumb for anonymous attributions is that no responsible reporter will relay information unless he believes it to be true. His choice of code words reflects his ability to back it up; but if he has any serious doubts about the story, he won't write it. The reader's best protection is to know well the newspapers and publications he normally sees. He should learn their policy on anonymous quotes—if any—and be able to identify their source words. He might also keep track of by-lines that regularly appear until he learns which reporters have been consistently well informed in the past. Above all, he should apply selective belief, checking one source against another, the same way correspondents do.

There is an unsettling caution to the whole question of sources. Even a multitude of sources, tapped and identified by the best of correspondents, can be wrong. When United Nations Secretary General Dag Hammarskjold flew to Ndola, in northern Rhodesia, in 1961 for talks on the Congo crisis, reporters were waiting at the airport. A plane landed, and they saw a man who looked like Hammarskjold walk down the steps and into a limousine. To be certain, they asked local airport officials if the man was the secretary general, and they were assured it was. Urgent dispatches were sent, and the correspondents returned to their hotels. They learned only later that the arriving passenger was a British envoy. Hammarskjold was dead in the jungle, the victim of a plane crash.*

---

*David Halberstam, then of the New York *Times,* was in the Congo, and he missed covering the Hammarskjold arrival by some quirk of fate. He wrote later that if he had been there he most likely would have made the same mistake as the others. Instead of going on to Vietnam and a subsequent Pulitzer Prize, he said, he might have ended up back in New York, discredited. He is probably right. Correspondents, with reason if not necessarily justice, are seldom forgiven such mistakes.

The Hammarskjold incident illustrates one of the most difficult aspects of foreign reporting. Obviously, no careful correspondent trusts a single source in any but the most straightforward story. And he will not write an eyewitness account of a battle or a disaster until he has seen enough of it to have a fair picture in his mind. But he must know when he has enough. Some reporters do more than is necessary —or wise—only to prove to themselves they are neither lazy nor cowardly. It might mean one more dangerous trip up a road. Or it could mean spending an additional day finding still more sources when it is time to move on to something else. Often the news value of the story does not warrant the effort; time might be better spent in other ways. Sometimes the medium doesn't require the risk: only an overdriven radio reporter can justify crawling closer to unseen gunfire if it serves no more purpose than background noise on a voice report.

Each correspondent must find his own balance between what he thinks is required of him—or what is too much. A reporter who later became a magazine editor caught the essence of the dilemma in a conversation with friends in Phnom Penh. Asked why he was not particularly aggressive about going up the road, he replied, "I'm not interested in having my legs blown away, so that when my kid asks me how it happened, and I say, 'In Cambodia,' he says, 'Where?' "

Some reporters who do too little are brought home; some who take too many risks are killed or wounded. Many, however, spend entire careers overseas without ever working out the proper balance. They are never quite sure of what is really expected of them, and it shows in their dispatches.

Correspondents who do shoddy work fall roughly into five catego- ries. The Modified Police Reporter is happy with his story if it is carefully attributed to authoritative spokesmen, however out of socio- political context it may be. He is usually new to the business and has yet to learn that there is much more to foreign reporting than getting the facts straight. He can work comfortably by telephone and from headquarters, since he can forgo a personal look if he can get a good description from officials. He leaves out interpretation, calling it editorializing, and he dismisses revealing detail as superfluous fluff. Often he is so busy collecting official accounts that he misses the overall point. Even in those few countries where the credibility gap is slight this is poor journalism.

His opposite is the Henry Morton Stanley Type, who has to see everything for himself, whatever the sacrifices involved. He eschews official comment and explanation, however elucidating it may be. While the successful Stanley type can come up with dramatic, gripping stories, he is seldom able to put them into proper perspective. Today's newspaper economics make it tough for this style. The original Stanley took two years to find Dr. Livingston; the new Stanleys try to find their quarry within the space of a single expense account. Any editor loves to boast that his intrepid reporter found the secret jungle headquarters of the Ismailian guerrillas. But most prefer to leave long, chancy investigations of obscure stories to low-paid stringers who are willing to gamble a poison dart in the thigh or indefinite captivity against a few days on the front page.

The Fleet Street Type is an offshoot of the Modified Police Reporter and the Henry Morton Stanley styles. He gets out to look for stories, too, but when his deadline nears—or the natives get overly restless—he simply makes up the remaining details. The Fleet Street Type is not common, and he is found mainly on staffs of popular British dailies. But a few correspondents for American organizations fall into the category. One Briton still swears at the mention of a colleague who now contributes to American media. The two of them had covered an African rebellion, and at one point they could get only as far as a wide river separating them from a town held by guerrillas. They agreed to limit themselves to writing about what they could see across the water. The Englishman kept to the bargain. His competitor, however, was splashed across the front page of the rival paper with a lurid account of how he breasted the crocodile-infested river, extracting himself from giant snapping jaws while fending off native spears. He described how he reached the other bank, watched the battle and then had to slug a few hostile guerrillas to escape back across the river. When confronted later, he told his irate colleague, "I couldn't help it. Something just came over me, and my fingers were writing by themselves."

Two other styles are direct opposites of one another. The Technocrat is a good reporter, but he is so overworked that he does not have the time to add the extra elements of depth and explanation to his stories. News agency correspondents in Geneva, for example, often work shifts alone, dealing each day with 200 press releases from international agencies, nine newspapers in four languages, non-stop radio broadcasts, visits by assorted chiefs of state, foreign ministers and financial figures, calls from tipsters and stringers and messages from the head office asking questions. If a terrorist attack happens to coincide with Rhodesian peace talks and a summit of socialist leaders, the lone man must handle everything until help arrives. A good reporter can produce an enormous amount of work under those circumstances, but he can hardly be blamed if it sounds like it spewed out of a human computer.

The How-Does-It-Feel Type spends little time at all in the office. He is out-seeking the disgruntled dropout or the farmer with banana blight to write an individualized story with human impact but seldom with enough overall information to fit his characters into a larger picture. Done well, a How-Does-It-Feel dispatch can explain a major problem with a single human example. But there is little room these days for stories which begin "Melvin Blatt leaned forward in his chair, rolled a thin cigarette between his pudgy fingers, swiveled once, looked out the window, scratched himself and said . . ."

It need hardly be said that a large number of correspondents abroad elude these categories. These are the talented individuals who are responsible for what effectiveness our foreign reporting has. The best ones combine the positive traits of these five styles, and they apply them with calm but speedy reason. They know when to concentrate on people and when to pile up statistics. They weave historical and literary reference into their copy and relate dispatches to their readers with bits of color and detail. A few approach a sixth style, the Bionic Correspondent, which is the nonexistent intellectual ideal of Philip M. Foisie, the Washington *Post*'s assistant managing editor for foreign news.

These styles apply equally to men and women correspondents. Editors who for years were reluctant to assign women abroad are finding they have the same strengths and weaknesses as men. Women often do a better job because they are still such a rarity that they must work harder to prove themselves. The biggest problem of most women correspondents is attitudes of their editors. "This is still a macho profession, and the editors—all men—feel they have to protect us or that they can't count on us," observed one woman working abroad for a newsmagazine. Although some American newspapers had more women reporters than men in their newsrooms at home in 1978, fewer than 5 per cent of correspondents were women, and they were concentrated in "safe" bureaus like Paris and London. Kate Webb, an Australian, covered Cambodia for UPI, going everywhere that men went and emerging unrattled after months of guerrilla captivity. But she was one of the few women reporters dispatched to Indochina during the war.

Editors tend to stick women with things like tours of presidents' mothers or filmings of new movies. "I think that women correspondents are still insecure about themselves and secretly hope for these easy assignments because they know they can handle them—there is a terrible pressure not to fall down," said one news agency correspondent who has reflected at length about her profession. "That aggravates the problem."

Sometimes the difficulties are more basic. A woman photographer who wanted to go on a B-52 bombing run over Vietnam from Guam was advised there was no pilot's relief for women. If her kidneys could hold out for twelve hours, she was told, she would be welcome. She made it.

But whatever the real or imagined difference between men and women reporters, their job is the same. If a correspondent is off base and uncovered when the king is deposed, he—or she—had better start learning a new trade.

4

Star Reporters and Unsung Helpers

The Bionic Correspondent has no ego, libido, mother, career drive, cultural snobbery, fallen arches or fear of flying. He persuades officials to answer their telephones and comment forthrightly. He speaks Urdu and Lingala in a gentle manner which charms shy villagers and melts the hearts of tyrants. He sends his uncensored dispatches to a desk which cherishes his every comma and adds only a few trenchant words from elsewhere to broaden his dimensions. And, just to keep his focus sharp, he returns home every so often to hobnob with Harvard dons and Virginia ham curers.

With that sort of correspondent and circumstance, says the Washington *Post*'s Foisie, American readers would be perfectly served. But while his ideal is only wishful thinking, he allows, a number of flesh-and-blood reporters do a damned good job.

A close look at some individual reporters abroad and at their own views on their work gives an idea of what makes a good correspondent.

One of the greatest prototypes of today's Bionic Correspondent, Homer Bigart, has already hung up his flight bag to raise New Hampshire primroses in splendid retirement. Bigart first set out to be an architect but washed out, he says, because he couldn't draw. Instead, he roamed the globe for three decades until 1972 for the New York *Herald Tribune* and then the New York *Times,* covering almost every clash of arms from World War II to Vietnam and filing dispatches in between on anything from Ping-Pong to polar expeditions. He won two Pulitzer Prizes and, more importantly, was highly regarded by his colleagues.

Bigart's direct manner—too witty to be flippant and too persistent to be ignored—got him answers to questions. He was a master at sprinkling his stories with telling detail and felicitous phrasing. (Bigart once referred to New York's East River as being littered with beer cans, cigarettes and "other debris of pleasure.") And he had a natural instinct for being in the right place when something happened. On one assignment, he flew to Haiti for the funeral of François "Papa Doc" Duvalier in April 1971, and the spot he selected as a vantage point was where mourners went into a sudden mysterious panic as the feared dictator's casket passed by. He wrote:

> It began inexplicably on the flower-strewn avenue. . . . It began not with a volley of shots or even a sudden scream. The city lay silent in the midday heat except for the dolorous music of the bands and the distant sullen banging of the "cannons of condolence." . . . But suddenly the street was churning in a wild melee of Haitians who ran madly about in search of escape. They were slammed against the metal shutters of closed stores. Two men fell out of sight down a manhole. Members of a marching band dropped their instruments and ran for cover. Militiamen with rifles and pistols at the ready ran about in circles, shouting orders at the crowds . . .

At seventy, with honest but unreasonable modesty, Bigart reflected on his success: "I thought I had instincts. And I figured that if a story was interesting to me, it would interest a lot of Joe Blows. I have average intelligence and only an average interest in news. I don't think I ever read a newspaper well."

For some, Bigart might have been the last great freewheeling "special." Today's correspondents, they contend, are far too hindered by the technology which puts them in close contact with demanding editors and niggling accountants. Bigart has not given much thought to the passing of the good old days, but he summed it up well in a single Bigartism: "That all ended when they made us ride economy on airplanes."

A few grand old correspondents have simply adjusted with the times and are as bionic as they come. One is Phil Foisie's own brother, Jack, of the Los Angeles *Times.*

Jack Foisie went into journalism in high school, he says, because he stuttered and was a bust at public speaking. If he was going to communicate, he decided, he had better learn to write. He rose through the ranks—copy boy, sports writer, police reporter, war correspondent—until he was a superstar for the San Francisco *Chronicle.* For the *Chronicle,* Foisie covered what he called the "three M's": maritime, military and missiles. He promoted overseas assignments, persuading his editors to let him cover the last of the Korean war and the beginning of the U.S. involvement in Vietnam. The Los Angeles *Times,* just starting to build its large foreign staff, hired him away to open an Indochina bureau in 1964, and he has stayed overseas since.

One colleague recalls: "When we hired Foisie [at forty-five], the boss asked, 'You mean you want to send that little old man over to Vietnam?' But Foisie is ageless and timeless. I was looking through the files and found an old story . . . about him covering World War II [for *Stars and Stripes* when he was in his early twenties] and he was described then as looking like a white-haired little old man."

Anyone riding in a jeep with Foisie, hearing him yell, *"Yaa-hoooo,"* at every jolt, knows that he is hardly ready for a geriatric ward. Once, with a group of weary reporters eager to return to Saigon after a hair-raising day at the front, some gunfire rattled up the road. "What's that?" asked an ingenuous new man. "That, my friend, is action, and unless you are a coward, you will advance," Foisie replied, calmly wheeling about and trotting back toward the noise.

In Dacca, as Indian and Pakistani jets soared and strafed low over the Intercontinental Hotel, most reporters tried to rationalize that the safest place was on the lower floors. Foisie, not one to miss a ringside seat for a dogfight, just curled up with his notebook on the roof.

Foisie's forte is finding the off-beat story which no one else has.

I've been trained, and the office has not discouraged my readiness, to go for the off-angle [he wrote in a letter explaining his philosophy]. I hate to be part of gang-bang coverage. If my colleagues head off in one direction in riot coverage, I try to conjure up a reason for going in the opposite direction. [The] question is, for me, when should I admit that I have lost all my charge, and the office is just letting me stay on overseas because they are kindly folk? I thought I had lost it in the Middle East, but in South Africa and Rhodesia [1976–77], I think I've demonstrated that I can still get up and go, however tough the situation might be. Much to my amazement, I was the only American "special" at

Francistown in Botswana when the parents of some 380 Rhodesian black teen-age schoolchildren who were either kidnapped or had volunteered to join the insurgents were allowed to come and try to talk their children into rejoining the family. Few more than 50 did—but it was dramatic stuff to see the parents and children reunited for a few minutes of persuasion and rejection. It took some doing for correspondents to get into Botswana from Rhodesia—the border clearance was, in some cases, a very nasty experience. But the story made it all worthwhile; I didn't know I still could underwrite pathos, for the drama was so intense the story didn't need adjectives.

Foisie's attitude toward his job is typical of the Bionic Correspondent: ". . . not only is the glamor of the job grossly exaggerated, but also our impact on events. Thus, I have never expected or wanted to be lionized, although I have other forms of ego, like liking to see the byline on a meaningful story, and appreciative comments from my editors when they think I have done well. . . . The moments of elation follow the triumph of being on hand for a dramatic story, of writing it well (there is no better critic than one's self)."

If Foisie is the archetypal action correspondent, Flora Lewis is the virtuoso of nuance. As European diplomatic correspondent for the New York *Times,* she unravels the tangled snarls of summitry, macroeconomics, North-South confrontations and multilateral disarmament to lay out a single thread for her readers to follow. That is not all she does. "I don't want to be typecast as a heavy," she puts it, and she proves regularly that she can man the riot barricades and interview goose liver stuffers with the best of them. But, whatever else she is, Flora Lewis is a cerebral reporter, and she pays close attention to the important stories which break one crack at a time.

One of Ms. Lewis' duties is running the *Times* Paris bureau, and she goes about it with typical thoroughness. She described her approach:

I believe in what I call a do-it-yourself mosaic. The individual pieces—stories—are each complete in themselves, but they are consciously made to fit into a larger picture. That way, the reader is not getting disjointed bits, like sections cut out of a picture postcard. You should be able to take a year's coverage and make a brochure which would give a pretty good picture of the country —politically, geographically, culturally. . . . Someone who reads everything in the Times about France, for a year or so, should be able to come here and not find anything surprising. He should have the same sensation as if he were to go to see the Mona Lisa for the first time after seeing dozens of reproductions of the same thing. The authentic thing in its own detail always has a special impact but he would not be surprised by the picture. That is what I hope we provide in terms of coverage.

Ms. Lewis' first job in journalism was on her third-grade newspaper. She worked for the Los Angeles *Times* while still in university, and she was with the AP in New York, Washington and London. In 1946, when the AP wanted her to return to the United States in a general demobilization, she decided to stay in Europe as a freelance. In the following years, she now jokes, she worked for every publication except *Pravda* and the *People's Daily*. She wrote a book on Poland and, eventually, did a syndicated column on foreign affairs. The New York *Times* would not hire her because she was married to a *Times* executive, but she contributed articles regularly. In 1972, after her divorce, she was made a full staff member and assigned to Paris.

With dignified gray hair and a resolute set to her jaw, Flora Lewis heads straight to the heart of a story. A president does not intimidate her in the least; she has been a reporter for thirty-five years, and she will still be a reporter when he is no longer a president. Some colleagues say she is too direct, that she intimidates sources to silence. A few call her a tough cookie. Ms. Lewis doesn't like the sobriquet, and those who know her soft side think it is unfair. She is generous with her equals and helpful to neophytes. "I suppose there is a toughness there," she said once, "but it is toward stories, not people."

Until 1977, her main competition in Paris was the Washington *Post*'s Jim Hoagland, as bionic a correspondent as an editor could want. Hoagland won the Pulitzer Prize in 1971 for a six-week reporting assignment on South Africa which produced enough copy to fill a small book. Hoagland is the antithesis of the hard-drinking, ill-tempered stereotype so popular in the old movies. He is affable, low-keyed, courtly and hard-working. He approaches his job philosophically—with an almost boyish dedication—but he can chortle cynically at the weak points of his profession.

Hoagland became a correspondent in textbook fashion. He was reared in Rock Hill, South Carolina, and he wanted to get into a bigger world. He decided journalism would give him not only mobility but also a chance to express himself. By the time he finished university, he was sports editor for the Columbia (S.C.) *Record,* a daily paper of 30,000 circulation. To study French and France, he spent two years at the University of Aix-en-Provence. After two years in the air force, based in Germany, he got a job as copy editor on the international edition of the New York *Times* in Paris. Hoagland soon learned that the old pros had locked up the political and economic beats, so he got into the paper writing about jazz and show business. He returned home two years later and joined the New York *Post* just as the paper was expanding its reporting staff. He covered metropolitan news and courts for the next two years, until he was awarded a fellowship to study economics. After that, the *Post* put him on the foreign desk and sent him to Africa.

"If there is anything I have that is useful to the paper," Hoagland said in an interview, "it is the ability to explain things clearly to the reader. You must start off with the presumption that the reader does not know very much about the story and then carefully explain things, breaking them down step by step, so that he is interested and that he can follow it. I try never to write sentences that I don't understand. That may sound funny, but I can read a story and know when a correspondent did not understand what he was writing."

Hoagland's contribution is more than that. His sensitive but dispassionate series on South Africa made an enormous impact in Washington, altering the way many people looked at the government and its apartheid policies. Administration sources said later the articles slowed down projected plans by President Richard Nixon to increase American communication with South Africa. His perceptive analyses of Eurocommunism and economic summit talks informed hundreds of thousands of people about subjects vital to their lives which they might otherwise have ignored.

Malcolm W. Browne just fell into the profession, but he trained himself with ascetic zeal. He was a laboratory chemist until the army turned him into a tank driver in Korea. Then, Browne recalled later, "the army, for reasons I never fully apprehended, decided I would be more useful to them as a reporter for *Stars and Stripes* than chogeying my beloved M-48s over the Imjin River Valley. So I became a correspondent."

Back in the United States, he went from the Middletown (N.Y.)

Daily Record to the UPI and then to the AP. He worked in the Baltimore bureau with a thin Vietnamese grammar in the back pocket of his familiar khaki pants, and in 1961 he finally persuaded the AP to send him to Saigon. Individualistic to the point of eccentricity, Browne went after stories by hammering, badgering and outwaiting. Some officials, fooled by his red socks and Dagwood forelock, at first thought him naïve. They soon learned better. In the AP's cramped, smelly office, Browne tacked to the wall a withered hand brought back from a battle to remind reporters that there was a war on despite the deceptive charm of downtown Saigon. He ordered his new reporters to the front before their bags were unpacked, and he covered the action himself as often as he could.

After his Pulitzer Prize and his book, *The New Face of War,* Browne quit the AP to try television reporting for ABC. He wrote freelance magazine articles after that, and then in 1968 he joined the New York *Times.* In a few years, he covered South America, Pakistan, Eastern Europe and Indochina, with side trips to places like Antarctica and the Spanish Sahara.

Browne can witness some complex bit of turmoil and, after 15 minutes of machine gun–paced typing, produce a 1000-word dispatch which most colleagues won't match after hours of reflecting and rewriting. He weaves in historical background, literary reference, poignancy and political analysis with hardly a pause between paragraphs. He explained his drive in a letter:

> I think the biggest motive force in all of us is a kind of neurotic compulsion coupled with personal (and often morbid) curiosity. We are all psychologically hounded by pervading guilt feelings —the implicit question from our employers, "Yes, but what have you done for me lately?" [In the AP's Saigon bureau, long after Browne, another compulsive reporter emblazoned one wall with the motto "You're only as good as your last biggie."] In a negative sense, we tend to go on doing it because we are not good enough (or at least feel we are not good enough) to do anything else. We may write long articles or books from time to time. But relatively few of us take the big jump and become *professional writers,* particularly in that most daunting of all writing pursuits —fiction. So we massage our creative itches with daily news stories. Sometimes—just sometimes—it seems to have real value . . .

Browne's first full-time assistant in Saigon, Peter Arnett, was already a respected correspondent when he arrived in Vietnam. Arnett, born in the old New Zealand whaling port of Riverton, found that reporting was the best way to see the world and still afford to eat. He started off on the standard route of adventuresome Australians and New Zealanders—to Southeast Asia, through India and on to London —but he settled for a while in Thailand. He worked for the Bangkok *World* until the publisher sent him to Vientiane, Laos, to start an English-language weekly. Arnett, then thirty, stayed until the government closed the paper a year later. In Laos, Arnett was a stringer for the AP and a handful of other organizations. The AP liked his work and said he could report for them from Indonesia if he got himself to Jakarta. He did, staying eighteen months until he was expelled. Arnett had been taken on as "local hire," an agency term meaning cheap help. He decided that if he was ever going to make it professionally, he had better let AP executives know who he was. He scraped together enough money for a trip to New York and so impressed the AP high command that he was sent to Saigon with a major pay raise and a boost in status. (He did not become a full-scale staff member, however, until he won his Pulitzer Prize in 1966.) By the time he left Vietnam eight years later, with a mountain of awards and a formidable Asian art collection, he was widely considered the best reporter of the war. He was assigned to New York as a special correspondent to write in depth about major world stories.

Arnett, short but tough, with a Dick Tracy jaw, commands attention by sheer force of personality. He speaks quickly in a room-filling voice, but he listens attentively and takes time to get to know people. He separates his intense feelings from his work in a machinelike manner. In Saigon, when word came at four A.M. one morning that a helicopter crash had killed John Paul Vann, one of the most important American advisers of the war, the AP bureau called Arnett at his hotel. He had known Vann for years as a close friend and had survived firefights with him. Awakened from a sound sleep, without five seconds' hesitation, Arnett began dictating a balanced but moving obituary, complete with dates, figures and a comprehensive analysis of Vann's significant impact on the war.

"I'm one of those who subscribes to the belief that some stories are worth dying for," says Arnett, without a trace of bravado. "A reporter should be able to determine his own destiny, but it is his responsibility to cover his story. That's why I stayed in Saigon after the North Vietnamese took the city. If at a forward position a company or a battalion was under fire and taking casualties, I felt it binding upon me to go. I never went out on the point or crawled out to machine-gun posts. But, there are times when you have to get out—you have to risk your life."

Part of a reporter's skill, Arnett adds, is knowing when to put your life on the line. You only lose it once.

Arnett looks the part of a dashing correspondent, but outward appearances mean nothing. James Pringle of *Newsweek* is a timid-looking Scot with rosy cheeks, Coke-bottle glasses and itchy tweeds. But he is an absolutely fearless reporter who digs into the most mundane of stories with the tenacity of a hammerhead shark. Pringle went with reporters to Kolwezi, Zaire, in 1978 after a rebel assault. He escaped the pack and managed to be alone with Zaire President Mobutu Sese Seko when he looked through a window at the bodies of thirty-five massacred European hostages. Other reporters provided only a clinical account of how the town looked. But Pringle said in his dispatch: ". . . the battle-hardened president, a former army sergeant, put his hands to his face and moaned: 'Mon Dieu, they have smashed their heads in.' "

Some correspondents are too erratic or idiosyncratic to qualify as bionic, but in their own style are excellent reporters. One of the most colorful was depicted by an English colleague, John de St. Jorre, in an article about covering the Biafra war:

> The archetypal American newsmagazine man: this one is in his mid-forties, has seen many wars (and appears to like them; or at least his office thinks he likes them); he is wound up, tight and bunched, ready to pounce, fly, run, fight (usually with his colleagues), drink, screw—even write—at a moment's notice; he always takes over the best suite in hotels and shouts at the waiters; he flies first class on aeroplanes; his magazine is rich and expects huge expenses which are offset against Federal taxes; money is no object. He charters planes in the way that lesser mortals order hot dogs—and did so from Cotonou in Dahomey to fly into Biafra; it was a DC-7 (four engines, 50 seats) and cost $2000. His equipment on this occasion was an updated version of William Boot's [of Evelyn Waugh's *Scoop*]: two steel trunks, camp bed, pounds of salt, a five-liter tin of whiskey, massive supplies of canned food,

hundreds of cigarettes. He is continually sending cables, and giving messages for people to pass on.

"When you get to London, do me a favor, buddy. *Please* telephone my pseudo wife . . ." He files *frantically* when on a big story; his style of journalism works on the principle of saturation bombing; he can work all day, food, whiskey and cigarettes at his side, sweating like a lawn sprinkler. He writes thousands of words but appears content with a half a dozen good pieces in the magazine annually.

"He's off his trolley, isn't he?"

"Well, I wouldn't go as far as that, but he burns brightly, all right."

The man whom John de St. Jorre described was not off his trolley, however brightly he burned. But he was almost a caricature of the paradoxes of his profession. Under pressure, he was very much as depicted. And yet the words he produced, after all the sweating and snorting, read with grace and precision. On the surface, he appeared sometimes insensitive and hardly humane. But he had a respect for African and Asian cultures which few missionaries develop in a lifetime. For all of his bombast, he listened carefully and understood what he heard. He was as generous with favors as he was demanding. And the vast stores which he habitually brought into Biafra usually ended up as gifts.

He was hardly typical. Still, he demonstrated the one totally safe generality about foreign correspondents: they are not your average workaday drones.

All correspondents, good or bad, rely heavily on stringers to help them keep up with events. Stringers are infinite in their variety. Bionic stringers are rare; there are a lot more of the other kind. String correspondents are often hired casually—or in desperation—by passing correspondents who have few means of checking their dependability. One agency reporter needed a new stringer in Burundi, a landlocked speck of Africa next to Zaire, and he only had two days to find one. The U.S. Information Service staff had a few suggestions, but all of the candidates were too closely linked to the Burundian government. No one else wanted to risk working for an American news agency, since it was obvious that almost any story of interest out of Burundi was likely to involve embarrassing conflict or disaster. One agency stringer had already been jailed for his contributions. Finally the correspondent settled on an articulate Greek headwaiter who, if nothing else, was jolly and fearless. The man's first and last dispatch was a rambling letter in Grenglench—his inimitable melding of his own tongue with English and French—detailing which authorities' wives were doing what and with whom. (Like most stringers' copy, it went first through a correspondent—it didn't reach the news wire.)

As regular staffs shrink, the problem of finding good stringers increases. Foreigners are often reluctant to risk expulsion, and well-trained nationals are sometimes hard to find. This is particularly serious in Middle East oil states, where highly qualified nationals can make so much money doing something else that stringer earnings would hardly serve to light cigars. News organizations take who they can get. Sometimes they are lucky, but often they are not. One agency used a man named Mohammed, who was seldom heard from except when the Beirut police called the bureau for bail. He periodically came over to Lebanon to catch up on his carousing, and routinely he ended up in custody for overdoing it. One stringer filed an important oil story with no hint of a source. When asked where the information came from, he replied, surprised at the question, that his good friend the oil minister told him. Where else would it come from? And why, he wondered, was it necessary to say so in the story; didn't anyone trust him? Another was a gay European with close ties to the nobility of the country he covered. He regularly sent long reports by mail, in flowing handwritten script, about some fascinating aspects of court life.

In Africa, one stringer sent almost no news, but he kept up a steady stream of messages asking, among other things, that the agency settle his tailor bill. In one important Latin American capital, stringers for American newspapers included young travelers and spouses of regular correspondents who had firm political beliefs but little economic training. One, during a complex and important financial crisis, had to be told there was a difference between export earnings and international loans.

Nonetheless, a great many stringers provide skilled and responsible coverage at bargain rates. A few are eager young Americans who head overseas after university, too impatient to wait to be discovered and assigned abroad on a staff basis. Others are accomplished correspondents who have resigned, for one reason or another, and have stayed abroad as freelancers.

Some nationals exhibit far more loyalty to their unknown bosses thousands of miles away than do many of the correspondents who supervise them. A few in Africa and Asia risk jail terms and persecution of their families to file cables which won't earn them enough to buy groceries for the evening meal. They are driven by the same professional ethic and pride as regular correspondents but without the rewards of a good salary or of seeing their work in print.

One of the best stringers abroad is Santosh Basak, a Bengali who covers Calcutta for the AP. When a story breaks, Basak borrows time from his generous employer, the *Daily Statesman,* and goes to work. After East Pakistan rebelled, Basak spent dawn after dawn shepherding a constantly changing stream of AP men over back roads to remote border crossings. Once he almost had to wrestle a bear in the AP's service when the beast wandered into his room on a stopover as he was heading to Sikkim on a story.

The sacrifice was greater for Mean Leang, Sun Heang and Saing Hel. Known as the "Big Three," they were three Cambodian stringers for the AP who stayed in Phnom Penh as it fell to the advancing Khmer Rouge in April 1975. As the conquering armies moved in, Leang messaged on the teletype line to Hong Kong:

I ALONE IN POST OFFICE, LOSING CONTACT WITH OUR GUYS. ONLY GUY SEEING ME IS MOONFACE [a photographer] AT 1300. I HAVE SO NUMEROUS STORIES TO COVER. ONLY CALL FROM HEANG STILL AT HOTEL LE PHNOM. HEANG TOLD ME BLACK-JACKETED GUYS [Khmer Rouge] WANT HIS BIKE.

I FEEL RATHER TREMBLING. DO NOT KNOW HOW TO FILE OUT STORIES. HOW QUIET THE STREETS. EVERY MINUTE CHANGES. AT 0630 LOCAL MY WIFE CAME AND SAW ME HERE AT POST OFFICE SAYING THAT MONATIO [Khmer Rouge National Front] THREATENED MY FAMILY OUT OF THE HOUSE. . . .

APPRECIATE INSTRUCTIONS. . . . I, WITH SMALL TYPEWRITER, SHUTTLE BETWEEN THE POST OFFICE AND HOME. MAY BE LAST CABLE TODAY AND FOREVER.

There was one more cable. It went out on the AP wire like this:

WHITE FLAGS AND BANNERS OF SURRENDER FLUTTERED FROM
EVERY BUILDING IN DOWNTOWN PHNOM PENH ON THURSDAY
TO WELCOME THE BLACK-ROBED KHMER ROUGE VICTORS.

THE FIRST REBEL TROOPS CAME IN FROM THE NORTH. THEY
PARKED THEIR ARMORED VEHICLES BY THE MUNICIPAL STADIUM
AND WALKED TRIUMPHANTLY SOUTH IN GROUPS OF THREE OR
FOUR ALONG A BOULEVARD BY THE TONLE SAP RIVER . . .

Despite efforts to locate them for years afterward, that was the last
the AP heard from, or about, the Big Three.

5

The Photographers

One of the most dramatic photographs of the Vietnam war showed a nine-year-old girl running hysterically down Highway One, her clothing burned off by billowing napalm. That picture, ironically, almost didn't make it to the newspapers.

AP photographer Nick Ut was near Trang Bang when South Vietnamese skyraiders dropped napalm too far behind front lines and burned civilians. He brought back dozens of pictures showing women and children trying desperately to escape the inferno while others watched in horror. Ut left them at the bureau and went back to work. Four correspondents (I was one, I admit reluctantly, but I'll spare the others) each suggested the ones they thought should be radioed to New York for distribution. No one chose the picture of the girl, Kim Phuoc. Horst Faas, the photo editor, picked it out immediately as the first of a series of four. We argued, and several correspondents accused Faas of selecting a secondary picture because of jealousy; one warned that editors might think the girl was too old to be shown naked. Faas insisted, and the picture was sent. The photo not only won every major photographic prize—including the Pulitzer—but also Senator George McGovern adopted it to dramatize his anti-war campaign for the presidency. So much for correspondents second-guessing photographers.

Photographers and photo editors, a whole different bunch of madmen, are as important to the system as reporters. Their job is often harder; and frequently they have greater impact. A lingering prejudice against photographers still remains from the earlier days of domestic reporting when many of them just tailed along behind reporters to shoot what they were told. That stereotype never fit the photographer working overseas, and, as more and more cameramen operate independently of correspondents, it is even further from the truth today.*

A responsible news sense is as important in selecting the right photograph to tell a story as it is in choosing the right words. Pictures can lie, exaggerate or distort in the same way as stories. Sometimes a photograph is the only means of relaying information accurately— or powerfully. Reporters in Nigeria during the civil war wrote about starving babies time and again, but they evoked little interest in the United States. Then *Life* magazine carried a photo spread showing the infants' distended bellies and matchstick limbs, and suddenly the war was headline news. Ancient Chinese wisdom noted that a picture is worth a thousand words; in today's international reporting, a good picture can outdo 100,000.

Unlike correspondents, there are only two types of photographers. There are the good ones, who consistently get the pictures which tell the story. And there are the mediocre ones, who spend a lot of time looking for work. Individual motivations and inner reactions differ widely, of course, but the nature of their work automatically weeds out the inept, the timid and the dishonest.

A reporter who is not present at a major event, for whatever reason, can always get by with sources, clever writing and generous colleagues. But a photographer who misses the picture has blown his assignment, and no excuse can cover the failure. Photographers use their cameras in the same way reporters use notebooks. All impressions are recorded—not just the obvious ones with immediate impact —in case they may be of value later. A reporter, though, can always sit down over a Jack Daniels and reconstruct things in his mind, expanding on his notes. A photographer cannot. Beyond that, a photographer must build his story in the same way as a reporter. He has to visualize what he wants to say and how he wants to say it. But while a correspondent can cast about in his lexicon, without moving from the typewriter, to come up with the right words, a photographer must go out and find his "lead paragraph" and major points.

---

*"Cameramen" usually refers to television crews who shoot news film rather than photographers who take still pictures. Since their problems are so different—and so closely tied with the general problems of television news coverage—they will be discussed separately in Chapter 9.

A photographer must know how to deliver the right pictures, whatever that might mean. If the story is too big for him to handle alone, he has to know when to stop and to act as an editor. Instead of just shooting, he then has to marshal stringers, buy pictures from local newspapers and agencies or scrounge up whatever he can from amateurs. If he does his own shooting, he must surround the story. Film is cheap, and some photographers shoot 100 rolls on a one-week feature assignment. And each frame must say something, with attention to expressions, background and overall effect. Professionals make pictures; amateurs take them.

News organizations usually keep a separate staff of photo editors. Editing pictures and making them are separate skills entirely. (Some people do both, but seldom at the same time.) Often photographers do not even know what they have in their cameras when they finish an assignment, and only an editor with experience can skim over hundreds of frames to find what he needs. On big stories, an editor might handle film from a half dozen photographers and photo stringers. But, however good an editor might be, if the material is not there, he will not find it.

The best photographers have at least two things in common: they are deeply moved by the worst part of the world, and they can detach themselves enough to treat it irreverently.* But, whatever their surface callousness, it does get to them.

Faas and Michel Laurent won a Pulitzer Prize in 1972 for pictures of Bengalis bayoneting and applying lighted cigarettes to terrified Bihari prisoners in Bangladesh. Pushed so close by crowds that they had to use 21-mm wide-angle lenses, they crouched near the murderers and torturers waiting for fleeting moments which depicted the horror most dramatically.

"My hands were trembling so much I could hardly change film—but we had no time to think about it," said Faas, a stolid German with a thick veneer of gruffness. "The shock came later. It was terrible." Laurent, a gentle Parisian with none of the Faas-type bravado, said

*Legend tells of the well-known news agency photographer who returned to his hotel in Calcutta and remarked, "God, it was awful. There was this horrible-looking old lady, bent and covered with sores. She kept reaching her hand out to me." "What did you give her?" "About f/8 at a 500th of a second."

he was sick to his stomach and had to force himself to keep working. The Bangladesh pictures raised an important issue for news photographers. There were suggestions that the photographers' presence was the reason for the torture. One French cartoon showed the incident, with one photographer shouting, "Not so fast." Faas and Laurent just shrugged off the charges, but both were hurt by them.* Each told me independently that as the brutality started they at first covered their lenses and turned away; the torturers did not even notice them. It is a professional—and a human—responsibility for photographers to be certain that they are not affecting the scenes they are picturing.

Such questions of ethics and professionalism are as important to photographers as they are to reporters. The ideal Bionic Correspondent has a counterpart with a camera. Faas and Laurent come as close as any to the category.

Both Faas and Laurent decided as teenagers to be news photographers. Faas got a job in his native Berlin with the Keystone photo agency, and then, in the early 1950s he went to work for the AP, based in Frankfurt. He produced dramatic pictures of turmoil in the Congo and Algeria, and by the time he reached Vietnam in 1961, he was respected among fellow newsmen. Two Pulitzers and a trunkful of awards later, after covering every type of story on four continents, he was perhaps the best-known news photographer in the world.

On assignment, behind twin black Leicaflexes, Faas thinks of nothing but the picture he needs—and how to get it. Once at a summit meeting in Singapore, he had to share a small raised platform with a number of others covering airport arrivals. Crowded out of position, Faas calmly left a wake of sprawling, bruised photographers wondering how such a lumbering hulk could move elbows and hips with such deft and deadly accuracy. Later, tailing Edward Heath's yacht in a bobbing sampan, Faas produced exclusive pictures of the austere British prime minister disporting with a bikini-clad lovely. When necessary, he barks orders in his Kissingerian accent with all the tactful grace of a grizzly bear heading for his first lunch after hibernation. When the work is over, Faas can become someone else entirely. He does not even have a camera of his own, and he doesn't talk about pictures. He is an art-loving bon vivant who, in the right mood, can

*Laurent did not carry his pain for long. He was killed in the final days of the Vietnam war, going up one more road.

shrug when his cat knocks over a rare Chinese vase.*

Faas's formula is obvious to anyone watching him. He gets up early, works hard and takes five times more pictures than most others. When he can, he stands far back, unnoticed, and shoots with a telephoto lens. "The main thing," Faas says of his profession, "is to always be on top of a story, to be a part of it, without getting involved in it. There is no good concerned photographer. But no photographer is good if he is unconcerned."

Michel Laurent wandered into the AP's Paris bureau as a fifteen-year-old kid who had trouble at school and wanted to make pictures. He was hired as an office boy. Laurent worked his way through the photo library, the darkroom and the transmission desk, scraping together enough money for cameras and selling the AP freelance pictures on the side. At nineteen, he was hired as a photographer.

No one knew what to make of Laurent when he showed up on a story. He looked like an underfed underage urchin, with the face of a Botticelli cherub and the hairdo of an uncombed Angela Davis. At first glance, it looked as though a loud "boo!" and a gust of wind would undo him. But that impression never lasted long. Laurent had nerves of magnesium, and he would go anywhere his fertile imagination suggested might produce a picture. In Dacca, Pakistani troops putting down an uprising with massive gunfire ordered all newsmen out of the country on pain of death. "If I can kill my own people," one officer said, "I can kill you." Laurent quickly yanked his registration card out of the hotel file and hid in the kitchen to stay behind. He was discovered and expelled twenty-four hours later, but he managed to sneak out the only pictures of the assault. In Ceylon, when everyone else speculated about young rebels somewhere in the

---

*Faas's split-level personality sometimes throws people off track. Once, during a customary lengthy liquid lunch at Saigon's Hotel Royale, a British journalist asked him why he liked to cover the war. The reporter was a serious-minded but beautiful young woman, and Faas was in top form. He replied, "I like the boom-boom," with a suggestive motion and a wink to friends that made it clear he was not referring to incoming artillery. The reporter had seen him at work, and the remark made sense. Missing the double entendre, she quoted him in an article. When Phillip Knightley wrote his book on war correspondents, *The First Casualty,* the quote came back, "Vot I like eez boom-boom, oh yes," as an indication of Faas's presumed bloodthirstiness.

bush, he hopped in a canoe and found them. He didn't look like other newsmen, and many teased him mercilessly. But no professional ever disparaged his work.

In the early 1970s, Laurent accepted a share in the French photo agency Gamma. He was shooting pictures for his new agency when North Vietnamese troops, making their final advance on Saigon, sprayed him with automatic weapons fire as he went out to photograph them.

The war also killed Kyoichi Sawada of UPI, one of the most talented and best-liked photographers to work in Indochina. Sawada won the 1966 Pulitzer Prize for a picture of a woman refugee struggling to get her children across a swollen river in Vietnam. Afterward, he tracked her down and shared the prize money. Sawada first worked in the photo shop at a U.S. Army post exchange in his native Japan during the occupation. In 1960, he got a job with UPI in Tokyo and was soon a picture editor. He was assigned to Vietnam in 1965. He was captured by communist troops in Cambodia in October 1970, but was released without explanation eight hours later. A few months later, Sawada was killed going up the road.

The AP's Neal Ulevich became a photographer in Vietnam because, he says, it was the easiest way to avoid starvation. He was drawn to Indochina as an aspiring reporter and a dilettante Asia scholar. But he could only find work taking pictures. Driven by a professional sense and a distaste for mediocrity, Ulevich threw himself into his new job. He would lug a bagful of Nikons with him on brief rest trips to Singapore and Hong Kong, snapping pictures constantly because, he said, it relaxed him. The AP hired him in Saigon and then sent him as regional photo editor to Bangkok, where he won a Pulitzer for pictures of lynching and violence during the military coup in 1976. Ulevich, with slightly rounded lines, a friendly mustache and scholarly wire-rimmed glasses, fits no one's stereotype of a hotshot news photographer. But, with the best of them, he scampers atop cars, sneaks through doorways and bulls through crowds when the job demands. "It does not take brilliance but rather hard work and attention to detail," he says of a photographer's work. "You have to do all the little jobs yourself if you want to see it done right."

The changing economics of newsgathering are sending foreign-based staff photographers toward extinction. Major news stories break too infrequently, over too much of the world, for any organization to keep a large international staff abroad. Were there a sudden coup d'état in Brazil, editors might welcome the work of any amateur in town with a reasonably able body and a Kodak Instamatic. But under normal circumstances, no organization distributes more than a handful of pictures a month from Brazil.

News organizations have found different ways to assure coverage. AP and UPI, which produce most of the foreign pictures published in the United States, depend heavily on locally hired photographers. Neither agency keeps more than a few American photographers or editors based abroad. Each uses some foreigners on an international staff who might be transferred from bureau to bureau. And each uses proven regulars who hurry out of American cities for big stories. But most of their photographers are nationals of the countries they cover. It is more practical to let local photographers or stringers handle the first hours—or even days—of a breaking story until help can arrive from the nearest headquarters bureau. In any case, chances are that the best pictures will come from local cameramen, who know the customs, language and the people involved in a breaking story. For scheduled events, staff photographers can be dispatched in advance. Even with locally hired photographers, less than half of all foreign pictures distributed by AP and UPI are made by people on the payroll. A majority comes from subscribing newspapers, government or independent agencies, stringers or other sources.

The newsmagazines and major newspapers all subscribe to AP and UPI, but they often prefer to have their own photographers cover major stories. They can count on the news agencies to deliver the standard pictures—chiefs of state shaking hands at a summit, the fallen leader in his casket—but often agency photographers don't have the time to step back for the dramatic sidelight that adds a different perspective to the story. When the agencies do produce especially moving pictures of an event, the same photos go to everyone, and some editors want exclusive material. When magazines and big papers have a staff photographer nearby, they will send him. But, more and more, they depend on specialized photo agencies and top-quality stringers. Organizations like Magnum in New York and Gamma and Sygma in Paris have dozens of expert photographers available for special assignments. For between $75 and $200, these agencies provide exclusive coverage. The work is often better than what might be expected from a staff man at a fraction of the cost. Also, the special agencies keep vast libraries of negatives supplied by free-lancers in every part of the world.

Not only the specialized agencies but also AP and UPI depend to a great degree on an irregular army of travelers with cameras who show up in trouble spots and major news centers. These photographers might be talented young professionals out to prove themselves or they might be impoverished adventurers hoping for disaster to befall the country they are touring so they can scrape up enough earnings to go on to the next. Sometimes they are the only newsgatherers of any type to cover little-known stories in remote places, and they may be the only ones willing to gamble the time and money. It is a hard life. News agencies might pay as little as $20 for even an exceptional picture, hardly covering a day's film costs, much less plane tickets, lodging and time. One of the first persons to travel with the Eritrean guerrillas in Ethiopia was a South American photographer of proven ability. He spent five months lining up the trip, ferreting out contacts among exiles in the slums of Khartoum and slogging through the bush just ahead of government troops. His ticket and expenses came to $3500. When he returned to New York with a mountain of exclusive pictures, one newsmagazine photo editor gave them a brief glance and observed, "This stuff looks like basic training at Fort Dix. Sorry, we can't use it." He didn't sell anything.

Freelancers work in a variety of ways. Some sell to the highest bidder whenever they can. Others try to supply a single agency to build their reputations and establish continuity. Normally, news agencies pay a fixed amount—perhaps $15 to $50—for a usable news photograph. If someone catches the Eiffel Tower toppling, there are few limits; but most pictures are routine. Often freelancers are contracted by the day or the week to shoot only for one organization. One enterprising photographer in Vietnam was hired to cover for *Time* and *Newsweek* at the same time, but he did not bother to advise either of the arrangement. He simply put two cameras around his neck, each with a large, clear label: "Time" and "Newsweek." When the *Newsweek* correspondent happened to see him, he jerked the label with the name of his magazine off the man's camera and growled, "Not any more."

Often correspondents are pressed into service as photographers. Some know what to do and come up with excellent pictures. Others are sent out with a loaded Nikon and the famous Horst Faas instruction: "Just give it 500 at f/11 and I save you in the darkroom."

As a group, photographers earn respect for courage alone. More than sixty newspeople have been killed since 1954 reporting abroad, and most of them were taking pictures or shooting news film. Prudence is seldom a factor in deciding how best to picture a story. In a riot, the camera range is generally shorter than the distance a rioter can throw a rock. In battle, if a photographer keeps his head down all the time, it means he must also keep his lens down. A telephoto lens poking over a roof ledge looks like a bazooka to soldiers on the ground. The privacy laws which bedevil photographers in the United States do not normally apply abroad; instead, in many places a reluctant subject simply has soldiers or political thugs thump the photographer.

Photographers never know when they might run into trouble. An agency man taking some background pictures of public buildings before an African summit in Kinshasa was arrested by soldiers. He argued that no sign prohibited photographs. "In the Congo," replied an officer, "if there is no sign saying pictures are allowed, they are prohibited."

Typically, photographers don't talk about death or risk. Those are constants which each handles in his own way. Faas spent eight years in Vietnam plowing into action which terrified lesser men. When he decided he had reached the point where he was pushing his luck, he left the war for other assignments. Photographers do not always have the choice. Stories break without warning, and they must be off in minutes, with portable darkrooms and enough film to stay for months. Larry Burrows, *Life* magazine's old Asia hand, was working leisurely in Calcutta making pictures of museum pieces for a story on the British empire. He was sent suddenly back to Vietnam and, almost overnight, he was lying dead in the smoking remains of a helicopter.

At times, assignments are far less dangerous than they seem. A photographer can never be sure of his subjects' reaction to the camera. Rick Merron, illustrating a story on GI drug use in Vietnam, was prepared for weeks of risky surreptitious work to get a single picture of illicit dealing. But on his first day, at an infantry barracks where heroin was being passed around like chewing gum, he decided to go for broke. He nervously revealed a camera and, before anyone could grab him, quickly suggested he might photograph only hands exchanging cellophane bags. He assured that all faces would be thrown far out of focus. One of the men protested: "Why, man? No one'll be able to see me then."

In most cases, the danger of making pictures is less of a problem than the difficulty in getting them back to editors. The more urgent the story, the more acute the difficulty. On feature and background assignments, photographers can carry their work back themselves or airfreight it to the nearest bureau. If they must forgo some pictures, they can get by with others. But important news pictures have to be rushed off immediately, and that means, if at all possible, transmitted by radio or satellite. Photographs can be sent over regular telephone circuits, from anywhere to anywhere, using simple equipment which relays electronic impulses in the same way that voices are carried. It takes fifteen minutes—or less—to send a picture. The catch is that a photographer needs a transmitter and a reliable telephone line. Major bureaus have their own sending equipment with full-time leased circuits, and many cities have commercial facilities for transmitting pictures just like regular telegrams. Often photographers carry their own portable transmitters, and they can usually persuade local engineers to help. But many times a photographer has no way to send his photos, and he must spend hours or days getting his film onto an airplane headed toward the nearest transmitter. Chartering planes and charming stewardesses are the easy ways. Sometimes dispatching film can mean driving under heavy shellfire, smuggling exposed rolls past belligerent soldiers or persuading strangers to alter their travel plans.

On the biggest stories, the problems multiply and intensify by geometric proportion. When the army moved against Chilean president Salvador Allende in 1973, every newspaper in the world was screaming for pictures. The news agency correspondents, who were busy enough trying to cover the bloody coup d'état and get word to the outside over blocked communications channels, had to find some way to provide photos as well. Neither had staff photographers. UPI had a full-time contract stringer who had just arrived from Argentina, and he photographed part of the dramatic assault on Moneda Palace from the bureau window overlooking a main plaza. But, before he could develop his film in the strange darkroom, bullets began peppering the office, and the staff was pinned to the floor for hours. Once inside the lab, the stringer couldn't find fixer for his film. When a faltering phone line was finally established to Argentina, and he reported his predicament to the photo editor, the editor yelled, "Piss on it! Just piss on it!" He did, and that solved at least one problem.

Then, when he had prints ready to transmit, he could not get a line, and it was days before he could send anything. Meanwhile, AP bureau chief Bob Ohman, from his office farther away, dodged tanks and bullets to get photos from Santiago daily newspapers. One paper, expecting a coup, had kept photographers for weeks in a room overlooking the official residence. They produced vivid pictures of the palace in flames and of firemen carrying Allende's body from the building. Like the UPI man, Ohman had a working transmitter and pictures to send—but no line. Finally, the photo editor in Buenos Aires charmed the overnight telephone operator into giving the AP one of two barely functioning circuits over the Andes to Santiago, giving him priority over 2000 other requests. Ohman held the line for two hours, transmitting four fuzzy but graphic pictures of the siege. The next day, a Buenos Aires photographer flew to Mendoza, in the Andean foothills, with a portable transmitter. With the help of a local newspaper's radiophoto receiver, he engineered an emergency relay system, and Ohman moved another seventeen pictures during the next twenty-four hours.

After the initial assault, picture taking was extremely hazardous because of trigger-happy soldiers, and photos were sometimes poorly focused. Each was processed hurriedly, and whenever a line opened it was sent to Mendoza over a failing line across the snow-covered Andes. It was received on aging equipment and then sent again on a portable machine to Buenos Aires. From there, it was transmitted a third time, going by satellite to New York. A sleepless technician in Buenos Aires kept the system working, marveling at the quality under the circumstances and praying that the precarious set-up—defying all logic and government intention—would not suddenly collapse. UPI still had not been able to transmit a single picture, so the photos were exclusive. Things were fine until a New York editor, used to receiving crystal-clear pictures by high-grade channels from Tokyo and London, cut in: "These are lousy. Why don't you hang up and call the guy back?" After an ear-rattling barrage of bilingual abuse, he decided he had better take what he had.

Although AP won that round, the UPI stringer got his own back on the next coup—in Argentina. Military officers carried Isabel Perón away from the pink official mansion in a helicopter that was parked on the roof. Almost every photographer crowded in close to police lines to try for a shot of the president boarding the helicopter. But the UPI man moved far back, and he produced the most dramatic photo of the coup. He showed Argentines in the foreground waving to the departing helicopter. Everyone else had only a meaningless helicopter and a roof ledge.

The frantic pace of news photography sometimes causes monumental mistakes. One classic case involved Dennis Lee Royle* of the AP and a UPI man. They were assigned to cover the Dalai Lama as he emerged from Tibet in 1959 after its unsuccessful rebellion against China. Both had chartered planes and set up motorcycle relays for a frenzied race from where the spiritual leader would first cross the border out of Chinese territory to the nearest transmitter in India. The Dalai Lama appeared, after a long wait, and the mad scramble began. It was a close finish, but the UPI photographer won. He immediately began sending picture after picture, tying up the only available line for hours. By the time Royle could transmit to New York, the first UPI picture was already in print in the United States. Royle checked into his hotel, dejected. Suddenly he got a cable reading something like "Opposition's Dalai Lama has long shaggy hair. Yours bald. How please?" And he messaged back, "Because my Dalai right Dalai." The UPI man, in his haste, had assumed that the hirsute interpreter was the Dalai Lama. He wasn't.

Like so many others, the Dalai Lama story depended upon logistics. Barring mistakes, the "winner" is the one who gets to the story first and gets his material to a relay point. It is as true for correspondents as for photographers. Logistics—travel, communications and general resourcefulness—are a cornerstone of the system.

*Another first-rate professional who was killed on assignment; he was in a helicopter which crashed off Britain.

6

Getting to the Story— and Getting It Out

Richard Harding Davis did not mess around when he went off to cover a battle. In one war, his kit was a large cart, two oxen, three Basuto ponies, one Australian horse, three servants and 400 pounds of supplies and baggage, including, of course, his collapsible rubber bathtub. Today's correspondent would love to travel that way—if only he could get it all under an airline seat.

In 1897, ample stores were essential, Davis explained, to ease access to staff officers and to placate censors: "If, when a man halted at your tent, you could not stand him whiskey and sparklet soda, Egyptian cigarettes, compressed soup, canned meats and marmalade, your paper was suspected of trying to do it 'on the cheap,' not only of being mean, but, as this was an unpopular war [the particular campaign he was describing], unpatriotic." These days a correspondent can entertain with a small plastic card, and all he really needs is a passport, a few extra socks, some antibiotics and a telegraph charge plate. If he cannot get from place to place in a hurry and then quickly dispatch material to an editor somewhere, he is in the wrong business.

For tourists used to Pan Am schedules and telephone booths, a correspondent's logistical problems are almost unimaginable. But these difficulties exert an enormous influence on what eventually gets reported, and allowances must be made for them when trying to make sense out of coverage. Some cases are obvious. A hijacking in which an airliner hopscotches across desert airfields can only be covered in

79

bits and pieces. But, at least in some small way, virtually every story is affected by the problems of getting to it and getting it to an editor.

To begin with, correspondents are always pressed for time. Deadlines are stipulated in hours and minutes. On the biggest of stories, an agency man endures shame if he trails his competitor by seconds. A resourceful reporter shaves time every way he can. At airports, he figures out where to sit on the plane and the shuttle bus to beat everyone else through customs. His distracted gaze moves like a minesweeper, taking note of telephones in cafes, taxi stands, corner policemen and one-way streets. During moments of calm, he lavishes flowers and tall drinks on the telephone operators who might later have to be persuaded to stay up half the night trying to clear a line to London. When it comes time to move fast, he'll bribe, cheat, lie, scream or make a pact with the nearest devil without a moment's pause.

During the Biafra war, two radio correspondents with urgent stories were stranded in a backwater town when they suddenly saw a plane circle to land. They rushed up to find it was an ambulance plane piloted by an old mercenary they knew from an earlier war. "Hey," yelled one, "got room for a couple of reporters?" The pilot boomed back, "Sure, we always got room for a couple of reporters. We'll just offload a few wounded." (The correspondents, who accepted the ride, insist that they saw no one left behind.)

A correspondent learns quickly that impossibility is a relative concept. With enough determination, imagination and money, almost anything can be done. It might mean flying 8000 miles to Europe and back to travel between Bangui and Kampala, two African capitals separated only by a few hundred miles of jungle. Or it might require talking a lot of people into doing things they are not happy about doing. To a correspondent, the first few "no's" are seldom final.

Reporters are pushed not only by their own competitive manias but also by their editors' obsessions with being first and fullest, however that may affect the overall reportage of a breaking story. Ethics require a correspondent to wait long enough to be certain of his basic facts, but there is no rule about understanding the background. When a major story develops in a remote area, readers and viewers can expect truncated bits and pieces, which should be absorbed only tentatively until correspondents have a chance to catch their breath and write wrap-ups. Logically, a reporter should stay with a story until it reaches some definable denouement, and then he should explain it at length before going on to the next stage. Some newspaper and magazine correspondents have the luxury of doing just that. But often reporters must snatch whatever they can and then devote their full energies to getting something out in time for the last editions.

A vivid example was the Green March in the winter of 1975, when 350,000 Moroccans gathered on the Spanish Sahara border. King Hassan II had announced that his people would march in and seize the phosphate-producing colony if Spain did not accede to Morocco's territorial claim. Civilians were trucked down a ten-foot-wide tarmac road to the desert frontier, where they waited in makeshift tent camps. To cover the march, the AP put 7500 miles on seven different rented vehicles over four weeks. Photographer Michel Lipschitz drove 600 miles round trip, weaving through truck convoys the whole way, to transmit a single photograph. Reporter Paul Treuthardt took a full hour to dictate a six-paragraph story, letter by letter, to a colleague at the other end of a shaky radiotelephone line. Engineers put a faltering telex circuit in from the fly-blown border outpost of Tarfaya, but, among other problems, a sandstorm covered a relay station. Treuthardt heard about a telex line in Tan Tan, 150 miles away, and he rushed there just in time to dispatch his stories before it went out of service, never to function again.

Newsmen had to crash through roadblocks and blaze trails in the sands. Coverage was especially hard for television crews, who had to get news film back to their networks. The networks had teamed up for a relay system: a car from Tarfaya to Tan Tan, a light plane to Agadir and then a chartered Boeing to take film to London at $9000 a trip. They were undone by their own ingenuity. The Moroccan television man entrusted with driving the film to Tan Tan did not believe that anyone could organize a charter flight from there to Agadir. He decided that, instead of wasting time driving out to the Tan Tan landing strip, he would race the film straight to Agadir in his car. The airliner did not wait.

Under those sorts of conditions, reporting reflects more the inventiveness of news people—and the acts of God—than the news itself.

The off-and-on mercenary wars of the Congo provided countless examples. At one point, in 1967, white rebels led by a Belgian planter had occupied the lakeside town of Bukavu, and the only way to reach them was through Cyangugu, across the lake in the neighboring country of Rwanda. To get to Cyangugu, reporters had to fly to Entebbe, Uganda, and then catch a twice-weekly milk run to Kigali, capital of Rwanda. From Kigali, bush charters could be hired to fly to Cyangugu for a few hundred dollars. The trick was getting by the Rwandan border guards, who had orders to let no one pass. Some crossed the cold, treacherous waters at night in inner tubes, risking fire from guards on both sides. Others managed to sneak by the border police as they dozed after lunch. One enterprising Belgian reporter took the band off of a Corps Diplomatique cigar—a gold-embossed "CD"—and pasted it to his briefcase. He walked smartly up to the border post, pointed to the tiny paper emblem and said, "Diplomat." The guard saluted and waved him through. For months, only a trickle of reporters made the Rwanda run. But when the Red Cross suddenly announced that the mercenaries had surrendered and were in an internment camp in Cyangugu, there was a frantic scramble.

At the time of the announcement, virtually every foreign correspondent based in the Congo was on a guided tour in Katanga (Shaba) Province, which, they realized later, was a diversionary tactic by the government right out of Evelyn Waugh's parody. They were bottled up far from Kinshasa, from where the only flights to central Africa were possible. The AP man first heard about the surrender on a one A.M. radio broadcast. In desperation, he woke up the hotel clerk to see if he could suggest any way to reach Rwanda. As a matter of fact, the clerk replied, the man in the next room was piloting a chartered cargo flight to Kigali in four hours—the first flight between the two cities in months. By daybreak, the correspondent, straddled across a crate of cigarettes, landed in Kigali. He had no health card or luggage, and it took several hours to convince authorities he was not a diseased spy. But he soon found a charter pilot willing to go to Cyangugu despite a raging storm. The plane grazed a mountaintop and was briefly forced down on an emergency jungle strip, but the reporter reached the border town by late afternoon.

The first person he saw in Cyangugu was an AP photographer who had been hanging around hoping to cadge a ride out. The photographer, a stocky Frenchman with a tough-looking mustache, had managed to sneak into the internment camp and stay there, pretending to be a mercenary. He had taken pictures with a Leica hidden under his raincoat until a snarling Belgian officer in the Rwandan army walked up to him at random. "We understand there is a photographer in here," he said. "You seen the bastard?" The photographer, pressing the concealed camera tightly against his stomach, promised to be on guard for the sneaky son of a bitch and then he beat a hasty retreat.

The correspondent and the cameraman spent the night outside after missionaries and local residents refused to let them in for fear of reprisals by authorities suspicious of strangers. At daybreak, they persuaded the airport control tower to radio for their charter pilot to return from Kigali, and they headed for Entebbe, the nearest point where they could telex stories and ship film. They climbed into their plane just as the first batch of their competitors arrived from Nairobi. The reporter ended up staying in Uganda for another story, going on to Kenya for a conference and then flying farther north to Ethiopia for a visit by the Shah of Iran before returning home to Katanga three weeks later from his overnight trip.

Unorthodox displacement is routine. A photographer covering the 2500th anniversary of the Persian throne in 1973 found that the erratic shuttle service between the press camp and the main pavilions made it impossible to get pictures out fast enough. So whenever he needed to make the trip he simply hot-wired a handy Mercedes-Benz and stole it. Since he took a different car each time, no one caught him —and no one could figure out how officials' cars kept ending up at the wrong end of the road.*

When Bengali rebels declared their separation from Pakistan in 1971, authorities in the eastern wing reacted with bloody repression, sealing off the capital, Dacca, to all travelers. Hordes of reporters waited around Calcutta, in neighboring India, making sporadic forays across the border but grumbling at not being able to get to the real story in Dacca. Dennis Neeld and Michel Laurent, a redoubtable correspondent-photographer team for the AP, decided to go overland. They spent two days in rickshaws, canoes, borrowed trucks and on foot, playing hide-and-seek with Pakistani soldiers who had orders to shoot on sight. They finally reached Dacca, spent the night looking

---

*This particular photographer was not timid. In one capital, the blaring noise from a garden party at his hotel kept him awake, and he complained. The desk said it was a royal ball, with the monarch himself as host, and nothing could be done. He took his insulated pliers, sneaked down to the garden and snipped off the power supply, thus ending the party.

over the city and talking with sources they felt they could trust, and then made their way back. Even though nearly a week had passed, no one else had made it in. Their words and pictures were the first real evidence of the atrocities that were going on in what was about to become Bangladesh.

If he is lucky, a correspondent can travel and report at the same time. When General Antonio de Spinola left Portugal after a coup attempt in 1976, word circulated that he was expected to pass through Brazil, perhaps en route to Argentina. As everyone else speculated on ways to interview him at the airport, Dennis Redmont of the AP figured out what airplane the general would have to be on and bought a first-class ticket on it from Rio to Buenos Aires. He boarded the plane and found Spinola sitting there with two aides. As soon as the aircraft took off—and it was too late to throw him off—he walked over and introduced himself in elegant Portuguese. By the time he landed, he had an exclusive story ready to dictate to the bureau in Buenos Aires.

Major exclusives can take considerably more sacrifice. Little was known about guerrilla operations in Angola during 1977, so Leon Dash of the Washington *Post* set out to fill the gap. He walked for 505 miles, over six weeks, until he found the headquarters of Jonas Savimbi, leader of the Union for the Total Independence of Angola (UNITA). Dash, a thirty-three-year-old black who spoke fluent Swahili, joined the rebels and emerged seven months later with vivid accounts of battle and life among the leeches and razor-sharp elephant grass.

Sometimes a correspondent outsmarts himself. During one round of Cyprus troubles, an agency reporter hurried to the seaport from where he expected the Turkish fleet to sail. He got there in ample time for authorities to confine him to his hotel room, with no phone, and he watched helplessly as Turkish ships steamed past his window. And that was just the first blow. A late-arriving competitor saw the fleet's departure and reported it. The first man's desk, desperate for a matching story, phoned the hotel long distance and asked to talk with anyone who spoke English. The hotel clerk obligingly passed the phone to the correspondent of the rival agency who was only too happy to help: Ships? What ships? I didn't see any ships.

Getting to a story is only half of the problem—and not always the easier half. The story must be sent somewhere. At times, that can mean waiting for hours to have a dispatch transmitted, with misspellings and dropped words, over a faltering Morse code circuit. Filing copy, as sending stories is called, can be simple. Some foreign bureaus have computerized consoles; reporters write directly onto an electronic screen and, by touching a few buttons, send their stories instantaneously to their editor's desk thousands of miles away. (Of course, reporters can also hit the wrong button and erase two hours' work in a split second.) In other big bureaus, news agencies lease 24-hour circuits to their headquarters, and they often share them with special correspondents. Operators punch the copy, so a correspondent need worry only about typing clearly and remembering a Christmas gift. For brief items, many cities have direct dial telephones and automatic telex exchanges. But modern technology can be deceptive, and even the easy ways to file can send peaceful men into fits of rage. The unwritten Law of Communications is that failures invariably occur during breaking urgent stories. Computer lapses can send scores of thousands of words disappearing forever into the vapor. Lines can suddenly break or cause unreadable garble. Writing about general strikes in Rome or Paris is no fun if one of the struck services is telecommunications.

Away from major bases, correspondents never know what to expect. China's Chou En-lai once gave a surprise news conference during a visit to Katmandu. The Nepalese telegraph clerks, used to the odd ten-word cable from a relaxed doper or an easygoing businessman, suddenly found themselves awash in reporters, all pounding the table and demanding that their 1500-word dispatches be rushed off immediately. The clerks were so flustered that, instead of telegraphing any of the stories, they baled them all up together and put them aboard a slow plane to New Delhi. Several correspondents got home before their stories did.

When the African republic of Equatorial Guinea was about to become independent from Spain, an agency correspondent was delighted to find the post office could transmit stories. It had a dot-dash sender with an antenna strung across nine palm trees out back. He filed a leisurely, rambling piece, rich in history and local color, and found out only later—from a ranting editor—that the cost was a dollar a word.

And at one African summit meeting, an agency laid out great sums to lease a full-time circuit to Brussels which transmitted at the painfully slow rate of 15 words a minute. The lone correspondent was so tired at the end of the day that he punched his main story on perforated tape and left it coiled partly on the floor, running through the transmitter by itself while he went home to sleep. Four minutes after he left, a janitor came through and, muttering something about sloppy foreigners, picked up the roll of tape, unwittingly ripping it off the machine, and the story was lost.

In the Congo, one correspondent couldn't get a telex for an important story, so he paid an enormous amount to duplicate his dispatch by cable at the urgent rate, twice the regular cost. The clerk counted the words, charged him and went to the pneumatic tube to send the cable upstairs for transmission. The vacuum system had broken down long before, however, so engineers had run a string through the tube with a clip at the end. When the clerk had a telegram, he banged on the tube with an otherwise useless carrier. That was Friday night. The correspondent happened to walk by Monday morning, and he found his urgent message still dangling at the end of the string.

Communications people in underdeveloped countries are not the only ones to screw up transmissions. When Saigon fell, one correspondent sent ten takes—successive pages of a cabled story—from the communications center on an American evacuation ship. He did not learn until it was too late that only the last five reached his newsroom.

Sometimes a correspondent can make a slipshod system work in his favor. In Laos, one reporter slipped his copy ahead of a huge stack of waiting cables by giving it to the operator one paragraph at a time, with a crisp banknote wrapped around each page. The harassed clerk was almost as happy to get the short, easily dispatched takes as he was to get the money.

During political upheavals, communications can be impossible. When reporters heard that one well-known Latin-American president was about to be overthrown, they scrambled to set up protective communications. Two agencies considered buying a small clandestine transmitter but decided that it would be better to be late with the story than to have someone shot as a guerrilla. U.S. embassy officials told correspondents that they could not accept copy on their special channels. But one kindly officer agreed to a compromise. He would send a message reading, "Your man advises he cannot transmit copy because new government under General Whomever has shut down all communications." With that, an alert desk editor could write a 500-word story.

The Lebanon civil war was a supreme test of ingenuity and courage. For a while, Palestine guerrillas were operating the post office as usual. The only hitch was that correspondents had to dodge sniper fire across a 200-yard open field of fire to get there. One French reporter made the run so fast that he spun out his car on the far turn and crashed into the post office building. Later, communications between Lebanon and Western Europe remained open, but local lines to the transmission station were out. An enterprising businessman found a way to make the link, and he charged correspondents a usurious rate. He softened the blow by installing his gorgeous daughter as cashier.

Even carrier pigeons are still occasionally pressed into service. One British reporter who tried using pigeons for the first time on a story in South Africa hurriedly thumbed through his copy of *How to Use Pigeons* (or whatever), stuffed his microscopically written dispatch into the bird's leg capsule and threw him into the air. The pigeon plummeted to the ground and began walking slowly toward home. The correspondent chased after it, waving his arms and shouting and, finally, throwing rocks at the bird to get it to take flight. He discovered later that he had skipped over the page about feeding. Pigeons home, among other reasons, to eat; they fly on empty stomachs. The reporter, figuring the bird had a long way to go, fed him an enormous feast prior to take-off, and the bird could hardly flap its wings.

Today's correspondents don't normally mean birds when they refer to pigeons; they mean people. Anyone going anywhere who might carry stories, film, supplies or a bottle of sour mash is known as a pigeon, and he is a treasured commodity. Often reporters have no other way to evade censorship or to send any kind of message at all. Strangers are often pressed into service at airports or hotels, and the best correspondents can spot a trustworthy pigeon with unerring skill. Naturally correspondents regularly act as pigeons for one another.

One radio reporter was about to leave Bangkok for Vientiane when a Thai stringer for an American television network asked him to carry an envelope to his boss, who was on a story in Laos. The reporter didn't know either of them, but he thought nothing of it. In Vientiane, he learned that the correspondent was staying at one of the two hotels, so he just left the envelope in the man's box. Later, the correspondent thanked him and added, "Do you know what was in that? Ten thousand dollars in hundred-dollar bills. Operating expenses."

The system doesn't always work. A handful of correspondents are still wondering how the lone reporter who flew back from the

Nigerian warfront they were covering managed to lose everyone's copy but his own.

Correspondents with copy to file are desperately dependent on the whims of fate—and of other people. Once when communications failed from Saigon, George Esper of the AP spent hours trying to place a phone call to New York. Known as "Telephone Man" because of his skill in working miracles, Esper arranged some patchwork routing and finally got through to his desk on a weak but audible circuit. It was the only link out of Saigon in the midst of heavy fighting. The desk man who answered listened for a few seconds and said, "George, it's hard to hear you. Call back." And he hung up the receiver. Another agency man spent half the night trying to get a call to London from Calcutta. Finally, a man answered and explained that everyone was on a tea break. "But," the correspondent pleaded, "this is urgent. You have to take this down." The London man, conscious of his union rights, replied, "I don't have to, y' know, mate."

If I had any doubts of how the powers of world communications giveth and taketh away, they were dispelled the day the Nigerian war ended in 1970. As Biafra appeared to be collapsing, I stayed up late listening to the secessionists' radio and heard, about three A.M., that President Odumegwu Ojukwu would address his crumbling nation at six A.M. I went down to the government cable office, not trusting my own telex at home, and gave all clerks, operators and intermediaries handsome gifts to make sure nothing interfered with my call. Ojukwu came on as scheduled to announce that he was speaking on tape. He said that he had already left the country "in search of peace." What he meant, it was clear, was that it was all over. I sent a long urgent story and got confirmation of receipt. As I was chatting on the machine with London about which reporters should fly to what cities to search for Ojukwu, the telex died. There was a general power blackout —nothing unusual for Nigeria—and it lasted for the next four hours. By the time electricity was restored, each of my competitors had a mountain of rockets awaiting them. The AP was alone with the story for all that time. But the perverse thrill of victory was slightly numbed by the memory of situations when I had been at the wrong end.

Besides trying to move quickly and find communications, correspondents must constantly solicit visas, entry permits, special passes, accreditations and various documents which make no sense even to the most convoluted of bureaucratic mentalities. Reporters assigned to the Congo in the late 1960s could get only six-month visas which had to be renewed regularly. One American counted seventeen separate trips to the foreign ministry and five to the secret police headquarters, involving dozens of hours of waiting around, for a single visa. Even after he learned whom to bribe, he was only able to cut the waiting time by half. And in the 1970s, visas became harder to get.

Each country has separate requirements. In Western Europe, most of Latin America and much of Asia, correspondents can enter as tourists with no visa at all. In some other countries, visas can take a year of intense negotiation—if they are granted at all. A correspondent in Africa was so fed up with waiting for a visa to Guinea that he booked passage on a freighter which stopped over for a few days in the Guinean capital, and he got in that way. Another managed to look at Brazzaville, capital of the former French Congo, by booking a flight to Paris from across the river in Kinshasa. He was allowed to cross over in transit but, clumsy tourist that he was, he missed the flight and had to stay around another day.

The speed and ease with which visas are granted often depends upon the individual consulate or embassy. An unofficial network passes along information on which diplomats are the most enlightened, and correspondents fly thousands of miles out of their way to apply for visas. Friendly immigration officers are cultivated and treasured as much as any news source.

Getting a visa is no guarantee of entry. Most correspondents have suffered the sinking feeling of watching a scowling airport police officer come upon their name on a blacklist. More than once, reporters have gotten off planes to find that the ambassador who granted their visa has just been arrested for treason or that the consul forgot to deliver the essential documents which must accompany the visa.

For television crews, the problems can be triply frustrating. A newspaper correspondent can arrive in plaid Bermuda shorts with an innocent look and a pencil buried in his suitcase. But a television crew must travel with mounds of odd-shaped silver trunks stuffed with expensive gear and unprocessed film. After the dreaded and inevitable question "What's that?" they may spend weeks trying to get their cameras out of customs, or they may have to take the next plane out.*

*One television reporter artfully extracted himself from a "What's that?" predicament after a customs inspector pointed out that regulations permit-

A correspondent has enough troubles finding a way to get his words to an editor, but a television crew has to ship out sound and film. Correspondents sometimes risk their lives and spend fortunes only to have a customs official confiscate their material at the airport. As Indian troops were taking over East Pakistan so it could become Bangladesh, American networks filmed the action in Dacca. Cameramen on the roof of the Intercontinental Hotel had to use wide-angle lenses because the aerial dogfights were so close to their tripods. They filmed some of the most dramatic footage ever shot of jet fighters in battle. A gunner's slight miscalculation could spray them with machine-gun fire, they knew, but they kept filming, calming their nerves with gin and tonic sent up from below. When it was over, the correspondents persuaded Pakistani authorities to provide a light plane to fly the material to Bangkok, where it could be processed and sent to New York by satellite. Film cans were bundled into a trunk and onto the plane, and the crews watched in triumph as their material took off on its way to millions of American living rooms. Their glee subsided when they learned what happened next. The plane stopped to refuel in Burma, and authorities immediately seized the suspicious-looking trunk. It stayed there for months, long after the story died.

One skill required by correspondents and cameramen of all types is the ability to pass through closed doors and then remain omnipresent but invisible at the same time. When Viet Cong representatives began arriving in Saigon for peace talks in 1972, Tan Son Nhut air base was closed to all but military personnel. Newsmen risked imprisonment to sneak onto the base. One agency photographer put on big white noise-killing earmuffs so he could hang around the flight line like he belonged there. He had no problems except that a lone jogger in an air force sweatshirt kept passing him and casting suspicious glances. Finally, the man trotted directly up to him and asked, "What outfit are you with?" The photographer, figuring the jig was up, replied, crestfallen, "AP." The jogger grinned, stuck out his hand and said, "CBS." Later, when Vice President Spiro Agnew was arriving at Tan Son Nhut and reporters could not get telephones, an agency reporter pleaded with a uniformed air force sergeant for brief use of

---

ted entry of only one camera. He glanced at his dozens of camera bodies, lenses and accessories and wrote down, "One composite camera."

his portable telephone equipped with alligator clips for tapping onto a line. Finally, the sergeant broke out laughing. He was a television reporter.

Being a woman sometimes helps open doors. Jurate Kazickas, an attractive and enterprising AP reporter, talked herself on board Libyan president Muammar el-Qaddafi's plane for a state visit to Yugoslavia, and she stayed close to the action for days. She told the Yugoslavs she was with the Libyans. The Libyans thought she was with the Yugoslavs. When authorities finally asked her to leave, one Yugoslav officer remarked, with obvious admiration, "We don't know what you are up to, Miss Kazickas, but we will never forget you."

One plain-spoken woman correspondent put it this way: "I find that once a woman gets through the door, a man has a harder time throwing her out than he would another man. I'm no twenty-two-year-old cutie any more, so I don't do it by flirting—I'm more businesslike and crisp—but it makes a difference. There are some women who would trade their bodies for a good story, but that's not really necessary. . . . Of course, I'm not talking about emergency situations. On a fast story, police would just as leave kick me in the ovaries as you in the balls. I've been roughed up with guys on an equal footing."

Often, she added, it can be harder for women. "Sometimes I've got to do a little tap dance to get people to realize I'm not just breezing in from the fashion page and I actually know something about the foreign policy of Lower Slobovia."

Most often the problems are the same for men and women alike, and getting a story is a matter of ingenuity and energy. On whirlwind tours with U.N. ambassador Andrew Young, for example, the reporters who jog with aides at 5:30 A.M. or play tennis after midnight get the best briefings. Covering earthquakes in Peru, correspondents who watch the surface of their bottled water have an early warning of tremors. UPI reporters in Cambodia found a way around American briefers who refused to discuss combat helicopter damage; they just called around to the military repair shops. And in Argentina, a correspondent learned to determine whether muffled nighttime rumblings were bombs or thunderclaps by listening to the pitch of his dog's bark.

The need for resourcefulness extends to all areas. One constant problem, for example, is how to take notes quickly enough to preserve intact complicated quotations—particularly in foreign languages. A few American correspondents have studied shorthand, but most rely on their own special shortcuts, which are unintelligible to others (and sometimes to themselves). Experience helps. During the Vietnam peace talks in Paris, one reporter asked North Vietnamese spokesman Nguyen Tranh Le if his country's troops were fighting in Cambodia. Le replied, "The Nixon administration must cease the American war of aggression, withdraw rapidly, totally and unconditionally all U.S. forces and those of its allies, and accept a coalition government in South Vietnam according to the ten points of the National Liberation Front and the Provisional Revolutionary Government." The reporter wrote only, "Nixad mus cease am agg." He could reconstruct the rest by memory, having heard it before so many times. Similarly, each time Nelson Rockefeller used the phrase "fatherhood of God, brotherhood of man," reporters who knew him well just wrote, "FOG-BOM."

In many difficult situations, the most brilliant displays of resourcefulness can only get a correspondent closer to the story. He may still have to leave out vital elements. Responsible reporters signal these gaps to their audiences, and readers and viewers should take heed. A dispatch on an African rebellion sent with an exotic-looking dateline automatically suggests the reporter was a firsthand witness. But if it says, "Reporters could not approach the disputed area," and it quotes fleeing refugees and pro-government officers, it is obviously not a definitive account. If a dispatch about a coup d'état says, "Normal communications were interrupted, and there was only an intermittent telephone link to the outside world," the reader can assume that the whole story is yet to come. Even without such clear signals, readers should be wary of dispatches from remote places. In many such stories, logistics cannot help but cause at least some inadvertent distortion, and suspended belief is doubly essential.

Often communications and travel are restricted deliberately by governments in attempts to control the news. But that is another problem—an extremely serious one—and it requires a close look.

7

Censorship and Government Pressures

We are pleased to announce, the Nigerian government was pleased to announce, that we are lifting censorship.

Does that mean, asked a correspondent, that we can send a story saying so?

No, replied the officer, because it was never announced that there was censorship.

The measures contrived by authorities to influence news about their countries go far beyond the old-fashioned censor with a pot of black ink and pinking shears. Direct and indirect pressures in scores of countries make it impossible for casual readers and viewers in the West to have a balanced view of world events. Not only are correspondents often prevented from reporting vital information, but also they frequently cannot—or do not—warn their readers that they are providing only a partial picture. Some correspondents practice self-censorship without even realizing it; others are artfully conned by official propaganda and managed news.

In the most extreme case, Cambodia, not a single reporter or traveler was allowed inside the country for a long time after the Khmer Rouge took power, and the few diplomats in Phnom Penh were under severe restrictions. The world's knowledge of Cambodia was limited to official radio broadcasts and accounts of embittered refugees who could speak only of the small areas in which they had lived. Background stories were based on the thinnest of details. In 1977, the

French press discussed at length the relative importance of two Cambodian leaders, until someone realized the two leaders were the same person; he just had a long name. North Korea, Albania and several other authoritarian countries allow journalists in only on the rarest of occasions and then under careful surveillance. All but a few countries in the world make at least some effort to convince correspondents to report things in a favorable light—or to prevent them from reporting anything at all.

Some direct measures are casual enough to be circumvented easily. In the late 1960s, when Congolese authorities decreed that all news dispatches had to be sent in French, reporters simply cabled things like, "Les mercenaires sont holed up en Bukavu avec beaucoup recoilless rifles, anti-aircraft guns et Scotch whisky." One British journalist in Nigeria dictated a coup d'état story in Welsh to his wife back home. From Sri Lanka—then Ceylon—reporters covering a rebellion chatted from hotel telephones about the weather and the local curry until the censor hung up, bored with what he considered to be tourist prattle.*

But sometimes action against correspondents is brutally direct. Reporters have been beaten bloody; some have been found dead in mysterious circumstances. Many reporters have spent at least a few nights in jails, military barracks or confined to their hotel rooms. Expulsions are almost routine.

The situation is worsened by the general imbalances of the system. One such problem is that some countries are reported more sympathetically than others, despite news organizations' efforts to be evenhanded. If a country has a favorable image in the United States, and its authorities are hospitable and helpful to correspondents, it is usually given the benefit of any doubt. This was illustrated when Lebanon imposed censorship on outgoing dispatches in 1976. When the measure was announced, agencies and newspapers carried long stories about the harsh new restrictions. Most dispatches from Beirut carried editors' notes warning that the contents had been censored. But for

---

*One classic censorship evader was Floyd Gibbons of the Chicago *Tribune*. When General John J. Pershing arrived at Liverpool in 1917 after the United States entered World War I, the British censor refused to let reporters name the port where he landed. Gibbons cabled, "Pershing landed at a British port today and was greeted by the Lord Mayor of Liverpool."

years the same organizations have accepted without comment a more subtle but equally effective censorship by Israel. Under the Israeli system, correspondents must submit to the censor all dispatches on specific subjects, including military, oil and nuclear matters. Censors sometimes hit the "garble button" which obliterates outgoing dispatches on sensitive issues. As a result, reporters avoid certain forbidden stories. For a long time, for example, they could not say Israel imported oil from Iran. Until the mid-1970s, news organizations could not even say that a story had been altered by censors. Few correspondents protest, since the censors are usually reasonable and sometimes can be persuaded to change their minds. But readers are often not given the full picture, and they are seldom warned about it.

News organizations respond differently when direct measures are imposed. When former Indian prime minister Indira Gandhi insisted that Western reporters sign a list of guidelines for coverage, there were three reactions. Some refused to sign and left the country in a blaze of integrity; some signed and respected the restrictions; and others signed and paid no attention to them. Correspondents who stayed and ignored the guidelines say they pulled no punches. But some editors who followed events closely said they detected a slightly tempered tone.

The imposition of self-censorship can be more damaging than direct measures. Many authorities will let correspondents file whatever they want, but they react harshly if they are unhappy with what is reported. This was called the "File now, die later" policy in Chile after the 1973 coup. Faced with undefined threats, reporters may inadvertently withhold sensitive information by convincing themselves that their perfectly reliable sources are not good enough. And the more timid deliberately omit material that might well have gotten by an official censor.

A number of foreign editors tell their correspondents to ignore pressures and report frankly. Should they get thrown out, they will be reassigned somewhere else. But other editors prefer that their correspondents do not risk getting thrown out except on the biggest of stories. An expulsion is not necessarily a badge of honor. Often authorities will not allow news organizations to replace ejected correspondents. News agencies can be particularly sensitive if they sell their news and photos to local papers in the country. AP and UPI policy is to report the news, whatever the consequences, but local bureau chiefs and correspondents are sometimes reluctant to jeopardize agency income by risking having their offices closed down. Regardless of an organization's policy, correspondents know that if they provoke the wrath of hard-line rulers, they could suffer a fate worse than expulsion.

When borders are sealed, the usual result is either that the country is ignored completely or that it is reported almost totally in the negative with scant mention of any possible saving graces. The level of international concern about a particular country determines whether reporters will go through the time-consuming process of finding alternate sources of information outside of its closed borders. In either case, the reader is left ill-informed.

Idi Amin Dada of Uganda and Francisco Macias Nguema of Equatorial Guinea are both absolute despots responsible for mass murders, torture and whimsically imposed prison terms. Macias' record is far worse than Amin's. He has killed a larger percentage of his population, and he has imposed virtual slavery on a wide sector of his tiny nation. And yet, while almost everyone in the United States knows about Amin, hardly anyone has heard of Macias. Because of the vagaries of the system, Amin and Uganda are "good stories"; Macias and Equatorial Guinea are not. Amin decided for his own reasons that he wanted publicity, and he learned how to get it. His antics attracted attention among the most casual readers, and editors knew it. The slightest reference to Amin got into newspapers around the country. Also, by geographical coincidence, Uganda is next to Kenya, where many correspondents are based. The official radio can be monitored in Nairobi, and telephone calls are often easy. Since Uganda has "news value," reporters seek out refugees, churchmen and defectors for accounts of depredations. Under Amin, newsmen could not move freely in Uganda to report on whether the regime accomplished anything positive, so the picture which emerged for an eager audience was one of unbridled bloodshed. By contrast, Macias has shunned publicity, withdrawing behind his tightly sealed borders. No demand has been created for news about him. A number of exiles live in the Cameroun and in Gabon, but those countries are off the normal itinerary for reporters in Africa. When correspondents do write about Equatorial Guinea, the name rings no bell of recognition, and the stories are soon forgotten.

Some countries become inadvertent victims of their own openness to reporters. One good example is the Philippines under Ferdinand Marcos. The government violates human rights on a grand scale, but it also allows correspondents in to travel with relative freedom to write about what is happening. Reporters can interview victims and conscience-stricken security officers. Marcos himself is accessible to reporters, who can ask do-you-still-beat-your-wife questions. As a result, correspondents are able to write detailed accounts of government abuses, rich in quotes and color. Other governments commit more flagrant violations of basic rights, but they escape public censure by closing their borders to reporters. If they are not of sufficient interest to merit intensive coverage from the outside, they are hardly mentioned at all. This results in the lasting impression that countries like the Philippines are the worst of a bad bunch.

Even if there were no restrictions or pressures on correspondents, some countries would still get more attention than others. But, ideally, correspondents would be able to apply some standard yardstick so that readers could evaluate the actions and the conditions of one government in light of others. The present system, however, gives the reader only scattered fragments of the whole picture.

Obviously, there are differing reasons why a government seeks to control what is written about it. (The growing confrontation between Third World countries and the Western press requires special attention, and will be discussed in Chapter 16.) No government welcomes reporters poking around in its affairs, least of all foreigners. In the United States, officials have little choice. But only a handful of nations share the philosophy of America's First Amendment. One African nation, with no overabundance of reverence for the press, has a cabinet post of Minister for Information, Broadcasting and Prisons.

If leaders can get away with controlling information—for personal ego reasons, for internal politics or for international image—it is only logical to expect them to do it. Soviet policy flatly states that the government determines what news reaches its people, since the wrong sort of reporting can cause unrest which is harmful to the society. Some governments see themselves as victims of plots by big nations to subjugate them economically and politically, and they suspect reporters of sowing discord and stealing secrets. Government control is more the rule than the exception in many regions. A Jordanian censor apologized to one correspondent, after reading his dispatch, and said, "We don't care ourselves what you write, you understand.

But the press is so controlled in the Arab World that our neighbors think that anything you say has our approval, and we must be concerned with our relations."

Censorship is often haphazard and arbitrary. The same correspondent in Jordan wrote about a cabinet change, saying, "The minister of information was charged with improving government coordination." A censor held up the dispatch with no explanation. The reporter finally got hold of the minister himself, who later explained, laughing, "The censor thought you meant I was criminally charged with something."

Readers can correct for some distortions caused by government measures as long as they know what the measures are. More subtle censorship requires more subtle reading. Sometimes reporters can provide all the information they want to get across. But they must phrase it carefully and parcel it out sparsely throughout a dispatch. Correspondents under rigid controls routinely stick with basic "safe" material while in the country they are covering and wait until they can file from somewhere else to do a full situation report.

To guide readers, reporters try to say in their dispatches if pressure has been applied against them. Newspapers often carry stories announcing when countries impose new press restrictions. Those who are seriously concerned can find specialized reports: *Index on Censorship* magazine and the International Press Institute, both based in London, make studies on press freedom, country by country. But it is helpful enough to know the main types of pressure and how they are applied to correspondents.

Official interference with news flow can be grouped largely into four attitudes. The "Blackout" approach is based on the theory that no news at all is better than what might be expected by an open policy, so stringent controls obstruct reporting. "Reluctant Coverage" governments feel they must allow reporters in for their own reasons, but they restrict correspondents' activities. Some governments practice the "Subtle Squeeze," appearing to allow free coverage but exerting indirect pressures. Finally, others rely on "Friendly Persuasion" to try to influence reporters in a positive way, without restrictive measures.

Governments in the first category—mostly in Africa and Asia—are generally in a tenuous domestic political situation and are vulnerable to outside influences. They prefer to choose who writes about them, even if it means they are seldom mentioned in the Western press. By granting visas on a highly selective basis, they can determine who is likely to report sympathetically. If they guess wrong, and a reporter writes a story they don't like, they can refuse him or his organization permission to return. They often allow news organizations to keep stringers, thus avoiding any charge that they forbid all reporting. But stringers are easily intimidated and are not likely to send dispatches that are overly blunt or embarrassing. Under such circumstances, the government does not have to impose censorship.

The Blackout attitude is extremely dangerous for correspondents who do manage to get in. Although a country's United Nations representative can debate the values of a free press on an intellectual level, an unschooled soldier from an up-country village is not so detached. He hears that Western reporters are the enemy, and he knows only one way to deal with enemies. He seldom understands— or cares—that thumping a correspondent might bring the wrath of Midtown Manhattan executives on his shoulders, and he most certainly has never read the Bill of Rights. Every correspondent working in such countries has his own set of horror stories.

In Angola, Ed Blanche and Horst Faas of the AP were thrown into a windowless cell splattered with blood. At one end, someone's bloody fingers had clutched far up the wall and then left marks which continued downward, trailing off more and more faintly toward the floor. Blanche nearly panicked when Faas was carried off without explanation. Then an officer stuck a 9-mm automatic pistol between Blanche's eyes and told him he had two minutes to confess he was a CIA agent. Blanche said he had nothing to confess and waited, petrified, to see what would happen next. Finally Faas was brought back, and both were released. Fortunately, officers did not search their hotel rooms, where they had $4000 in cash for expenses and some damning notes on the situation in Angola.

A correspondent never knows when or why he might end up in trouble. John Burns of the New York *Times* was held for two days in Mozambique until a visiting congressman helped to get him out. It turned out that authorities thought he worked for *Time* magazine, and they were mad at *Time*. They had never heard of the New York *Times*. Once a Congo correspondent was arrested simply because his office mentioned Moise Tshombe in a cabled message to him. Police officers could not read English but they recognized the name of the hated former president.

Reluctant Coverage governments make it as difficult as possible for correspondents to collect and report solid information. The Soviet-dominated countries fall into this category. China now allows American correspondents to set up bureaus, and other Western newsmen live in Peking, but China should be included in this category. A number of Third World countries, like Yugoslavia and Indonesia, share the attitude, although obviously there are degrees of severity.

The Soviet Union carefully screens correspondents seeking visas, although most American news organizations are allowed to keep bureaus in Moscow. The U.S. State Department assures that a rough balance is maintained so that there are not many more Soviet correspondents in the United States than American reporters in Russia. If an American is expelled from Moscow, the State Department almost automatically retaliates in kind. Since Russian correspondents often double as intelligence officers, authorities are reluctant to lose them, and they are slow to expel American reporters they don't like. Instead, they use other means. Some correspondents have been denounced as homosexuals, spies or general layabouts in the Soviet press. Examples are made of correspondents when it is convenient to pick on them. Robert C. Toth of the Los Angeles *Times* was just about to leave at the end of his assignment when authorities detained him. He was interrogated brusquely for a week, with his exit visa ominously denied in June 1977. Toth had written several articles about Anatoly Shcharansky, a jailed Jewish dissident and a computer specialist. Toth recalled, "They resurrected every science story I've ever done from here—genetic engineering, sociology, linguistics—and some I didn't do but that I was interested in doing. Every story they had, including dates." Eventually, Toth was allowed to leave. Reporters, in general, find that if they stand up to pressure in the Soviet Union, the government backs down.

Correspondents are constantly harassed by bugging, surveillance and isolation. They live in state-approved compounds under the eyes of special guards. One reporter found the only way he could get heat in winter was to complain into his office wall tap about the lousy heating in Soviet buildings. Another once ordered a photographer to go take pictures of a mountain of snow left for weeks in front of the American embassy. By the time the photographer got there, bulldozers had already cleared away the snow.

A greater problem is the lack of sources and information. Press conferences almost never happen, and interviews with even middle-level officials can take weeks of bureaucratic busywork. There is almost no such thing as private Soviet sources except for a courageous few dissidents who might talk under guarded circumstances. Western reporters can meet ordinary citizens from time to time to get the flavor of life in the Soviet Union, but such contacts are difficult and dangerous. The reporters' major Soviet sources are Tass and the state-controlled newspapers. Authorities discourage the reporting of disaster stories, saying that plane crashes and fires have no news value other than to satisfy morbid curiosity. Reporters, they say, should concentrate instead on increased soy bean crops and official ceremonies. This purposeful dearth of accurate, official information can cause serious misinterpretation. A veteran Moscow correspondent recalls that until Soviet scientists began cooperating with Americans on space exploration, correspondents had regularly reported that the two space programs were neck and neck in technology. They made assumptions on the scant official data available and were misled by propaganda. As it turned out, correspondents discovered, the Soviets were far behind the Americans.

There is no censor for television film, but ABC senior vice president William Sheehan told a U.S. Senate subcommittee, "Anything beyond the most casual street-scene filming requires a tortuous trip through bureaucracy to obtain permission to visit a farm or travel to Leningrad or whatever. . . . The permission never comes in any instance where the Soviets suspect they might not be presented in any but the most flattering light."

Until 1979, news from China was even harder to come by, and it was less reliable. It is still far from complete. Correspondents in Peking can provide a valuable context of atmosphere and mood, but little hard information is available beyond the official press. The picture is clouded by false reports circulated by Taiwan agents and by fabricated accounts from some Hong Kong dailies in need of a headline. When word is received of civil strife or political turmoil, reporters have few means of determining its extent. Late in 1976, a few American newspapers carried a brief front-page item from the Reuters correspondent in Peking about a mystifying rebellion south of the capital, and then almost nothing else was seen again. An uprising in China is big news, but no editor can write a large black headline over a story that says, essentially, "We heard something is happening, but since we cannot go check it out, we have no idea what the story is." If the authorities then put a clamp on any mention of the incident, it disappears.

When an earthquake struck the Chinese city of Tangshan in July 1976, authorities noted only "a great loss of lives and property." It was 11 months before the quake was officially acknowledged as China's deadliest in four centuries. The news was filtered through two Mexican researchers who were not allowed to visit the destroyed city but were given access to data. The Chinese provided no casualty figures, but they did not deny a figure available only from Nationalist Chinese intelligence sources: about 650,000 dead.

The selective release of official information is a pressure tactic which spans all four attitudes. Experienced information officers know that most correspondents will relay dutifully most government statements, even preposterous ones, since that is part of "balanced reporting." Some reporters will point out inconsistencies in government declarations, or they might try to tip off readers with words like "claimed" and "purportedly." But information officers know that most readers skip right past the clues, retaining only the basic exaggerated or erroneous statement.

Certain governments develop specialties. The Thais, who by custom tend to avoid direct answers, can be masters of waffling. Often, different officials will say different things on the same subject, thoroughly confusing everyone and committing no one to any embarrassing positions.

One of the most skilled manipulators of official information is President Mobutu Sese Seko of Zaire. Mobutu used elaborate flimflam, complete with Pygmies and Cubans, to elicit world support for his 1977 battle with a small army of Lunda exiles which invaded Shaba (formerly Katanga) Province from Angola. The raid was intended to cause enough momentary turmoil in the country to enable anti-Mobutu elements in Kinshasa to topple the president. To mask the political character of the invasion, Mobutu steered attention to the military aspects. If he could enlist foreigners to help his own troops put down the rebels quickly, he could place the focus on combat rather than political intrigue. And he could show his people that he had powerful friends abroad. Mobutu launched a public relations campaign by taking correspondents on a carefully guided tour of the front. After that, correspondents were banned until he could demonstrate he was winning. And to keep interest high without battlefield reports, he produced the Pygmies.

The president knew that if anything turned on Western editors more than cannibals and slavery, it was Pygmies. The image of tiny warriors, naked to the waist and with long bows slung across their backs, illustrates perfectly a war in Storybook Africa. So, when charges of Cuban involvement elicited only lukewarm interest, Mobutu announced he was sending crack Pygmy bowmen into the fray. Some news organizations leaped upon the story with glee. One newsmagazine had it as 300 Pygmies at five feet each; another, coming up with similar total footage, said there were 400 Pygmies at four feet each. The "jungle-wise Pygmies" were reported as deadly shots, with rare valor, feared because of their magic talismans. When reporters began pressing for details about how the Pygmies were faring, Mobutu's information people removed them from the scene as deftly as they produced them. The grass was too tall for their arrows, the uniforms did not fit and the army training was too different from what they were used to. They were, so to speak, strategically withdrawn.*

Mobutu, like many other proponents of Reluctant Coverage, did not stop at managing news. Seven correspondents were arrested for trying to get to Shaba without permission. One reporter who made a factual error was put on nationwide television to confess his mistake to the nation. When a Europe-based agency correspondent reported there was little support for the president at a public rally, Mobutu threw him out of the country for the fifth time.

Expulsion is a popular device among Reluctant Coverage countries, and each government adds its own touch. When Nigerian authorities were angered at a correspondent for the British agency Reuters, they put him aboard a dugout canoe with his family and sent them paddling across a wide estuary, without passports, to neighboring Benin.

*Some short warriors were actually produced, but they were not, as a few news organizations pointed out, Pygmies. The real Zaire Pygmies are timid, peaceful people who seldom venture out of their corner of rain forest. The "Pygmy" bowmen were Batwa pygmoids, not particularly warlike—and lousy shots. At least one newspaper didn't fall for the gambit. Ronald Koven, at the time foreign editor of the Washington *Post,* said, "I told my people not to say anything about Pygmies in the first paragraph of any story. We just didn't believe it."

The third category, the Subtle Squeeze, is deceptive. Its tactics are not obvious to the reader—sometimes not even to the correspondent —but they can cause more distortion than many direct measures. The methods used by the Argentine military government which deposed Isabel Perón demonstrate this clearly.

Before the coup, officers had decided they needed a moderate image in order to attract international credits and investments for the crippled economy. They courted the press energetically. Selected correspondents were briefed on plans even before the coup took place. During the takeover, communications remained open, and spokesmen were available for comment. But their approach was soon clear. One official told reporters privately, "We will not interfere with your work —you are free to operate. But we will do everything we can to keep you from finding out things we don't want published." Press officers gave barbecues and cocktail parties, everything but information. Major sources were muzzled subtly but effectively—officers, civilian officials, churchmen. Each time correspondents asked about evidence linking the "mysterious right-wing death squads" to the government, press spokesmen would lament that, alas, some elements were holdovers from the past and impossible to control. But almost no official action was taken against the death squads, whose targets included, among others, journalists. When a squad called at the empty office of an Italian correspondent early one morning, the reporter complained to the chief press officer. He was advised, "Stay away from your home for a while." For a long time after the coup, Argentina retained an image of moderation and tolerance of the foreign press. But many correspondents were running scared, and it was clear that authorities wanted it that way.*

Prime Minister Lee Kuan Yew of Singapore, who detests criticism, is a master of the Subtle Squeeze. Since he values his international reputation as a defender of democratic freedom, he reserves his toughest measures for the local press. But correspondents who are based in the bustling crossroads republic are scrupulously careful about their immigration and tax status, the pure content of their medicine kits and their personal proclivities. Access to Singapore is vital for anyone covering Southeast Asia, not only because of the news sources there

*The effects of this on reporting are discussed more thoroughly in Chapter 15 on human rights reporting.

but also because so many flights transit the tiny island. Singapore authorities know that if they hold a technicality over the head of a correspondent, he is not likely to be too rough on Lee.

Angola has hardly been subtle with some correspondents, but one ABC television team found on one trip they were censored by excessive hospitality. The government told them they were so welcome that they need not stay in a hotel or rent a car. They were obliged to settle in a government guest house, with a chauffeur-driven car. Their movements, naturally, were carefully supervised.

In one classic squeeze, Peter Arnett found himself trapped in a remote Indonesian island town for three weeks, and he had no idea of what was happening. A friendly general had invited him to fly to Manado on the northern end of the Celebes, an important provincial outpost. The two flew out on the general's plane, host and guest each in his most affable and expansive mood. They discussed politics and stories which Arnett might like to cover. In flight, the general received a mysterious message. Suddenly he closed up like a clam, ending the conversation and ignoring Arnett. On the ground, Arnett found himself aggressively cut off from everything. The local airline told him all flights were booked solid, although he could see planes were going out half empty. Post office authorities said he had no permission to use the telephone or telegraph. Finally the sympathetic captain of an oil tanker took him on board and dropped him in Borneo. He never did find out what happened and could only surmise that someone had messaged he was some kind of enemy agent.

A tight squeeze can come where it is hardly expected. President Jomo Kenyatta was relatively tolerant of correspondents throughout his long reign. But during a dinner for visiting U.S. Vice President Hubert Humphrey, a waiter accidentally dumped a bowl of soup in Kenyatta's lap. The bearded leader, nearly 80 at the time, shot upright and sent the man to the floor with a single punch. Kenyan officials hurried to the lone correspondent there and told him he would be out on the next plane if he reported the incident. No one read about it for years afterward until Jim Hoagland mentioned it, quoting witnesses, in an article on how Africans censor the news.

Friendly Persuasion is used, to some degree, by almost every government in the world, including American administrations. Elected politicians and dictators alike want to be seen in the best possible light, and it is accepted practice to employ information officers to accentuate the positive. Some governments do all they can to help correspondents gather information—even if it might reflect failure or embarrassment—on the theory that a free flow will eventually work in their favor and establish their credibility.

But however open a government may be, there is a natural temptation to keep the lid on anything that makes authorities look bad. The most popular excuse for suppressing embarrassing details is national security. Britain, generally enlightened on press freedom, has a handy "D-notice" system which puts involuntarily "voluntary" restraints on reporters. The government can put a D-notice on anything which it considers might endanger security. An editor can ignore a D-notice, but he risks the wrath of his colleagues and possible sanctions under the Official Secrets Act.

Frequently a government buries unflattering statistics in ponderous reports which require more energy to read than most correspondents are able to expend. Other times it packages the information in a positive light: a project might be either half a success or half a failure, depending upon how it is seen. And sometimes nothing at all is said about a particular subject in the hope no one will ask about it.

Leaders steeped in public relations and psychology can make an enormous difference in how their countries are reported abroad. One correspondent who covered Indira Gandhi's fall from power remarked later, "Mrs. Gandhi's main problem was that she took an antagonistic approach to the press and treated reporters as enemies. If she had called us in before her sweeping emergency measures and explained off the record what she felt she had to do and why, most of us would have given her the benefit of the doubt, even if unwittingly. If it had been Israel instead of India, she probably would have emerged as a hero, with world sympathy from the start, and she might still be on top."

The allusion to Israel was well taken. In sharp contrast to most Arab officials, Israeli authorities take great pains to provide basic tools for correspondents. Daily summaries of the Hebrew-language press are prepared in English. Interviews are arranged quickly. Documentation is swift and complete. Correspondents are often given background briefings, even on subjects they are forbidden to write about under the subtle censorship laws. The contrast was seen clearly when Anwar Sadat and Menachem Begin visited each other's countries in 1977. The Egyptian president announced his trip with only a few days' warning. Within 48 hours, Israeli engineers had installed about 150 telephone lines so correspondents could make instantaneous—and free—calls around the world from a lavishly equipped press room. The Egyptians had weeks to prepare for Begin's return visit, but on the day of his arrival, technicians were still struggling to finish a few working lines. These basic factors cannot help but influence coverage, no matter how objective correspondents attempt to remain.

One popular act of Friendly Persuasion—particularly among lesser-known countries—is the press junket. For these trips, information officers try to round up editors, columnists and writers with little experience in the country, so they will not know to probe in sensitive areas. Schedules are so loaded with activities that there is little time for random observation. The usual result is a sheaf of sympathetic articles, weighted toward the government. Any critical comments added from the opposition or from the visitors' own observations are generally modest, and they tend to lend an air of balance which fortifies the more positive information in the articles.

Some major news organizations have strict policies against paid trips of any kind. The AP, for example, forbids its correspondents to accept free rides or hospitality under any circumstances. If there is news value in riding on a presidential or a company plane, the agency pays the equivalent fare.

Governments attempt all sorts of con jobs, and they can be difficult to handle, even when the correspondent knows he is being conned. Once President Ferdinand Marcos of the Philippines was shown on television making an on-the-spot tour of a southern island threatened by rebels. Arnold Zeitlin of the AP discovered the film was made in the back yard of the presidential palace in Manila; Marcos had never left town. He wrote the story, and that was a major cause of his subsequent expulsion.

Occasionally fabrications are hard to miss. During the Nigerian war, a local paper printed a photo purporting to show a white mercenary fighting for Biafra. He had a World War I soup-plate helmet, a 1914 vintage rifle and baggy doughboy pants. When some jokester from London wrote to express delight at seeing his old friend "Millard Phillmore," whom he hadn't seen since the Great War, and wasn't that just like old Millard to become a mercenary, the paper carried the letter as proof of the picture's authenticity.

Sometimes, though, the attempted seductions are far more serious.

Several months before Indian troops intervened to help rebelling Bengalis separate East Pakistan into Bangladesh, Pakistani authorities took six correspondents on a week-long tour of the embattled eastern wing. Only reporters not based in Pakistan or India were invited. The correspondents were from the New York *Times,* Reuters, *Time* magazine, Hsinhua (of China) and the *Financial Times* of London. I went for the AP. We were treated courteously and assured we could write what we saw. But it was obvious at the outset that the Pakistanis had definite ideas about what we were expected to see.

Each day the group was flown by helicopter and light plane to a different town for what we soon dubbed "tea and atrocities." After the local commander served strong tea and cookies, we would be taken to hospitals, mass graves or blood-spattered concentration camps to be shown how cruelly the Bengalis had treated countrymen from West Pakistan before the army established order. Although the military authorities made their point, we were also able to see how viciously the West Pakistanis had acted at first and how brutal the army had been in putting down the Bengalis. At one hospital, a Pakistani officer grabbed a young boy's hair and jerked his head back to show how his neck had been cut. As he reopened the wound, and the boy's face contorted in pain, he invited reporters to reflect on what monsters the Bengalis were.

Whenever possible, we eluded our escorts to talk with neutral sources—diplomats and officials of international organizations—and with Bengalis. We looked behind the bamboo screens that lined the main roads masking razed homes and rubble left by the army's assault. We found eyewitnesses who had seen violent massacres and indiscriminate shelling of crowded rows of homes and shops. Sometimes reporters caught only snatches of words from Bengalis on the street before soldiers rushed up to shoo them away. "Turn right at the corner and go two blocks," murmured one young man before scurrying off, and we abruptly veered off to follow his advice. We found the crumpled remains of a two-story brick marketplace which looked as if it had taken direct hits from heavy bombing. (It hadn't; the damage was from shelling.)

When the Pakistanis realized their trip might backfire, they increased their ever-friendly escort. Finally, it became so hard to break away that we had to jump out of rolling jeeps at a prearranged signal to scatter in different directions. Since there were usually no more than three officers, and there were five of us (the Chinese correspondent did not take part in these particular operations), at least two of us could lose ourselves long enough to ask questions. Our escorts would run after us, shouting, "Wait, sir," and we would apologize later, explaining the tenets of balanced reporting. Once, for several moments, I was certain a flustered lieutenant was going to open fire at our disappearing backs. In one town, the local commander told us confidently, "You see, there was absolutely no damage here." Then we spotted a telltale bamboo screen and, jumping out of the jeep, we scattered. One of us reached the screen, peered behind and found the blackened hulk of a Hindu temple, its spire shot away by cannon fire. Each time we found such evidence, we asked for official comment. We were careful to look at whatever we were shown and to listen to the official side at briefings. Eventually, a balanced picture emerged, but it was not what authorities had intended to portray.

8

Gus and the Gatekeepers

A block-lettered sign over the Los Angeles *Times* foreign desk reads simply, "Consider Gus." And each afternoon a handful of copy editors in rolled-up sleeves sit down next to their small piles of gray pencils to make sure that Gus, the average reader, does not confuse the Rann of Kutch with the Shah of Iran.

Desk editors, obviously enough, are crucial. A ham-handed editor can wreak more havoc on a piece of reporting than a squadron of censors. A skillful one can save a reporter from making an ass of himself—or worse. Editors not only direct the movements of their correspondents, but they also decide whether to use their stories or to flip them into the trash bin. A correspondent's dispatch, if it survives at all, may pass through a dozen sets of hands at several stages before reaching the reader.

These gatekeepers operate in a slightly different manner at each agency, newspaper and magazine. But their goals are the same: to add information to dispatches by shortening them and to provide a rounded picture of the world while throwing away most of the material available.

Green eyeshades and hemorrhoid cushions went out with upright telephones, but desk editors still remain a breed apart. They sit in unsung anonymity, applying their talents to make others look good. They are usually well paid and always in short supply. Only a few of the biggest papers maintain separate foreign desks. The others combine foreign news with national—and sometimes state—news, so that the same editors handle everything. Papers which prize good desks might consider 100 applicants for a single opening. They value insight in world affairs as well as skill in handling the language. Other papers seem willing to hire anyone who can sharpen a pencil and tell a verb from a comma.

Good editors are horrified not by the smoking remains of a Boeing 747 but by dangling participles and split infinitives. Like veteran undertakers with the loved ones of strangers, they dispassionately touch up incoming cables, whatever the condition. The big by-lines may impress readers but not editors. A reporter who evokes the respect of millions might be to his desk just another manic depressive who can't keep his hands off the semicolon key. On the Los Angeles *Times* desk, one of the best in the country, editors spend at least an hour even on the smoothest dispatches from their most experienced correspondents. To the editors, it's all just copy—material to be read and put into English.

One master of the craft is Harris Jackson, "early" foreign editor of the AP since the 1940s. Jackson comes in before midnight, in opera dress or a ragged flight jacket, and begins electronically editing all incoming dispatches on a computer console. He and two deskmen select and prepare the foreign stories distributed each morning to afternoon newspapers around the country. Jackson is precise and brutal. If he can't supply missing information from his own trivia trove or from the reference shelf behind him, he fires off acid-laced "Jackson messages" to his correspondents. New men on the desk anxiously watch his moods, fearful of sarcastic abuse should they misspell the Court of St. James's or let a limp verb sneak through. Jackson is good because he understands the larger picture. He has kept track of the day-to-day events for decades and, with instant recall, he can add context and meaning to breaking stories. He can catch a reader's eye with a dramatic detail or a turn of phrase. And, as a former correspondent, he knows the practical problems at the other end.

Jackson is not easily impressed. In 1972, when President Nixon went to China, the AP sent along Hugh Mulligan, one of its best men. Mulligan was dazzled by the historical significance of the visit. From Shanghai, he wrote a compelling dispatch about that great city from which most foreigners had been banned for twenty-three years. With respectful awe, he waited as the Chinese telephone operator swiftly connected him with the AP's newsroom on Rockefeller Plaza, half a world away. Such communication had been unthinkable only months before. The phone rang on the other end, and he heard Jackson's familiar reedy voice: "It's Mulligan with more of that Peking shit. Who wants to take it?"

One night the London bureau wrote that the new Oxford dictionary included some dirty words. "What words?" Jackson asked. London replied they were too vulgar for the wire. Jackson insisted, and London demurred, saying there were ladies in the office. Exasperated, Jackson messaged, "Are they among the following, all in Webster's . . . " and he listed every obscene word he could recall.

Few editors are as good as Jackson. Most foreign desks, especially at news agencies, use a number of young reporters who are on their way overseas. They are usually enthusiastic and adept at editing and rewriting. But they seldom have the experience to bridge cultural gaps and to piece together the intricate workings of international affairs. Few have the background to question a story just on instinct because it has a funny ring. (For example, one correspondent quoted Zambian President Kenneth Kaunda as denouncing British Prime Minister Edward Heath as a "traitor" during a Commonwealth conference. That sounded far too strong to a seasoned desk editor, who asked that the reporter check again. It turned out that Kaunda, in his Zambian accent, had said "trader," referring only to Heath's defense of British commercial interests.)

Inexperienced desk editors often feel they must make some changes just to show they are there. And any alteration increases the chance for inadvertent error. One agency man decided that he liked the word "flights" better than "sorties" in a Vietnam story about B-52 bombing raids. But they are hardly synonymous. A sortie is a single strike by one plane; flight refers to all aircraft on a mission. As a result of the editor's changes, the story had three times as many of the big bombers as were in active service around the world involved in a single attack over North Vietnam. Another young editor decided to liven up a hijack story from Dacca by referring to the "plane glistening on the sun-baked runway." He had forgotten about time changes; it was pitch dark in Dacca at the time.

Editors can make mistakes on the most exacting of foreign desks. When Pope John Paul I died in 1978, a deskman on a major newspaper wrote that the pontiff was buried with a cross bearing "a skull and crossbones at its foot." Whether misled by an agency dispatch or a close-up photograph, he did not check back with his correspondent. He had mistaken the crossed keys of St. Peter and the papal tiara with the Jolly Roger.

Some agency desk editors are former correspondents who are waiting out their years for retirement. Although they can be the best of deskmen, they can also be the worst. Rather than using their experience as a base for understanding new developments and new approaches, some continue to see things as they were decades ago. Carefully written dispatches from Africa are sometimes rewritten as scorecards in a presumed power struggle between the "West" and the "East." Although there is obvious news interest in more offbeat stories, even if their news value is subtle, some old-timers pay no heed.

All editors are vital to the system because each can veto a story at any point. But by far the most important deskmen are those of the news services. Every overseas story with a syndicate signature—AP, UPI, New York Times or whatever—passes first across that organization's foreign desk. Since the agencies distribute stories by means of full-time teleprinters, sometimes operating at 4500 words a minute, there is less pressure to throw away excess wordage. Still, only about 20 per cent of the scores of thousands of words which cross AP and UPI foreign desks each day are relayed to subscribing newspapers. Some stories, judged to be unnewsworthy, are simply wiped out of the computer with the push of a key, obliterating words which may have cost a reporter three days' work at great personal risk. Others are stored in the computers for possible use later. Many of the dispatches sent on to subscribers are either sharply cut because of space pressures or rewritten completely for clarity and background.

This initial editing process is as important as covering the story in the first place. Only the agency's own desk has direct access to its correspondents and files to guard against mistakes. It can hold up stories that appear erroneous, libelous or superfluous. It can request further information about specific points, and it can ask bureaus elsewhere for reaction and more details. These desks must be especially careful, since reporters often do not see edited versions of their stories, even at the earliest stages. Some correspondents have suffered because sloppy desks gratuitously attributed to authorities information which had been specifically identified as coming from non-official sources. At times reporters are made to look moronic, and readers are misled.

There was a classic case in 1960 when some French residents in Algeria rebelled against President Charles de Gaulle's plans to grant self-determination to the colony. As the tense situation threatened to explode into a small civil war, De Gaulle broadcast an emotion-charged speech. The Paris bureau of one agency sent a dispatch reporting his appeal to the French to cease their resistance. Farther down, the dispatch noted a recurrent theme: De Gaulle again urged the army to wipe out the Moslem Algerian rebels who wanted immediate independence. A faraway desk editor decided that he knew more about the story than the correspondents. He put the secondary angle at the top of the dispatch and gave it the highest urgency priority. And he got it wrong. The agency, as a result, reported that De Gaulle had urged his troops to wipe out the recalcitrant Frenchmen.

Editors and correspondents often disagree over what belongs in a story. One news agency desk insisted on adding "former cabaret dancer" to every mention of Isabel Perón when she was president of Argentina. Finally the chief correspondent in Buenos Aires fired off an angry memo. He argued that unless Mrs. Perón leaped onto the table at a cabinet meeting in a pink sequined dress, or banned cabaret dancing, it was irrelevant to harp on her dancing career. But the desk has the final word, and he made little impact.

To attract readers, desk editors think in terms of declarative head-lines or a catch phrase which gives an immediate mental image. News is seldom black and white, but they do not like to deal in grays. Subtlety eats up a lot of words, and space is precious. Often desks harden up dispatches couched in guarded language. A correspondent might spend an hour finding the right phrasing to say what he does know and does not know about a complex situation. And in minutes an editor, grumbling about fuzzy writing, can turn it all around into a forceful, clear account which distorts the meaning. Sometimes, if the information cannot be stated directly, dispatches are simply tossed out.

Along with a clear-cut presentation, most desks want basic facts attributed with such comforting terms as "police said" or "according to an official communiqué." To some editors, it makes little difference if the police and army are in disorder—or may be deliberately lying —and the correspondent explains that any figures from them are unreliable. Certain things should be attributed to officials, these editors argue, or they don't sound right.

In purely competitive terms, the agency desk editors are right. News services measure their success by "play"—which dispatches are selected for publication in subscribing newspapers. Few papers will print a murkily phrased story if another agency delivers a crisp account of hard facts on the same subject. The newspaper editor has no way of assessing which is closer to the truth; he usually assumes that if one dispatch is more direct, its author is better informed—and is a better writer.

This can be maddening for responsible correspondents who refuse to hype stories for play. Desks do not ask their reporters to distort dispatches, but they can only judge their people's performance in terms of what the opposition produces. If an editor thinks his correspondent has been beaten, he will message urgently asking for a "matcher," and the correspondent must either match the story or show why it is erroneous. In one extreme case, an agency correspondent in Indonesia sent a dramatic account of an uprising on a remote island, with details and color. The rival agency's desk was frantic, sending rocket after rocket to its correspondent for a matching story. When the reporter replied that he did not file because it was completely false—his competitor had been given wrong information—he got back a message reading, "Grateful your explanation, but we still lost the play."*

The need to zero in on dramatic essentials causes a type of distortion when applied to quotes. Tightly edited stories allow only enough room for fragmented excerpts of someone's words, and sometimes the intent is lost. U.S. Ambassador to the United Nations Andrew Young, for example, was often reported as calling people "racists"—former presidents, world leaders, the populations of Sweden and the New York borough of Queens. In context, Young actually said that people who did not take into account cultural differences among societies and ethnic groups were practicing a form of racism. But that abstract thought, translated into headline terms, comes out "Young Calls

---

*Some correspondents are less intimidated than others by desk messages. As tension was building during one Middle East crisis, a British reporter was asked by an editor, "Canst file thousand words on will Egyptians fight?" He replied, "No, no, a thousand times no."

Whomever Racist." That is what Walter Cronkite of CBS labels a "malquote." It's not a misquote, because the words are correct; but it is a distortion. Cronkite coined the word in criticizing television, but newspapers and agencies malquote people as well.

Another distorting factor in news stories is the "today angle." Old news is out, even if it is significant, unless it can be doused with journalistic embalming fluid. A reporter arriving late at a disaster with no new development must cover himself with cliché: "Rescue workers today sifted through the tangled debris of . . ." Normally, an important speech can be reported only on the day it was given, unless its contents can be folded into a more general story. Readers who are aware of this can learn a great deal by looking at the actual information presented rather than the way in which it is introduced.

When news agency dispatches are edited and polished into publishable stories, they are distributed to newspapers in tidy packages, timed whenever possible to coincide with deadlines across the country. As new information arrives, the stories are brought up to date—"topped" —with newer beginning paragraphs designed to lead newspaper desk editors directly to whatever material is still applicable in the earlier versions. This requires careful construction so that most background information, which is unlikely to change, remains intact despite later tops. Because of this, readers can often find important explanations of breaking news down at the bottom of a long story.

AP and UPI each put out "budgets" twice a day—one at midnight for afternoon papers and one at noon for morning papers—to help guide editors. The budget lists about a dozen of the day's top national and foreign stories. They help newspaper editors shuffle quickly through the pile of dispatches they must digest between their first cup of coffee and the news conference with other department editors to decide what goes onto the main pages. Even the fastest speed readers have time only to glance at the first few lines of each cable, making mental notes of their contents and lengths and, from time to time, scribbling down a remark. Budget lists have an enormous impact on what gets into the papers. News sense is highly subjective, and editors are often insecure. An indecisive deskman knows his colleague in the next city has the same doubts and budget lists, and if he sticks to what the agencies say is important, he runs less risk of passing over a story given major display by the competition.

The selection of stories for the front page is far more subjective than even most professionals realize. In 1977, Los Angeles *Times* press writer David Shaw supervised a 155-day study of what appeared on the front pages of the New York *Times,* the Washington *Post* and his own paper. Checks were also made of fifty other prominent American newspapers. Only twenty-eight times in five months did all three of the major papers agree on the most important story of the day. Twenty per cent of the time, there was not a single story that appeared on the front page of all three. Only 60 per cent of the time did the front pages have at least one or two of their eight or ten stories in common. Shaw observed from the study:

> Newspapers other than the New York Times, Los Angeles Times and the Washington Post seem especially indifferent to all but the most cosmic of foreign news events. Of the major foreign stories published during the first five months of 1977, only the defeat of Indian Prime Minister Indira Gandhi was the lead story in virtually every American daily newspaper. Two months later, when Israel's ruling Labor Party suffered a shocking and historic defeat at the polls in an election that could have a profound and far-reaching impact on Mideast—and world—peace, the story didn't even make page one of the Atlanta Constitution, Dallas Morning News and the Portland Oregonian, among others. [The Israel election, which brought Menachem Begin into office, was buried on page nine of one important Southwestern daily.]

Many editors argue that they must concentrate on local news, since their readers get foreign and national news from television. But television news coverage is limited severely by time and scope. And, as Shaw notes, "what it does provide is largely influenced—often virtually dictated—by what the major newspapers play on page one. Thus, whether people get their news from television or from newspapers (or both), the residents of one city may have a considerably different perception of a given day's events than the residents of almost any other city."

Few readers realize this and make allowances for it. In fact, when Shaw presented his findings to the highest-ranking editors of the major papers he studied, they all expressed astonishment.

This subjective, often haphazard, selection process leads to an overall distortion in the presentation of world news. Only a few newspaper executives insist that their desks keep a close watch on the world from a long perspective. The best papers treat news in a world context and choose stories with major significance for their readers. They keep track of which areas and subjects are left uncovered for long periods, so they can bring them up to date whenever they have a little extra space. Obviously, if a reader happens to be rafting down the Snake River when a crisis is resolved, he will have to bring himself up to date. If he misses a situation report on Nepal, he may have to wait eleven months before Nepal's turn comes around again. But at least the material was presented. Other newspapers—the majority of them —plan their contents on a day-to-day basis with little thought about the past or future. In some cases, there is hardly any thought given at all. If an editor has a nine-inch hole on page 5, and he can quickly put his hands on a nine-inch story from practically anywhere on almost anything, he looks no further.

The most sensational newspapers select stories for immediate impact, and often drop them while they are still hanging. In August 1977, for example, a major afternoon tabloid carried a huge headline reading, "New Angola War; 5000 Cuba Troops Rushed to Battle Zone." A story, not attributed to any correspondent or agency, told how civil war had erupted again two years after it officially ended.* Nearly fifty white mercenaries had been killed, the dispatch had reported. The major news agencies could find no evidence to support the story, so they did not pick it up. The next day, the paper carried no mention of its mysteriously exclusive war. In the following days, with a crazed murderer calling himself the Son of Sam taking up newspaper space, the subject was dropped.

Sometimes when newspapers print inadvertently distorted stories from abroad, they follow them up with corrections or denials. But these are seldom given the same prominence as the original mistaken account. A news agency erroneously reported that 36 persons were killed in a freight train crash near Guadalajara in 1977, and one paper carried the news on its front page with a scarcely veiled sneer at Mexican freight trains full of non-paying passengers. When a new story reported the death toll was actually four, it was printed in brief form on page 4.

What gets into the paper depends largely on what else is also

---

*An editor explained later that the credit line had been dropped inadvertently. The source was a stringer in South Africa for a small syndicated newspaper service.

happening at the same time, whether local, national or international. After advertisements and regular features are situated on page plans, editors determine how many column inches are left for the "news hole." Since the early 1970s, when newsprint and productions costs rose sharply, newspapers have tended to be thinner, with smaller news holes. As a result, editors have developed new ways of dealing with foreign news as briefly as possible. One popular device is a newsbrief column, a few single-paragraph items which might be used to kiss off any story short of a major war. Remaining space is given to shortened dispatches from the agencies' budget lists and fillers selected for size to plug odd holes on the page. From time to time, there are long by-lined analyses or news features to assuage editors' consciences and to satisfy more serious readers.

To kill several birds with a single stone, news agencies often produce round-up stories which touch on a number of countries at once. With a single story on wars in Africa or inflation in Latin America, editors can discharge their responsibility without carrying a number of dispatches describing each country separately. This is often overdone. A "European round-up" on practically anything means little except in the most general terms since the viewpoints of seventeen nations, from Swedes to Turks, can hardly be covered in 600 words. Asia, Africa, Latin America and the Middle East are handy geographical groupings, but each is made up of individual peoples, often with little in common.

Another space-saving device is synthesizing the news in predigested packages. The giant Gannett newspaper chain employs a specialist to condense foreign news for its more than seventy papers. He writes wide-ranging articles which combine major trends, sparing editors from having to cover each separate element. Each paper uses what it wants. Some print the special analyses as well as a full range of foreign-dated items, and others don't even use the catch-all articles.

To help space-conscious papers, the AP and UPI sometimes send advisory messages on their wires calling attention to stories considered to be of particular value. But even that brings spotty results from editors with little room for anything. As background to the violent South Africa racial disorders late in 1976, the AP provided a graphic, thoughtful story on the black youths who rioted. It focused on Hector Petersen, a thirteen-year-old "child of apartheid" who was the first to die, and it discussed the new generation's changed views toward the blacks' lot. The story was sent out several days early to give editors time to look at it and was scheduled for the afternoon papers of Tuesday, ordinarily a day with few ads and more space for news. The AP checked its usage in twenty-seven major newspapers which care enough about news content to subscribe to both AP and UPI; of the twenty-seven, only one had used any of the story—a cut-down version buried on an inside page.

Agencies often move background and feature stories in advance on their wires. They give a suggested release date, with a minimum embargo, and editors usually stick to it to avoid being beaten by competing papers which subscribe to the same agencies. But sometimes stories are left around to fill holes on quiet days. One agency sent out a report on the fast-changing politics of France, explaining that the major parties of the left might split before elections because of internal discord. An important California paper ran the story six weeks after it was distributed—and almost a month after the left had split completely.

Most editors seem to have an informal Top Ten list in mind of currently popular subjects. If a story does not figure on the charts—whether it is on energy, human rights, détente or whatever—it probably won't make the paper. "You can easily see it down here," observed one veteran Latin America correspondent. "When Latin America is up, you can get the Asunción weather report into the papers. When the cycle is off, you can't get in anything about anything."

Many editors, like their correspondents, cling tightly to clichés, selecting stories which comfort their readers by reinforcing stereotypes. Alexander Cockburn, the press critic of the *Village Voice,* touched on this in an essay for *More* magazine. He picked on a columnist, C. L. Sulzberger of the New York *Times,* but his remarks were general, applicable to editors as well as writers: "C. L. has divined the central mystery of his craft, which is to fire volley after volley of cliché into the densely packed prejudices of his readers. There are no surprises in his work. NATO is always in crisis. There is and always has been an opening to the left in Italy. He never deviates into paradox. His work is a constant affirmation of received beliefs. . . . C. L. Sulzberger is much too experienced a hand to avoid the obvious when he has a chance to consort with it." Any correspondent who has tried to write something which contradicts a general belief knows what an obstacle this cliché barrier can be.

New stories can be edged onto the Top Ten list, and clichés can be overcome, but it is often a wearing process. One correspondent in India used to con his editors whenever he saw a major story with no immediate angle. If there was a famine in the south, for example, he would not rush down and write about it. First he would send a few three-paragraph stories about reports of famine. Eventually, some alert editor would message, "Grateful check reports of famine in . . ." That way, the editor would be delighted at his own ability to second-guess his unimaginative correspondent, and he would give the story prominent display.

Obviously, certain types of stories have general priority over others. Anything which involves Americans or the United States is tops on the list. Korea, for example, is seldom in the news unless U.S. troops tangle with North Koreans or a secret agent bribes a congressman. Often editors stretch for an American angle. The *National Lampoon* struck close to home in its newspaper satire in 1978 with a lead story beginning "Possible tragedy has marred the vacation plans of Miss Frances Bundle and her mother Olive as volcanos destroyed Japan early today."

The Vietnam war was an excellent example of these factors. When U.S. troops pulled out, there was no more American angle. Editors, like readers, were tired of the story, and it was off of everyone's Top Ten list. And the cliché belief was that the war was over. Suddenly the story that had commanded page 1 attention for years slipped back to the bottom of page 23.

Some stories are used purely because they are well written. On a trip to the Soviet Union with Richard Nixon, the AP's Hugh Mulligan was all over the papers with stories having little to do with the president. He wrote in one story, "The sleek looking Russian jet made its usual landing, which sounds like a stack of pizza plates toppling over onto a tile floor." Another said, "Yalta is where the czars built their ornate palaces that for centuries kept the Russian taxpayers feeling baroque."

Occasionally a dispatch is shaped to satisfy some editor's bizarre idea of what is news. Once Pope Paul VI made a historic flight to Colombia, the first visit of a pontiff to that devoutly Roman Catholic nation. A reporter covering the trip received instructions: "Downplay religious angle."

Occasionally correspondents can get marginal stories past the gatekeepers by using a familiar name or catch phrase. A reporter in Africa during the 1960s joked that he never wrote anything from Ghana, not even a brief traffic accident story, without mentioning Kwame Nkrumah in the first paragraph. Even today, Charles de Gaulle in the first sentence of a story from Paris increases its chances of play.

At times, correspondents can't give their editors enough. Appetites are voracious, for example, for sensational stories about celebrities and royalty. Some stories just catch on, and editors keep them alive with artificial respiration. When the Paris peace talks on Vietnam settled down to a single weekly meeting, one agency cut its coverage to a preview story before each session, a quick story during the day's talks, and a wrap-up afterward. The other American agency insisted on daily stories all week long, whatever was happening. Correspondents had to scrape for bits of news, sometimes whipping up out of proportion remarks of low-level aides, just to comply with orders.

Coups and earthquakes are still perennial favorites of all editors. But their coverage often presents special problems. Editors like their coups to be clear-cut, dramatic and, if at all possible, with an immediate and distinct turn to the left or right. No one wants a headline reading, "Confusing Coup in South America; No Deaths Yet and Political Slant Unclear." Unfortunately, political upheaval is seldom tidy, and always difficult to follow in those remote places which are rarely covered in between uprisings. When leaders were abruptly changed in the peaceful little island nation of the Seychelles, most editors reached for their globes to find the place, and then set out to present the story in clear—and misleading—terms for their readers.

For years, political support in the Seychelles had been divided between two young lawyers with slightly differing views about how to maintain prosperity without undue strain for the 60,000 inhabitants of the string of islands off Kenya in the Indian Ocean. Early travelers wrote that the Garden of Eden was definitely in the Seychelles and that today's tourists off chartered jets paddled among coral reefs. The dominant figure was James (Jimmy) Mancham, who as chief minister resisted independence from Britain as unnecessarily expensive and adventuresome. When independence came anyway, in 1976, he was elected president. He geared the economy toward tourism and private foreign investment, entertaining lavishly abroad on what he called publicity missions. The other leader, France Albert René, also favored tourism, but he argued for economic diversification to avoid control by foreign financiers. He was concerned that outsiders owned prime land and held important concessions, which, he said, forced islanders into a subservient role. When Mancham went to the London Commonwealth Conference in June 1977, René announced that he was taking over.

The coup was reported as a move by rebels under a leftist dictator to overthrow the pro-Western government. Stories focused on an order that anyone venturing onto the street would be shot on sight. A small band of "enforcers," which René had brought in just in case the island's police force did not readily shift loyalties, was described as a communist guerrilla army. Analysts immediately blamed the Russians for engineering the coup as part of their plan to control the Indian Ocean. It was widely seen as a clear-cut win for the Soviets and the fall of another defender of the West, with hints of widespread bloodshed and upheaval in paradise.

On the first day, none of these elements was clear. Few organizations had stringers in the tiny country. The Seychelles was too far away and too quiet for regular visits by correspondents. Word of the coup came in an unsigned and unsolicited cable, obviously from René's office, to news agencies' London bureaus. With that, and with sketchy reports from a few scattered sources, editors assembled their stories. The cabled communiqué said the move would make the Seychelles "free of capitalists and foreign countries." In Cold War terms, that was an admission of communism, and it smacked of Russian involvement. René was a socialist, so the label "leftist" was legitimate even if it conjured up an image closer to Trotsky than, say, George McGovern. He had brought in armed men, trained by radical African governments, and there was a shoot-on-sight order. But, as Mancham himself admitted, "Twenty-five people with sticks could take control of the Seychelles." From London, Mancham blamed the coup on the Soviet Union, but later diplomatic reports said the Russians were so surprised that they thought the Chinese were responsible.

The need to rush into print with something had produced a skewed picture. Only those readers who waited until the dust settled and read later dispatches understood what really happened.

Even earthquakes, without politics and personalities to obscure issues, are often presented with unconscious distortion. If an earthquake kills 1000 people in northern Italy, it is covered in graphic, gripping detail, and fresh stories are printed with each new discovery of victims. Some of the dead are named, and their destroyed villages are eulogized. A year later, stories are written describing the aftermath. But if thousands are killed in Guatemala, the reporting is different. The dead are vague round numbers. Emphasis is likely to be on American aid for victims rather than on the victims themselves. And the story, generally, is given less play.

This double standard exists partially because Italy is easier to cover than Guatemala, and more reporters are immediately available. But it is mainly because Italians are seen as individuals, with physical and cultural characteristics familiar to Americans. Many editors and readers have been to Italy, and they recognize place names in the stories. Guatemalans are seen, on the other hand, only as faceless residents of the underdeveloped world. The standard is part of the unwritten but well-understood sliding scale: a hundred Pakistanis going off a mountain in a bus make less of a story than three Englishmen drowning in the Thames.

Cultural favoritism is hardly particular to American editors. A British press lord typified the historic and still lingering attitude in a memo posted in his London daily's newsroom some years ago: "One Englishman is a story. Ten Frenchmen is a story. One hundred Germans is a story. And nothing ever happens in Chile."

Most types of stories are covered according to the sliding scale. When the late Francisco Franco of Spain was about to put to death four Spanish guerrillas, the story was on the front page of newspapers for days on end, with editorials and outraged letters from readers. At the same time, hundreds of Latin-American guerrillas—and suspected guerrillas—were being executed without trial by government-linked groups with scarcely a mention.

Obviously, editors are motivated more by their sense for what matters to the world than by any feeling for social justice. Less blood was shed by students pitching paving stones at the Paris police in May 1968 than in similar riots elsewhere in the world. But political turmoil in France has a greater effect on most Americans than a total revolution in Bolivia.

These judgments are difficult to make, however. And one of the worst problems of the system is that this sensitive selection process is in very few hands. The New York *Times* by itself plays an enormous role. Even at the AP and UPI, night editors anxiously await early editions of the *Times* to see what foreign stories the paper saw fit to print. If anything shows up in the *Times* that wasn't on the wire, hasty messages are sent to correspondents. Often agency correspondents are asked by their desks for stories which they did days earlier; some editors automatically assume the *Times* is first, and they don't bother to check back before asking for matchers. Occasionally, agency correspondents send stories which are not used on the wire, for one reason or another, until the *Times* carries a similar story and it becomes news. The television networks seldom break stories on their own. They are guided mainly by the news agencies—and the New York *Times.*

Nicholas von Hoffman, a commentator for King Features stressed this point in his syndicated column in mid-1977. He noted that few American newspapers paid any attention to a report on Israeli torture published in the Sunday *Times* of London. He wrote:

> The . . . team which did the story is universally respected in the business and has been copied by papers like the Washington Post. The lack of interest on this occasion may be explained by the New York Times covering the torture investigation with an 86-word article, if you can call a piece that short and appearing on page 13 an article. . . .
>
> To some extent all news in America is what the New York Times calls news, but even more so with foreign news. In part this is because the Times spends the money that other papers, the magazines and the networks won't spend on foreign correspond- ents; but it is also because so few print or broadcast editors are able to make independent judgments on the news. They simply lack the character and stature to have an opinion of their own and prefer the safety of letting the nation's most prestigious papers do their decision-making for them. This is particularly easy with an issue like Israel where any adverse publicity is likely to win an editor vociferous abuse from one of the nation's best organized lobbies.

Although the *Times* has an enormous influence on deciding what is news, AP and UPI have a greater role in determining how news is written and presented. In a sense, a handful of men and women in Midtown Manhattan shape the general picture which Americans have of their world.

In practice, it is not as pernicious a situation as it may seem. News organizations compete fiercely among themselves. If one neglects to report an important development, the others may not be so careless. Newspaper editors, even if they do not have their own correspondents abroad, can demand more coverage from the agencies on any story they feel is being underplayed. Several factors guard against any intentional meddling with the news. Newspeople at all levels have a strict sense of responsibility about news, and there are many individuals involved in the handling of each story. If someone tried to change the essence of a dispatch—or suppress one—others would sound the alarm. This happened in 1970 when an AP executive decided to hold up a story about looting by American troops in Cambodia. All troops loot in battle, he reasoned, and therefore the story was belaboring the negative. Such an uproar was raised within the AP that the executive reversed his decision within hours and acknowledged that he had made a serious error. The incident was reported in *Time* magazine, and, years later, critics still harp on it, because they can find no other such cases of tampering.

There is yet another consideration which has little to do with the people involved. The physical aspects of the system are so complicated that sometimes simple accidents cause significant errors. One news agency produced a long profile of French President Valéry Giscard d'Estaing, concentrating on his position in crucial legislative elections. The writer said the president had become "Giscard the grind" because of his long hours. A typographical error in the editing process made it "Giscard the grin," and the desk distributed the story that way. One newspaper used the piece under a huge headline, "Giscard the Grin," although the poker-faced president was distinctly sparing with his smiles.

Most of the editing and distribution process is too far out of reach for the reader to make his own assessments. Few non-professionals regularly see a full-service news agency wire. Editors are mostly anonymous, and readers can only guide themselves by a newspaper's general reputation for careful handling of copy. But a lot can be learned —about the news and the newspaper—by the way stories are displayed and headlined.

The discerning reader should look carefully at each item, no matter where it ends up in the paper. In American newspapers, stories which editors think are most important are displayed on the top half of the front page—above the fold—where they can be seen on a newsstand. The biggest story goes in the upper right-hand corner, where, according to general belief, the reader's eye first falls. After that, there are few rules. In some papers, like the New York *Times,* foreign news is concentrated mainly on the same few pages inside. In others, like the Washington *Post,* it is sprinkled liberally throughout. A number of papers use indexes or summaries, but most just fit stories in wherever they can. Editors must work around awkward advertising layouts and regular daily features, so they must often shoehorn dispatches into unlikely corners. Often vital stories appear in odd-shaped spaces deep inside simply because last-minute local news forced them off the front and onto a catch-all page.

Headlines are valuable only as a guide to subject matter; their information is often misleading. The number of letters in each headline is dictated by space, and copy editors must fit the substance and drama of a story in as few as a half dozen words. No matter how good the headline writer, there are bound to be distortions, misunderstandings and overstated assertions. A correspondent might take five paragraphs to explain how a country's worsening political crisis, coupled with an economic crunch, could cause militant sectors to use terrorism against the government. To a headline writer, that might mean: "Civil War Imminent." Although many headlines turn out to be brilliantly worded synopses which catch the essence of a story, readers can never be sure, and it's a good idea to look beyond them.

Datelines are a vital part of any story. Almost every foreign dispatch starts with the city from where the story was filed. If the dispatch is from the country the story is about, readers at least know that the correspondent—or a stringer—was there. Often stories must be written long distance, and readers have to evaluate them carefully. Coups, for example, are customarily covered from the next country over, or from a major European city, until borders reopen and communications are restored. In such cases, correspondents explain whether they are basing their information on monitored radio broadcasts, diplomatic reports or refugees' accounts. Readers must assume that the details, and possibly even the basic facts, are subject to change.

On some breaking stories, readers cannot expect more than emergency minimum coverage; they must guide themselves by the datelines and the source code words. In late 1977, German terrorists hijacked a Lufthansa airliner and leapfrogged across the Middle East. Reporters could not get visas or flights fast enough to follow the action, and when German commandos stormed the plane to free hostages, the news came from Bonn. Obviously, it was the official German version. News analyses about Third World countries are often written from London or Paris by correspondents who normally travel in remote countries and in the meantime keep up with contacts from a distance. These can be valuable stories, but readers should try to identify the writer and the organization and, if possible, the circumstances in which the story was written. This might appear in an editor's note with the story. The by-line might be familiar. If nothing else, a reader can always telephone the newspaper copy desk and ask.

Stories which carry no datelines are somewhat suspect. Sometimes they are responsibly written combinations of news agency reports. But if they bear no mention of the city of origin or the source, readers must add a few grains of salt.

Articles on foreign affairs written in the United States are a particular problem. The biggest news organizations keep specialists in New York or Washington to write about visiting leaders and international matters. But such stories written by regular domestic reporters are often uninformed and ingenuous. Few local reporters have the time to keep up with the finer points of foreign news. When assigned to cover visitors, their research is frequently limited to a quick flip through an incomplete library folder. They seldom know which questions to ask or how to evaluate answers. Obscure professors and politicians with slanted views are quoted at length with no balancing comments or general context. Astute foreign leaders understand this, and many send envoys to American cities where they are assured of uncritical coverage in the local papers. There are exceptions, of course, but readers never know whether a local reporter has done his homework. This also applies to reporters in most domestic bureaus of the AP and UPI. One night in 1977, a newsman in the Philadelphia bureau of one agency telephoned his foreign desk and asked, "Are the Philippine Islands still an American colony?" No, he was told, they have been independent since 1946 under the name of the Philippines.

At most newspapers, there is little coordination among the various departments that handle articles on international subjects. The deskmen who edit dispatches from abroad do not see foreign-related stories by staff reporters at home. Editorials and op-ed page articles come from different desks.

This creates confusion for the reader. A newspaper might carry a long article describing terrorist violence in a country, while on the travel page it runs a puff piece on the same day about the carefree natives. Editorials are written by specialists who try to stay close to the news, but sometimes they contradict information in the news columns.

The small unheadlined column fillers are a particular problem. These brief little items are prepared by syndicated feature services for editors who find they have an odd bit of space left over as the pages are being prepared for the presses. They are churned out from whatever sources are available—including press releases from governments and public relations companies. If a news agency reports that a country's inflation was 200 per cent, the dispatch might get no farther than the first editor's wastebasket. But a one-paragraph item based on a government communiqué claiming inflation was 15 per cent might well show up on page 2.

Stories written on junkets are another problem. A newspaper might not find room for a careful analysis on a troubled Latin-American country written by a correspondent who has studied the place for a decade. But if an executive of the newspaper happens to stop in that country for lunch, the paper might run a column of not necessarily well informed reporting by the executive who feels he must justify the trip.

Of all special categories of foreign items, the easiest to spot and the hardest to evaluate are editorials. An ever finer line separates the reporter from the editorial writer. In past decades, correspondents were ordered to set forth the facts and let the reader draw his own conclusions. But how, editors realized, can a sales clerk in Salt Lake City decide what is going on in Angola when he knows only how many tribesmen are fighting on two sides of a power struggle involving a dozen nations? In any case, objectivity is a subjective concept. Any choice of facts, words or structure amounts to judgment. Correspondents still give readers as many sides as is practical; but the wording is likely to lead an open-minded reader to the same conclusion the reporter reached himself, as objectively as possible, before writing the dispatch.

In some situations, dispatches marked "news analysis" go further, stating conclusions reached by the writer. But there is still a sharp distinction. In reporting—even in news analysis—a correspondent is bound by ethics to accept whatever conclusion the facts suggest to him; his personal viewpoint should play no part. The editorialist states an opinion on how things should be, and he can stretch any point he chooses to support his case. If the editorialist is well informed and thoughtful, he can suggest new ways for the reader to see a situation. If he has not done his reading, and his counsel is clouded by a particular prejudice, he can mislead readers badly.

In some ways, an uncoordinated array of international items in a newspaper can be an asset to the reader. Different sorts of editors can present information from varying angles, and the reader is protected from any one gatekeeper with too many blind spots. For example, the Washington *Post* on a typical Sunday in 1977 was stuffed with diverse material from abroad. The "Outlook" section had stories from Brazil on the threatened Amazon and from Greece on the ten-year aftermath of the coup. There were stories on Lago Argentino, a glacial lake, and the Mayan ruins of Chichen Itza. An article from Nice told about landslides scarring the Riviera. Another, from the *Guardian* and dated from London, was about white South African farmers moving to Bolivia. There were foreign business stories, situation reports from the Middle East and Southeast Asia and a number of brief items. And there was the normal foreign reporting on page 1 and the inside pages. The day's paper was by no means a complete picture of the world. But it was a good piece of the puzzle, and anyone who read other such pieces regularly would be on the way to keeping track of global affairs.

The newsmagazines have a different way of working than news agencies or newspapers. Their desks deal with far fewer stories, and they have much more time to work. Editors take a more active role in shaping and writing stories and in generating ideas. Editors at *Time* and *Newsweek* balance coverage of major stories with short reports on places not normally in the news. But the magazines have strict space constraints, and the selection process is rigorous. The biggest stories are included automatically, often with separate sidebar pieces to cover related aspects. The remaining space is allotted by an informal committee of editors. Each week, correspondents suggest a number of possibilities for stories; editors, in turn, throw out their own suggestions to bureaus. And then specific assignments are made. To be included, a story needs some sort of "peg"—a single event like an election, a riot or a major speech—on which to hang a general article.

In preparing each separate report, the newsmagazines try for the same sort of objectivity as newspapers. The aim is to inform readers so they can draw their own conclusions about events. But the tight format—for content and for style—adds an element of subjectivity. One *Time* editor explained his magazine's approach: "We have certain attitudes. For example, we basically believe that détente is a good thing [he was speaking in 1977]. If for some reason we change that attitude, rather than just abandon it we try to explain to our readers why it no longer appears to be the right course." Readers are not specifically told of these attitudes, but perceptive observers can distinguish them over a period of time. This does not make the newsmagazines unreliable, but it is one reason why readers should rely on a variety of sources for news.

At the newsmagazines, the role of the desk is so important that when *Newsweek* began giving by-lines it listed the writers in New York first and then followed with the correspondents who actually reported the story. (The same policy was applied to domestic stories.) After the story selection is made, each separate report is given a specific number of lines. Correspondents send long reports, covering all possible angles of the story, and writers on the desk produce a final version. Writers are selected more for syntactical skills than experience in reporting. They work with research staffs and elaborate libraries for background and details. The finished product often bears no resemblance in wording or style to what the correspondents originally wrote, although, ideally, the facts stay the same. *Time* uses a double system of checkpoints and playbacks. Correspondents are asked to confirm questionable information or to provide more details on certain points. Then, when a story is written, it is cabled or telephoned to the correspondent for comment. *Newsweek* uses a similar system of checks but plays back finished stories only at the correspondent's request. At the same time, *Newsweek* does less rewriting and often uses unchanged correspondent reports with brief editor's notes explaining the circumstances of the report.

Although newsmagazine correspondents complain less than in the past about distortion and mistakes from the rewriting process, sometimes New York can hear the screaming from Beirut, Hong Kong or London without the aid of a telephone. Last-minute rewrites can put quotes in the wrong mouths and sneak in clichés which have not applied for years. Distortions, of course, are not always the editors' fault, and the desk serves as a safeguard against sloppy reporting. One correspondent yelped into the phone on hearing a playback, "That is hyped way out of proportion." He calmed markedly when told the passage in question was exactly as he had written it.

Because of the time delays, newsmagazine editors are often forced into the unenviable role of seers. Just when Egyptian President Anwar Sadat made his surprise visit to Israel to negotiate a settlement, one magazine hit the stands with an article about how far away peace talks seemed in the Middle East.

Every major organization has an overall foreign editor who deals not only with correspondents' copy but also with correspondents. He is the main contact with home for his far-flung brood, calming their distraught relatives during dangerous assignments and defending their interests before insensitive personnel executives. But few foreign editors have the time to stay in touch, and correspondents must fend for themselves. One agency man, en route to Vietnam on his first foreign assignment, sat down with his editor, expecting advice on everything from finding the cable office to writing a thank-you note to the Pulitzer Prize committee. His editor pondered a while and finally said, "Don't take nylon underwear."

"Pardon."

"Nylon underwear. In the tropics you get sweaty. It binds."

9

Television and Radio

Television and radio have gatekeepers, too, but they work in different ways. When reporters learned that the body of Eva Perón was to be brought back to Argentina 23 years after she died of cancer, they scrambled to get ready. As a symbol of revolution and the subject of the rock musical *Evita,* she was perhaps the most famous woman in Latin-American history. Even in death, she was almost as important a political figure as her husband, President Juan Perón. When military officers deposed Perón, they spirited her carefully preserved remains to a secret grave in Italy so Peronists could not rally around their martyr. But Perón had returned to power after 18 years, and the beautiful waxlike figure of Evita was to be flown home. A television stringer telephoned her network desk editor and reported, "They're bringing back Eva Perón." He responded, "See if you can get an interview with her in English."

The editor may not have known much about the world, but he knew about television. Whoever Eva Perón might be, there was only one way to cover her—in person. His job was to make it possible for viewers to see news happening and to feel themselves involved in it. That they might come away with more impression than understanding was not for a desk editor to ponder.

As a rule, broadcast newspeople are solidly trained editors and reporters, and behind the show biz facade there are the same sweaty collars and coffee-stained ties as in any other kind of newsroom. But their subsystem of international reporting has its own particular failings on top of the problems of the general system. This is critical for Americans, since a majority of people in the United States get all or most of their foreign news from the air waves.

Television is, as former CBS president Arthur Taylor says, the Big Megaphone. Spoken, illustrated words sink in far more deeply than printed ones. When television is good, nothing can touch it. When it is not, it is an erratic headline service which often misleads more than it informs. Executives and editors naturally play to the medium's strong points—and the strong points are not necessarily suited toward solid reporting of world affairs.

Televised news coverage is at its best when stories can be shown live and are big enough to rivet viewers to their chairs. A blend of direct satellite transmission, historic film clips and correspondents' interpretation can give people a better grasp of a major story than if they were actually there watching it unfold. In such cases, editors* throw the gates open and devote as much air time as they can squeeze.

When Egyptian President Anwar Sadat put aside decades of enmity and addressed the Israeli Knesset in November 1977, American families watched and listened as it happened. No reporter or editor stood between them and the events. They could see Sadat's face as he called for peace, and they could observe—in dramatic close-ups—how Israeli Prime Minister Menachem Begin reacted to the speech. The two leaders met in an electronic handshake shared directly with the world.

But even at its strongest, television suffers from systematic failings. World leaders and newsmakers who understand American television can play it to the hilt. The Sadat-Begin encounter was planned essentially for television—a media event of enormous proportions. At one point, someone asked former Israeli Premier Golda Meir if she thought the two should get a Nobel Peace Prize. "I don't know about a Nobel," she replied. "But they should get an Oscar."

Coverage was so rich that many viewers, caught up in the dramatic moment, misled themselves. For them, it was not two leaders agreeing to talk; it was the coming of peace in the Middle East. When subsequent discussions broke down, these Americans were surprised and deeply disappointed.

---

*To simplify, the term "editor" in regard to television and radio refers to the whole gamut of producers, assignment editors and various production people who, together, tend the gates.

In routine day-to-day reporting from abroad, a series of problems causes more direct distortion. The most obvious of these is the lack of time—the network's and the viewer's.

An evening news program has twenty-two minutes of speaking time, not enough words to fill three columns of newspaper type. Although such comparisons are faulty—news film of Georges Pompidou, old and sick, has more impact than columns of words—limited time means that few items can be covered. The most avid viewer is not likely to see more than a few minutes of foreign news a day, even if he also catches a morning news show and takes a glimpse during lunch. That is enough to tell him whether Germany has marched on Poland again, and perhaps to show him a curbside view of the secretary of state's motorcade in Amman. It may even allow for a long instructive look at turmoil in southern Africa or inflation in Japan. But it can hardly give him a balanced report on the state of the world.

The time problem causes what Walter Cronkite of CBS calls "distortion by compression." In a speech to station owners in 1976, he said that just doubling the time for evening news would make a major contribution: "Give us at least a two-pound sack for our hundred pounds of news each night. . . . We would not have many more items . . . but we would take a little more time with each item—enough extra time for the explanatory phrase, the 'why' and the 'how' as well as the 'who,' 'what,' 'when' and 'where.' "

One vivid example was when the Carter administration cut military aid to Ethiopia, Argentina and Uruguay because of human rights abuses. It was Carter's first decisive step to show disapproval of governments which murder and torture, and it showed he was willing to risk losing friends abroad to defend a principle. The networks all but ignored it. One mentioned the story deep in its evening newscast, saying, "The Carter administration, concerned about violations of human rights in Uruguay, has cut its foreign aid money. Really cut it. From three hundred and twenty thousand dollars a year to twenty-five thousand. On the foreign aid list, that must put Uruguay somewhere near the bottom." It did not mention Argentina or Ethiopia, much bigger countries with worse human rights records than Uruguay; it didn't even say what Uruguay had done. It did not note that Secretary of State Cyrus Vance admitted to Congress that similar action was not taken against South Korea or Iran, because they were friends that the United States could not afford to alienate. The gesture was lost on most Americans, and very few understood its real meaning.

If the serious viewer who watches television regularly and pays close attention is badly informed, the casual viewer gets only a random smattering of news. With television, there is no way to go back and catch up. If the phone rings during an important story on arms talks, the story is lost.

A second major problem is competition at several different levels. There is a constant fight for larger audiences. However seriously news executives may take their mission to inform responsibly, if their ratings slip they are in trouble. Stories are selected not only for news value but also for general appeal. Unlike newspapers, television networks cannot include many items which are likely to interest only a portion of the audience. Most viewers will forgive a few significant but boring stories. But too many such items might move them to fire off the channel selector. Also, within each network organization, correspondents compete intensely among themselves for air time. In television, correspondents get ahead by corresponding, and that is not easy. They tend to push stories which are likely to get past their gatekeepers, and those are not always the most important ones.

Then, too, there are problems of production and format. Television is so highly visual that often stories are chosen or passed over on the basis of what color film is available to go with them. Some stories just cannot be filmed, however imaginative the cameraman. Often it is difficult to find people to interview in English. And in many cases film cannot be relayed back to New York within a day or two before a story dies of old age. Although producers will include important stories if there is no film, they will seldom give them much time; few stories will run a full minute with only still illustrations behind the anchorman.

To a certain extent, television has been victimized by its own technology. If something important happens in Spain, the New York desk can call London and get a crew on a plane within the hour. The correspondent can make a few phone calls, put together a usable piece and send it to New York by satellite in time for the evening news. But in such circumstances he is not likely to understand much of what he is reporting. Since it is possible to report so quickly from many parts of the world, stories die more quickly than they did before, and sometimes networks do not even try to go after news in remote places. In the past, networks had to keep more people on the spot, and reporters were more familiar with essential background. If correspondents had to rush off somewhere, they had an extra day or two to learn something about the story before explaining it to Americans.

Three facets of format and technique can be advantages or drawbacks depending upon how they are handled. Positive or negative, all are important to the system.

The first is the emphasis on personal rapport between newspeople on camera and the viewer. A survey by Oliver Quayle and Company in 1972 indicated that Walter Cronkite was the most trusted public figure in America. It established a "trust index"—showing a percentage degree of trust people said they had in different categories of public figures—and Cronkite finished first with 73 per cent. He was followed by, among others, the average senator, 67 per cent; the average governor, 59 per cent; and Richard Nixon and Hubert Humphrey, each with 57 per cent. With that sort of faith among his followers, Cronkite is taken at his word. To a lesser extent, this applies to all news readers and correspondents. If a trustworthy face on television tells people that something is important, they will probably listen. At the same time, if someone slips in a sly raising of the eyebrow at the mention of an African country, many viewers receive a clear signal that they need not treat the place seriously. Most television professionals try to control their non-verbal messages. John Chancellor of NBC says, "I'm so dead-panned they call me the Woodrow Wilson of broadcasting." But many people on camera reveal their own feelings with winks, grimaces and voice pauses in what amounts to subjective editorializing.

The second facet is the face-to-face interview. This can draw out significant information, allowing viewers to watch the impact of each question and to get a visual impression of the subject. But it can also give a very mistaken impression. Question-and-answer encounters allow a subject to exaggerate or lie outright. Few interviewers are well enough informed to make confident contradictions. In newspapers, reporters can go back to the files and write a story around the interview, interspersing direct quotes with balancing material. On television, if the interviewer does not break in at the moment, it is too late. Also, the newspaper writer can give a complete description of his subject, with good points and bad. Television interviewers are seldom prepared to start out by saying, "This dashing, beaming general next to me, seated with his dog next to a picture of his charming family, has just secretly executed 300 suspected terrorists without trial."

Barbara Walters of ABC conducted a highly publicized interview with Shah Mohammed Reza Pahlavi of Iran just as Jimmy Carter was outlining his human rights principles. Carter had not yet mentioned Iran, but there were reports that the shah's secret police were even harassing Iranians in the United States. "Death to the Shah" was written in flowing Persian script on subway walls, and magazines carried accounts of victims who had been tortured in Teheran. Walters broached the subject by asking the shah if he was a dictator. He flashed the smile of a good king in a fairy tale and replied that, if that meant was he taking firm steps to provide a better life for his people, yes, he was a dictator. With that, she let him off the hook and went on to an unrelated topic.

The third facet is the use of the camera itself. It can bring a viewer directly to the action, but it can also bring him too close to it. A camera zoomed too tightly on a noisy demonstration—showing contorted, yelling mouths and clenched fists without the empty spaces in between—can overmagnify the intensity and confuse the overall context. A high camera position, with the lens angled slightly downward, can make a sparse crowd look large and densely packed. By resting on one colorful and interesting element in a dull panorama, the camera can make a dull story appear colorful and interesting. Obviously, at times just the presence of the camera intensifies the action. When filming starts, demonstrators all of a sudden wave banners and shout with renewed vigor. Speakers and public figures seem to take on unusual eloquence when they notice that a lens is reflecting them into millions of American homes.

All of these elements combine to make television an extremely powerful and instructive medium. But they also give it a certain degree of unreliability.

At the very least, television is a basic index for someone who is interested in foreign affairs. It gives a valuable if incomplete table of contents for stories happening around the world, and it often provides the visual image so necessary for understanding. Armed with primary information and atmosphere, a viewer can then turn to newspapers, magazines, books or local experts to pursue stories which interest him. Sometimes television itself will provide the probing analyses and documentaries necessary to back up brief stories presented on the regular news programs. Done well, these accomplish more than a long well-written magazine article. But even with new emphasis on such background reporting, they are still rare.

Viewers can learn a great deal from televised newscasts despite the drawbacks, as long as they pay close attention. Information does not filter through by subliminal osmosis, and if a viewer's mind wanders for even a few seconds, the meaning of a story can be lost. Television and radio newswriters prepare scripts with the inattentive in mind, a practice which helps comprehension but limits still further the time available for new information. They approach the main point slowly, beginning with introductory words which may not be crucial to understanding. At the end of the item, there is often a brief wrap-up. But there is only so much a writer can do. Once something is said, it is gone.

With broadcast news, suspended belief is particularly important. Since spoken words appear to carry more weight than written ones, there is a natural tendency to take things at face value. At the same time, awkward source attribution is avoided whenever possible, and correspondents on camera try to sound as sure of themselves as they can. The result is a tight, dramatic presentation which can make the news seem larger than life; viewers tend to exaggerate stories in their own minds, distorting their meaning. Even when all the information is carefully qualified and presented in a low-keyed manner, the most attentive of listeners can miss a key phrase and hear something wrong.

Although the three networks' evening programs are the main newscasts of the day, foreign news is also presented in some depth on morning and late-night shows and on news programs of local stations. On some days, television provides a fairly wide range of stories for anyone with the time to sit still for them.

Some fundamental types of stories simply escape television's possibilities, and serious viewers must fill in the gaps elsewhere. International economics, for example, is practically a write-off. If French winemakers stone trucks carrying Italian wines to Bordeaux, that is one thing. But if economy ministers affect Americans' fortunes by deciding on a currency float and a paper-based standby system of credits—with SDRs and whatnot—there is almost no way to explain it on the evening news. John Chancellor, one of the most enterprising reporters in television, recalls that the Common Market bureau he opened in Brussels in 1963 was the toughest assignment he ever had. He said later, "It led me to realize that you have two choices. You can simply tell people that something is important to them, and that is not good journalism. . . . Something like 'We can't tell you everything about MIRVs and MARVs, but . . .' Or you can reduce yourself to visual stories; limit yourself to event coverage rather than covering the substance." For all networks, the situation has not changed since then.

Summit meetings are routinely presented as colorful entrances of the world greats into paneled rooms with little attention given to the vital content of the private discussions. The real news at such sessions comes from tireless probing at long-established sources, and the information must be hedged carefully and couched in qualifiers. For television, the emphasis is on winners and losers, with a summing up in concrete terms of things which are not at all concrete. Economic talks between industrialized and developing countries are even harder for television to explain because of vast cultural gulfs which must be ignored—even if they are understood by the correspondent.

For similar reasons, international politics is almost as difficult for television to present with any real meaning. Political stories require too many words, and they allow little opportunity for news film to justify the time. Elements must be reduced to the most rudimentary level. Opposing sides have to be presented simply, and their differences must be made understandable to American logic. Stock labels like "leftist," "right-wing" and "communist-inspired" are often essential, however subtle the real situation might be. Oversimplification is hardly peculiar to television, but the medium's format seldom allows for the occasional reminder that things aren't as simple as they may seem. Although television provided some excellent coverage of the fighting in Vietnam, for example, broadcast news was often shallow and misleading on the basic causes of conflict. After one coup, a skilled correspondent was carefully explaining what had happened in a call to New York when his editor broke in: "Hold it, Pete. Hold it. These Vietnamese names and parties are much too complicated. Can't you make them 'pro-communist general' and 'anti-communist general' or something?"

Since network news can only skim the uppermost surface, stories of quiet change and undramatic human suffering are rarely mentioned. Countries like Paraguay and Niger and Burma may go for years without being mentioned on American television. Even large and important countries like Brazil and Indonesia never seem to get onto assignment sheets. A filmmaker associated with one of the most popular weekly magazine shows said he tried for years to convince the producer to carry at least something from Latin America. He finally got approval for an item on Brazilian witchcraft, but it was canceled the next day. He recounted, "The guy told me, 'I frankly don't give a damn if South America is detached at the Panama Canal and sunk, and I doubt if anyone else does, either.' "

This superficial overlay seldom warns of imminent troubles, like oil boycotts, until they are major crises. Such stories, if covered in the newspapers, generally begin as brief items back among the classified ads. They gradually inch forward in the paper, swelling in size and appearing under bigger headlines. When they burst upon the front page, prompted by some dramatic act or declaration, then they suddenly make their television debut.

Each network keeps between fourteen and twenty correspondents overseas (compared with fifty-five to seventy-five in the United States), directed by assignment editors in New York. Reinforcements are rushed from American cities when necessary. Occasionally these correspondents develop stories on their own, but far more often they are assigned to do firsthand versions of stories sent by AP and UPI. This often causes friction. For example, in 1978 a network desk rejected a story from its correspondent in Beirut because it had not been reported—confirmed—by the news agencies; the next day, when the agencies carried the story, the desk asked the reporter to send his story quickly. He resigned. Earlier, also in Beirut, a news agency reporter noticed a fleeting rainbow on the morning of a ceasefire, and he mentioned it as a passing note of color in a dispatch. A half hour later, a television man showed up at the Beirut agency and demanded, "Where is your goddammed rainbow? New York wants it on film."

Because of the logistics involved, the network staffs are much smaller than they seem. In an average overseas bureau, about 15 per cent of the working hours are spent actually gathering news; the rest of the time is taken up by editing, typing and pasting labels, hanging around cargo offices waiting for material to come and go, waiting for visas and airplanes, arranging for satellite channels and looking for fresh batteries. And that is on days when correspondents are not losing time traveling. Television reporters must move constantly. During the Vietnam war, CBS's Haney Howell once changed countries seven times in three days—going back and forth among four capitals—and he filmed a story at each stop. (Some time ago, a network advertised that one of its Asian correspondents averaged 100,-000 miles of travel per month. At subsonic speeds, that would mean the reporter spent about ten hours daily aloft or going to and from airports.)

Under those circumstances, even the most perceptive and energetic correspondents cannot stay on top of all significant developments. Editors make their priorities and deploy their forces as best they can. If a network cannot get a correspondent to a story before it is old news, sometimes it can be ignored in favor of something else. If it is important, they might cover it by having the anchorman read a script written from news agency dispatches, using still photographs or graphics as illustration. But if the event is too important to be given such secondary treatment, editors will settle for reports on camera from stringers. This is a clear second choice for networks. Stringers are mainly used to assist visiting correspondents, leading them swiftly to "news"—something tangible which can be filmed—and filling them in on background for their narrations.

The value that networks attach to stringers, as compared to staff correspondents, is evident from their payment policies. When Isabel Perón was overthrown, one network could not get a staff reporter in quickly enough to replace its regular man, who was ill. Instead, they relied on their stringer, an American woman who was one of the best-informed reporters in Argentina. She supervised all the filming and editing, narrating on camera a balanced, colorful account. She was the only television reporter to note the veiled repression which soon came to light. Her story arrived in time for prominent display on the evening news after she fought heatedly with military authorities to get it transmitted by satellite. She was paid $64, less than one day's room charge at the hotel where a special correspondent would have stayed. Given time, the network would have dispatched a staff reporter—referred to as "talent" in TV parlance—with an average daily salary of three times that, and his ticket and expenses would have been at least $3000. And, without Spanish, local contacts or background knowledge, he would have had to rely almost totally on the stringer anyway.

This demand for familiar faces puts pressure on correspondents to justify the importance attached to them. Most of them squeeze all the mileage they can out of their stories within the limits of ethics. And a few don't stop there. Some correspondents lean toward doomsday predictions and touches of drama which lend a heroic light. One correspondent noted wryly, "Whenever I see a guy reporting from a trench on some battlefield, I alway look to see where his microphone cord goes. If it runs up over his shoulder, it means some sound man is up there taping, and no sound man is going to hang around exposed if there is real danger."

The temptation to hype is doubly strong because of the tight selection process of the gatekeepers. Footage with tension and emotion stands a better chance of reaching the air. One network man in Vietnam, famed for pushing the limits, set up a dramatic sequence by placing a microphone in a trench. As he walked by on camera, he leaped into the hole, as though gunfire had suddenly erupted, and he began a breathless narration. Unfortunately, his Vietnamese cameraman decided not to go along with the act. Pleading camera trouble, he made the reporter repeat the phony sequence three times, and then he dispatched the uncut film to New York. The correspondent received a message, thick with sarcasm, that two of his spontaneous leaps had been excised. Nonetheless, he kept his job.

It need hardly be said that reporting for television is often excellent. Even when it is not, it requires grueling work, courage and ingenuity. If newspaper photographers must get near enough to action to make pictures, television crews must stay there and keep filming. For television people, moving from place to place is a constant tangle of unwieldy metal trunks and fragile, expensive lenses. In many countries, crews find that, despite their enormous clout back home, ABC-CBS-NBC is just alphabet soup, and authorities do not take them seriously. Often cameras are banned from the most innocuous of public proceedings. On assignment, correspondents seem to be always looking for an English-speaking guerrilla, a lost soundman or a brief adjective which describes a political system about which six books have been written. They must be master planners and executors. ABC mustered a team of twenty-three reporters, production people and messengers to cover a trainload of hostages held in the Dutch countryside by Moluccan terrorists.

Since the visual impact of television is as important as the spoken words, a great deal of the burden falls on the cameramen. Correspondents frequently direct their crews on what to shoot, but not always. Overseas, most are non-Americans who travel from a fixed base, either as full-time staff members or regular stringers. However gentle they may be as human beings, they can invariably take on the properties of bulldozers when the need arises. Newspaper reporters sometimes have the impression cameramen are hired by linear foot and by the pound, with special bonuses for being able to elbow print journalists away from news subjects when they are filming them. One strapping British cameraman arrived in Dacca before Pope Paul VI was scheduled to stop off for an airport news conference. He carefully set up his camera position just opposite the papal dais. But when the pope landed, Italian photographers swarmed off the plane with him, and one of them planted himself in the narrow space between the Briton's lens and the holy father. The cameraman grabbed the photographer and, to the astonishment of the pope, a few feet away, he lifted him high into the air. "What do you think Monte Cassino was about?" he bellowed, invoking the wartime Allied drive through Italy, and he tossed the Italian into a far corner.

Somehow, cameramen can often manage to blend into surrounding woodwork, and their presence causes less effect on events they film than might be expected. At one African summit, newsmen were banned from a private session. But an agency reporter noticed that a television crew was setting up to film the meeting. He picked up a coil of wire, and, passing as a television technician, he listened to the whole thing. It had occurred to no one that television crews are newsmen too.

When correspondents and crews assemble their material, it is dispatched to New York, where gatekeepers package it into news programs. The networks each have about 200 affiliate stations around the country which broadcast the finished product. Affiliates agree to carry a certain number of hours of network programming for which they are paid—by the networks—a small percentage of what they would charge commercial sponsors for the same time. Although the networks have been pushing to expand the half-hour evening newscasts to an hour, a number of affiliates say they prefer to have their own local newscasts, which lead into the network programs. One major reason is that stations can make more money from sponsors for local newscasts than by giving the networks additional time at discount rates. In some cases, the lead-in news shows contain a number of foreign items from the news agencies to which the stations subscribe directly.

A number of prominent broadcasters argue that 30 minutes is just not enough time to give viewers the information they need to be informed intelligently about world affairs. Others say the gatekeepers of television can make a substantial improvement without more time; the common denominator should be raised, they contend, so the lazy and the unconcerned do not deprive the more interested citizens of vital news.

But most agree on one thing: television is not doing enough to report the world for America.

Radio news, often lumped together with television and forgotten in media studies, has a completely different set of possibilities, limitations and problems. It is immediate and pervasive, capable of delivering urgent news, complete with actual sounds and voices, at any hour to anyone with a five-dollar transistor radio. As a news medium, radio could be a constant source of reliable information about the state of the world. But, often, it falls short of that ideal.

It has strong points. Thoughtful commentators add insight and colorful background to breaking news. Papers like the New York *Times* and the *Christian Science Monitor* supply condensed spoken versions of some of their significant dispatches. But on the whole, radio news is a superficially written summary of the news agency wires, interspersed with brief voice reports from correspondents about whom individual news directors know little. Westinghouse, the last radio organization with staff people abroad, dismantled its foreign service in 1977. There are only a handful of full-time correspondents overseas reporting exclusively for radio. Correspondents for ABC, CBS and NBC often cover for radio as well as television, but as one insider explained, "Most of these guys are too busy worrying about TV to devote time to radio—they know that television will fire them, not radio." Correspondents for the AP and UPI also contribute to the audio services of their agencies. And all radio networks use casually hired stringers who are paid a fixed sum for each voice report.

About 90 per cent of the 8000 radio stations in the United States subscribe to broadcast news wires of the AP or UPI, or both. Roughly half of them use only local announcers to read from the prepared summaries, which come by teleprinter. (Some provide a complete, serious news service, and others are like the small station in South Dakota where an announcer remarked one morning, "Well, we usually have some news about now, but the fella that reads it isn't in yet, so we'll just play some more music.") The other half use canned newscasts and voice reports from one of the national networks in New York or Washington. The material is packaged by harried desk people who have little time to reflect on greater meanings. They are concerned much more with the what and where—and with the if-any-Americans-were-involved—than with the why and the what it means.

Affiliation requirements are more casual in radio than with television, and stations take a variety of approaches. In 1977, ABC had four separate radio networks going to 1400 stations. (CBS and NBC, with one network each, went to far fewer.) Many stations faithfully relayed the complete service—a five-minute hourly news summary, brief voice reports and special flashes to bring news up to date in breaking stories. But ABC's flagship station in New York used only about a minute of news per hour, generally local stories, along with some early-morning programming to fulfill network responsibilities. Hundreds of stations subscribe to audio services of AP or UPI which provide voice reports that are signed off only with the correspondent's name and the city. Announcers frequently begin reports by saying, "Our man in Caracas . . ." as though their small station kept a full staff of special reporters abroad.

Radio news is best heard during the "morning drive," the early rush hour when listeners are caught in traffic with nothing to do but listen. News directors try to pack that period with the most essential items, and they devote more time to such features as "mini-docs," brief spoken documentaries which delve more deeply into problems than the standard few-second treatment. The choice of stories is still likely to concentrate on the current international "celebrities" of hard news —an Idi Amin Dada of Uganda or, perhaps, a Pierre Trudeau of Canada—rather than the stories of substance which require careful explanation. The popular all-news radio stations give a better picture, depending upon the station, but most still concentrate on national and local news, with only passing mention of foreign items.

Listeners are best served when they can identify the disembodied voices speaking to them—and when they carefully choose their stations. National Public Radio and some commercial broadcasters concentrate on foreign news, and they look for people who report it with insight and accuracy. Some network commentators delve into world problems more effectively than columnists in newspapers and magazines. At the same time, astute listeners learn which popular independent commentators offer little more than personal opinion, often based on faulty information, rather than reasoned analysis.*

In general, radio is most valuable when a crisis suddenly breaks out somewhere. Listeners are immediately told what happened, and they can follow developments throughout the day and night. But this immediacy makes radio basically unreliable as a sole news source. Breaking stories are seldom clear at the beginning. There are often conflicting casualty figures and basic details. Politicians change their positions rapidly. Police and military officers jump to conclusions that later prove to be unjustified. And correspondents' first impressions do not always hold up after a longer look. News agencies and radio stringers provide a constant stream of reports on big stories from the moment they break. Although they carefully note, "First reports said . . ." or "According to conflicting accounts . . ." they say what is available.

With newspapers and even television there is usually time for events to clarify before they are explained to audiences. With radio, however, these initial reports are relayed immediately to listeners, who seldom pause to realize they are hearing only fragmentary bits of a picture which is likely to change. For example, during the Yom Kippur war in 1973, one agency erroneously reported that Cairo had been bombed. Its correspondent was on the phone to London when he thought he heard bombs dropped, and he reported an air raid. He soon discovered he was mistaken, but it took time to call back with a corrected report. This problem is not necessarily the fault of radio newspeople, but their medium suffers nonetheless.

But the radio format at least allows a listener to turn on his set at any time, listen for a few moments and know that his world is still out there in reasonable order. He will have an immediate warning of

*There is a range of subtleties for experienced listeners. For example, NBC uses a special system for establishing hierarchy. If a staff correspondent does a voice report, he signs off, "Arthur Airwaves, NBC News." If the speaker is a regular stringer, he says, "Arthur Airwaves, *for* NBC News." But if he is a casual contributor, he gives only his name, with no mention of NBC.

the most important news even if he must wait or refer to other sources to gather more information. That is no small contribution.

Radio news can be powerful and extremely effective when properly exploited, and its proponents defend it with passion. One highly placed professional put it: "One of the worst problems is that because everyone dumps on radio so much, it is considered the last resort. Kids going into journalism figure that if they can't do anything else, they can always go to radio. So no one teaches it properly and no one thinks about it. It has an enormous potential which is not being used."

There are a number of talented people in radio news, but some gatekeepers and executives care little about the substance of foreign news reporting. One correspondent, after spending fifteen hours trekking the Israeli desert, phoned his network to transmit an exclusive interview with an American woman wounded in a terrorist raid. He was so tired and hungry he could barely finish his narration. Afterward, an executive news editor came on the line. He was not concerned about the story; he wanted to check if the reporter was using a regulation-issue tape recorder. The correspondent asked him to amplify the line to full because he had something to add. Okay, his boss said, go ahead. And he thundered in the man's ear, *"Fuck you!"*

10

Digging Deeper

During 1974, little bits and pieces appeared in the newspapers which indicated that Iran might be something more than a graceful desert kingdom out there past Israel. The shah, after celebrating the 2500th anniversary of the Peacock Throne, had decided that the Persian empire should again take its place as a world power. And, with oil at $11.65 a barrel and Iran producing six million barrels a day, he had the wherewithal to do it.

Astute readers could see that Iran was important to the United States, politically, economically and militarily. What the shah had to say about oil prices, defense strategy, import sources and Middle East power balances had direct impact on their lives. But anyone seeking information in his newspaper or on television found little more than features on royal panoply and economic items laden with production figures. That was the time to dig deeper.

By the end of 1974, *Harper's* magazine carried a long article by Frances Fitzgerald which remains a classic on what made the shah run. *Fortune* had printed a major article by Louis Kraar discussing the depth and extent of the shah's plans for Iranian growth. *Saturday Review World* delved into other aspects. So did the *New York Times Magazine*. The shah himself was plumbed in *New Republic* by Oriana Fallaci, the Italian journalist-celebrity, and he was interviewed formally by senior editors of *Time*.

It was clear that 1974 was a year for catching up on Iran. Magazines had ignored it for years, and now its turn had come. The weighty coverage continued on beyond the first wave. *National Geographic* photographed the country in 1975, and Carl Rowan plowed through it for *Reader's Digest* in 1976. The Iranian poet Reza Baraheni described in such diverse magazines as the *New York Review of Books* and *Penthouse* how the shah tortures and torments those who oppose him. Commentary came even in books. Novelist Paul Theroux, in his 1975 best seller, *The Great Railway Bazaar,* dispatched Iran with saber strokes: "Money pulls the Iranian in one direction, religion drags him in another, and the result is a stupid starved creature for whom woman is only meat. Thus spake Zarathustra: an ugly monomaniac with a diamond tiara, who calls himself 'The King of Kings,' is their answer to government, a firing squad their answer to law. Less frightening, but no less disgusting, is the Iranian taste for jam made out of carrots."

The case of Iran shows clearly that a serious reader is not without hope. The background articles provided a sense of context for interpreting the precipitous events which sent Iran into upheaval during 1978 and 1979. On most countries, an enormous amount of information is available, not only in magazines and books but also in specialized publications like area newsletters, industry reports, government documents, think-tank and academic papers and the underground press. In every sizable town, there are professors, travelers and businessmen with valuable knowledge they are happy to share. The key, of course, is not trying to absorb it all but rather learning what to look for and whom to trust.

More-informed readers regard newspapers, newsmagazines and broadcast news as only a base from which to develop their knowledge of the world. Correspondents are under pressure to write quickly, as soon as the first information is available; and even if they do not make mistakes, their sources might. Overall patterns are not always clear from day-to-day events. Even in fast-changing situations like wars and political revolutions, the best reporting is often done by those who take months to write dispatches which must hold up for years. Many decision makers who depend upon an accurate picture of the world start with what they call a triangulation of sources. If, after a reasonable period, three different news organizations say the same thing about a particular situation, they believe it. Once satisfied with the basic facts, they prowl for sources which deal with foreign news on a long-range basis.

Supplementary sources not only give more details about news events but they also identify significant trends and international factors which bear on a specific situation. It is far less important to know how many persons were killed in a day's fighting in Beirut than to know who is involved and why and what it means to stability in the Middle East. Left-wing political gains in Italy mean much more when compared to European politics and history in general—and when there is some explanation of what "left-wing" actually means to Italy and to Italians.

The unhurried pace of a long background article is essential for explaining some stories. The same words and ideas often mean different things from one culture to the next, and the best of correspondents are limited in what they can convey in brief space. A letter to the Manchester *Guardian* in 1921 showed how tricky this can be. The writer was referring to England and France, two cultures which know one another well. He wrote:

> Words, like money, are tokens of value. They represent meaning, therefore, and just as money, their representative value goes up and down. . . . Some nations constitutionally tend to understate, others to overstate. What the British Tommy called an unhealthy place could only be described by an Italian soldier by means of a rich vocabulary aided with exuberant mimicry. Nations that overstate suffer from inflation in their language. Expressions such as "a distinguished scholar," "a clever writer," must be translated in French as "a great savant," "an exquisite master." It is a mere matter of exchange, just as in France one pound pays 46 francs, and yet one knows that that does not increase its value at home. Englishmen reading the French press should endeavor to work out a mental operation similar to that of the banker who puts back francs into pounds, and not forget in so doing that while in normal times the change was 25 it is now 46 on account of the war. For there is a war fluctuation on word exchanges as well as on money exchanges.

Digging deeper allows a reader a different perspective on situations which may seem simple and clear-cut in concise news dispatches. Walter Lippmann once pointed out, with characteristic irony, that a grocer usually has very clear, well-developed ideas about political conflict in Europe and the Far East. About groceries he is less certain, because he knows firsthand how complicated the subject can be.

As world leaders become more adept at manipulating correspondents and editors, supplementary sources—removed from breaking news pressures—grow increasingly important. During the celebrated Sadat-Begin encounters, each side played directly to world sympathies, through the press. Sadat granted a hundred interviews in six weeks, selecting television interviewers who could give him maximum exposure. Begin flew to Washington in a dramatic gesture to brief President Carter—and American reporters. Only long, thoughtful analyses, written from a distance, could separate the substance from the public relations tactics.

Some of the best sources for background are columns in newspapers and magazines, which most readers skip over for later and then forget. The New York *Times*'s James Reston, for example, wrote at length about what Sadat and Begin actually accomplished beyond their public displays. Newspaper op-ed pages usually carry a range of syndicated writers who dig deeply into foreign affairs. Columnists are not necessarily good just because they are in print. In fact, some occasionally write completely misleading and flatly inaccurate assessments of countries they have never visited. But a careful reader soon learns, by comparing forecasts with subsequent events, whose guidance he can follow. News analyses in the regular columns of newspapers are from correspondents who have had time to understand a situation, and most can be accepted at face value.

Newspapers and magazines from Europe add different perspectives, often with much more detail and interpretation, than those in the United States. One daily which concentrates on the world is the *International Herald Tribune,* published in Paris. It is owned by the New York *Times,* the Washington *Post* and Whitney Communications. Its chairman is John Hay Whitney, who published the defunct New York *Herald Tribune.* Since it has no hometown to cover, it is made up mostly of foreign news and analysis. The weekly *Economist,* published in London and widely available in the United States, delves deeply into global economic and political interdependence, with a clear, wry style. The weekly *Guardian* and the *Observer* from London and the English edition of Paris' *Le Monde* are among a number of European publications which circulate throughout the world. Anyone who reads German or French can find excellent news weeklies at specialized stores. Readers with special interests in Asia can find wide coverage in the *Far Eastern Economic Review* or the Asian edition of the *Wall Street Journal,* both published in Hong Kong. Any good library or foreign publications newsstand has a wide array of helpful alternate sources.

Readers in cities which are badly served by local newspapers can always subscribe to an out-of-town paper which covers foreign news more thoroughly. In many cities, the New York *Times* or the Los Angeles *Times* is available in coin machines by breakfast time. The *Wall Street Journal,* an excellent paper for foreign coverage, and the *Christian Science Monitor* circulate across the country. Even the paper from the next city over might be well worth the added cost. One journalism professor in a Western city observed, for example, "If I just knew what the papers print here, I'd be in total isolation. What do I do? Every morning I jog down to the drugstore and buy the paper from [the state capital]. It's not a lot better, but at least I know what's going on."

None of the general American magazines which touch on foreign affairs attempts to cover everything. But taken together they offer a wide range of timely stories which explain continuing news stories from a longer view. The answer is hardly in subscribing to them all; apart from the cost, the crushing guilt of a mountain of unread magazines is too much for anyone to handle. But it is easy enough to sample them. And library guides allow readers to find quickly articles on any particular subject. Magazine pieces can vary from close-to-the-news reporting to essays on cause and context which might remain valid for a decade. Either type provides a solid basis from which new developments can be interpreted.

Discerning readers learn as much as possible about each magazine they read—and about the individual writers whose articles they absorb. The down-the-middle objectivity of newspapers has little place in magazine journalism. Writers might not alter facts or slant their presentation, but they have a particular viewpoint. An article about human rights in Latin America in the *Nation* is not likely to heap praise on military governments. A writer steeped in Cold War diplomacy, whose personal opinion is that communism had damned well better stay where it is or disappear altogether, will analyze politics differently than would a fire-breathing radical at the other extreme.

The New Yorker is one of the few general magazines that uses a regular stable of contributors for covering foreign subjects. *New Yorker* writers are freelance, technically, but most keep a desk in the magazine's mustily elegant offices on 43rd Street and work for no one else. Over a year, ten or twelve of them will write from abroad, and a handful of outside experts will be asked to contribute specialized articles. The magazine has no particular pronounced point of view other than a slightly elitist—some say slightly arrogant—approach to life in general. It takes a single country at a time, often in the format of a "Letter from . . ." for a leisurely account of what is troubling the people and society. Sometimes it runs a hard piece of reporting; occasionally it includes an article on an obscure subject simply because it is written well. Faithful readers learn the by-lines and styles, and the articles sometimes come to be personal letters from friends. Those who followed the Vietnam war through the relaxed-pace dispatches of Robert Shaplen, for example, had a clearer picture of it than those who kept daily track of casualty figures and B-52 strikes.

"The intention, the desire is to cover the world," explains William Shawn, *The New Yorker's* venerable editor. "But not being a newsmagazine, we always take a long view." His approach is purely subjective; when a topic arouses his interest, he sends someone to write about it. "Sometimes we want to know about something—not because there is competition or because anybody is waiting for it, but because *we* want to know."

The *Reader's Digest,* too, has a regular set of contributors who write on current foreign issues, although their approach is totally different. The magazine favors brief articles, in direct style, on topics of major interest. It also reprints abridged articles from other sources, covering a wide range of subjects.

Magazines like the *Atlantic Monthly, Harper's, Esquire* and the *New York Times Magazine* buy articles from a relatively small group of freelance writers. Sometimes they want a particular story, and they commission someone they know to do it. More often they wait for the writers—or their agents—to advise that they will be in Greece or Burma and to suggest specific story ideas. Some writers are salaried foreign correspondents whose employers do not object to outside work. Others are authors between books. Still others are professional writers or travel junkies who have made names for themselves.

Each magazine takes a slightly different approach. The *Atlantic Monthly* editors, for example, say they welcome articles from experts who know their subjects well, even if the writing is not particularly elegant. *Harper's* editors prefer writers to tailor their pieces to fit the magazine's essay style.

Good magazine articles often include fresh reporting on new developments as well as general background. Claire Sterling's comprehensive and aggressive treatment of the sub-Saharan drought, in the

Atlantic of May 1974, brought to light revealing information on "how to spend hundreds of millions of dollars to help people starve." She described how poor planning, mismanagement, ancient habits and misplaced pride combined to hamper international efforts to save the 2.5-million-square-mile Sahelian belt for human habitation.

The range of magazines is enormous, from *Rolling Stone,* which often treats writers cavalierly and deals in psychocosmic themes from abroad, to *Foreign Affairs* and *Foreign Policy,* which count prime ministers among their freelancers but sometimes exhibit sedative properties. The *Stone,* in spite of itself, occasionally produces well-rounded articles on troubled countries and American foreign policy, and its kick-'em-in-the-ass approach lends rich color and atmosphere. *Foreign Affairs,* published by the Council on Foreign Relations, and *Foreign Policy,* associated with the Carnegie Endowment for International Peace, are the most serious-minded journals available on international politics and economics. They explore confrontations of power, transnational currents, macroeconomics and political change with bedrock detail and scholarly precision.

The *New York Review of Books* takes an intellectual approach, but it combines the specific with the abstract in superbly edited and often immensely moving pieces. Sometimes foreign themes are discussed in long book reviews, but often the magazine assigns writers to discuss any subject the editors feel is timely. The *Review* is particularly strong on international economics, which are explained in splendid simplicity by writers like Emma Rothschild, a regular contributor. *Penthouse* pays big money and devotes ample space to foreign subjects, attracting some well-known writers. It specializes in international intrigue, American blundering overseas and colorful personalities who upset establishments.

National Geographic, for decades a fascinating picture magazine which stuck to anthropology and sociology, has made a shift toward frank political and economic reporting. Its writers and editors use an elaborate system of rechecking facts to avoid rumblings among its conservative readership. But the new dimension allows the magazine, in its stilted but complete style, to provide richly done portraits of other cultures and societies.

This, of course, is only a partial list. Countless other magazines cover everything from general economics to such fields as dental tools and road building. Specialized magazines frequently go beyond their own areas. *Fortune* deals mainly with business, but when its staff writers turn toward general subjects, they provide an enormous amount of reliable information. Even *Computer Age,* a small industry magazine, took on Chile in a highly politicized article about the sale of American computers to police for political repression.

The obvious drawback to magazines is that sometimes readers cannot find the material they need when they want it. Some major subjects just aren't covered. The Lebanon civil war, for instance, almost pleaded out loud for treatment in *The New Yorker.* The magazine's discursive approach, with its almost unlimited space, is almost perfect for such an important but dizzyingly complex situation. Shawn said he thought often of assigning a writer to Beirut but each time decided against it.

"I didn't want to send anyone in there. I didn't want to risk anyone's life on that particular story," he explained. "The story wasn't worth the risk. We don't have the obligation of coverage the way the New York *Times* or the wire services or the newsmagazines do. When there is a situation like in Vietnam, we feel we have an obligation—it's our war. We take our chances like everyone else."

But there are dozens of ways to fill in the blank spaces. Editorial writers at major newspapers keep track of background publications, and most are happy to offer guidance to anyone interested enough to ask them. Groups interested in world affairs arrange for speakers and discussions in most big cities. A number of university resources are available to the general public. The U.S. State Department prepares a large amount of material on other countries, and officers in Washington and in embassies abroad can suggest sources of information on any nation.

It is not necessarily easy, but anyone who digs deeper into foreign news can find more material than he needs. And, although it is hard to believe, he might be better informed about the world than many of those in Washington making policy on his behalf.

11

The Washington Connection

Author Theodore H. White, who has spent decades stalking the corridors of power, has no doubts about the effect of foreign reporting on policymakers in Washington. Asked once if press reports from abroad carried much weight in official circles, he leaped to his feet, waved his arms and declaimed, "I would say the front page of the New York *Times,* what appears on it, is more important in policy-making than any CIA cable, or any State Department cable. And what appears in the L.A. *Times* when it gets to those forty-three California congressmen, or what appeared in the Chicago *Daily News* when it had a foreign service, or what the AP lands on the front page in Cheyenne, Chillicothe or Denver—that is what shapes the mentality of Congress. And you can't get anything through without Congress, which explains the presidencies' attempts to manipulate the press. What importance do press reports have? *Enormous,* for Christ's sake."

Hardly a correspondent—or a public official—doubts White's assessment. Some might not share his absolute terms, but few would question his basic premise. American foreign policy is based more on what most people think is going on rather than what is really going on. In a representative government, decisions do not necessarily reflect what officials think is best for the electorate. Leaders may try to convince the public that a particular course is necessary. But, in the end, they act according to what they feel the electorate thinks is best.

To a large extent, government people and the general public form their basic opinions from the same sources: correspondents' dispatches. President John F. Kennedy once remarked, "I don't think the intelligence reports are all that hot. Some days I get more out of the New York *Times.*"

The importance attached to general reporting in Washington is obvious to the most casual observer. In mid-1978, when the Washington *Post* reported the government had decided to freeze arms limitation talks with the Soviet Union, President Jimmy Carter delivered an angry personal denial of the story. He called reporters in to say, "It damages our country; it damages my credibility; it damages the prospects for the continuation of the basic policy of our government."

When major news is reported, reaction is often swift in Congress. Legislators sometimes vote with newspaper clippings in their hands, clearly their only source of information about the subject under debate. After Soviet police detained Anatoly Shcharansky, a Jewish dissident scientist who could not get an exit visa, Congress rushed to condemn the action on the basis of the first press reports without waiting for official confirmation. As it turned out, Shcharansky had been reported as arrested for treason when, under complicated Soviet procedures, he was only being questioned on possible treason charges. For most congressmen and officials concerned with the case, the difference was slight, anyway. Shcharansky, who typified the dissident movement, was being persecuted, and their prompt action signaled the Kremlin that he would not be forgotten.

Congressmen, who must face the polls periodically, are particularly sensitive to reporting from abroad. As White observed, their role is vital. On several occasions, they have restricted the president's ability to conduct foreign policy, and they control expenditures abroad. James Reston of the New York *Times* put it like this in a column during 1977: "Congress is not a creative but a negative power. It is not very good at starting things or foreseeing the future, but it is very effective at stopping things, especially when some thunderclap in the news . . . hits the headlines."

And rapid reaction to dispatches is hardly restricted to Congress. The Washington *Post,* the New York *Times* and, increasingly, the *Wall Street Journal* are on State Department desks by breakfast time. Anything important prompts an instant inquiry from the seventh floor. If an article contradicts reporting by an embassy's political section, the embassy must defend itself. In more than one case, an embittered diplomat has corrected an erroneous dispatch only to find that months later the accepted version in Washington was still the wrong one. Conversely, intelligent policy decisions have been made because officials in Washington acted on information from trusted correspondents rather than from embassies they knew to be weak in political reporting.

White House aides study the papers carefully, and staff members spend entire mornings checking out information and preparing statements of reaction.

Sometimes there is little difference between diplomatic and press reporting. Reporters and diplomats trade information frequently, particularly when they get to be friends. It is generally a give-and-take arrangement, with the reporter guarding his own sources and the diplomat holding back what he feels cannot be made public. But the balances can tip sharply in either direction. In one turmoil-troubled country, a news agency reporter found that he was listed as the source in so many embassy cables to Washington that he had to object to protect his independence.

Because of their unofficial status, reporters can move around more freely than diplomats. They can nurture contacts with dissidents and rebel leaders without compromising any official policy. They do not have to worry about channels of protocol, either within the government they are covering or within the embassy. Correspondents can hang out in the grubbiest of bars without worrying about sullying their employer's good name. They can be obnoxious at times if it is necessary for prying loose information. And frequently they are better at gathering news than a diplomatic foreign service officer trained as a bureaucrat.

Government people make use not only of basic facts from correspondents but also of interpretations and analysis. One top-level CIA executive, now in retirement, recalled, "We paid close attention to the press not so much for straight news accounts but for the analytical articles which suggested to us new ways of looking at things. For example, we found the articles by Bob Shaplen in *The New Yorker* [on Vietnam] to be of great use, not for the information they contained, which we normally had already, but for the way he saw things and the conclusions he drew."

The Washington crowd is not always so pleased at the helping hand. Harrison Salisbury, the distinguished senior New York *Times* correspondent, was invited to North Vietnam to witness the effects of American bombing on civilians. Salisbury, who had won a Pulitzer Prize in 1955, was respected for his reasoned and balanced approach to news. He had worked in the Soviet Union and understood how to gather information and avoid propaganda in a closed society. In North Vietnam, Salisbury found evidence that the bombs had killed civilians and destroyed residential areas. He was nearly the target of one deadly raid. His detailed accounts, exposing as lies the American assertions that only military targets had been hit, caused a storm in Washington. President Lyndon Johnson's aides began referring to his paper as the "Hanoi *Times.*" Officials scoured his past for something which might expose him as a closet communist. Salisbury recalls he made one slip which caused problems. The mayor of a small town gave him some casualty figures which were in line with other information he had, and he used them without attribution. Because of that, some officials challenged his professional approach. Salisbury said that at the time he was surprised that the figure was so low, considering the extent of the damage. In fact, three weeks later when the furor eased, officials were using the same figures they had denounced in order to show how few people were being killed.

Later on in the war, there were so many embarrassing dispatches about secret U.S. operations and official bungling that the Nixon administration organized the Plumbers to find information leaks. These "special investigators" went on to bigger things, and when they were caught in political espionage, they triggered the Watergate process which eventually forced Nixon to resign.

In a less serious case, a correspondent in Nigeria wrote how local soldiers were taking their girlfriends for midnight joy rides in jeeps provided by the American government for refugee relief. The embassy in Lagos was so furious that officers were forbidden to talk with the reporter.

Correspondents can be a safeguard against official reporting which is slanted for one reason or another. Sometimes ambassadors or embassy section heads take too seriously their responsibility to maintain friendly relations with the countries in which they are based. Other times, prejudices in Washington require embassies to angle reporting toward what is expected of them. At one stage in Uruguay, embassy reports on human rights were so much milder than press reports that

State Department officers concerned with rights had to do their own investigating. During the final months of the war in Cambodia, an official American information officer counted at least a dozen bodies after an airport rocket attack. He noticed the embassy was reporting only six dead, and he volunteered his eyewitness account. Thanks, he was told, but the embassy was obliged to stick with the authorized Cambodian version.

Despite the role played by foreign reporting, some policymakers pay no more attention to it than the average American citizen. "I just don't have the time," admitted one influential congressman from the Midwest active in foreign policy legislation. "I glance through the *Post* and the *Times,* but I don't really read them carefully. Do I read the [major paper of his constituency]? No, not really." Many congressmen and officials rely on brief summaries prepared by staff members who digest the most important newspapers and magazines. The Senate Foreign Relations Committee receives a daily summary, normally covering both sides of a legal-size sheet of paper, compiled from eight newspapers. It gives a handful of words about a few dozen top stories with reference listings to allow an interested senator to find details if he wants them. The well-prepared but brief report points out the futility of casual headline-skimming without understanding the sources. An item in September 1977 read, "Uganda did or didn't bar Britons from leaving. Amin is or isn't in Britain or Uganda. He either is or is not trying to attempt to disrupt or outshine the Commonwealth Conference in London (all media)."

Even those who watch closely, however, often find the press to be a toothless watchdog on foreign affairs. It is, once again, the system. There is a lack of coordination between foreign correspondents and their domestic counterparts in Washington that prevents a number of important stories from being discovered. One example was the CIA involvement in Chile until the early 1970s. No solid evidence of this emerged until Congress held an investigation. Correspondents in Santiago could not get a big enough piece of the story on the spot. Washington reporters tried from their end, but they did not have enough of a feel for actual conditions in Chile. And no news organization made enough of an effort from both ends at once. In Iran, the lack of hard interpretive reporting from Teheran and the hinterlands gave more weight to Washington-dated stories which tended to reflect the U.S. government's optimism about the shah.

Even veteran newsmen are sometimes amazed at the gulf between foreign bureaus and Washington. In one agency, a correspondent sent four separate messages over several weeks trying to get colleagues in Washington to answer a question on official policy toward Americans arrested abroad. He had prepared a revealing story, with full details and color and quotes, and he only needed official comment to finish it. No answer came, but weeks later a Washington reporter wrote a story on the same subject with none of the depth or flavor which the subject required.

When the two work at cross purposes, the foreign correspondents —closest to the action—are usually outshadowed. Washington reporters outnumber them, and they are closer to the editors. For example, in 1976, when Americans were evacuated from the Beirut embassy, President Gerald Ford set up a crisis center, and reporters around him wrote in lurid detail about the dangers of the operation. One agency man wrote that "Arab troops" guarded the embassy, and he gave the clear impression that Palestinian guerrillas posed a threat to American lives. In Beirut, correspondents for the same agency reported that the "Arab troops" were, in fact, Palestinians. The evacuation was orderly, and there appeared to be no danger at all. One quoted a German stewardess as saying she felt so safe she was coming right back for a holiday. When Beirut correspondents complained about the alarmist reports from Washington—and flatly contradicted official denials that Palestinians were providing security—they were told to just report their end and let the Washington people report theirs.

It is a double-edged problem. On one side, few foreign correspondents follow the nuances of news developments in Washington or in areas they do not cover. If the Secretary of State makes a significant remark about China while in Brazil, usually only the traveling Washington reporters understand the full implications. They are much better placed to detect policy changes and official contradictions. Washington press spokesmen who want to sell a particular viewpoint sometimes "leak" to correspondents during an overseas trip because they are easier to con.

On the other side, reporters from Washington seldom understand local background on the countries they write about. Reporters on official trips write their stories on the airplane or in special press rooms, following the guidance of spokesmen. Press kits prepared by

American information officers describe the political conditions and local color of countries they stop in. On the ground, instead of asking foreign correspondents for essential briefings, they often spend their brief leisure moments at Hilton hotels discussing American elections two years hence.

In January 1978, President Jimmy Carter visited France two months before one of the most crucial elections in French history. An alliance of the Socialist and Communist parties stood a good chance of being elected to govern France, a nuclear-armed power linked politically to NATO and a major Western industrial nation. The situation revolved largely around François Mitterrand, the eloquent Socialist leader who lost the 1974 presidential election by less than one percentage point. If the left won, he was the likely premier. Carter's visit, which had a major impact on the campaign, took on more importance when he agreed to see Mitterrand.

On the second day of the trip, one of the top White House reporters who had come along to explain all this to Americans paused to muse, "Mitterrand . . . Mitterrand . . . he's the Socialist, isn't he?"

12

How Foreigners
See It

The *Christian Science Monitor* in April 1977 devoted a full page to the reflections of a young Indian woman who had left her home to study in America. Though highly personal, the account is rich in insights on the way many foreigners feel about what Americans really know about them.

"I turned to catch a last glimpse of my family, standing bareheaded in the incessant monsoon rain, their faces dim with reproach," began Shallini Venturelli. She described what she felt she was running to, not the culturally deprived, traditionless "epicurean maypole" of her family's stereotypes but rather a land of intellectual freedom and opportunity where ideas and sensitivity could flourish. She traced her initial wonder and enthusiasm through stages of doubt and disillusionment as she saw how her fellow students in America seemed to be absorbed with dress and dating instead of the academic resources denied to most of the world's young people. And then she concluded:

> On an opaque morning in spring my dream came to its final, and lasting, end. I had been invited to address a ladies club. The club secretary had advised me that perhaps a dose of history with a pinch of politics and culture would be wonderfully suited to their taste. I obliged. After an excellent tea served on fine silver, I started to talk. I talked of the past, of struggles, of despair and poverty on the subcontinent; I talked of the present, of political battles and world maneuvers, of challenges that lay ahead; I spoke

of the right to learn, the right to self-awareness, of the chains of tradition and the poverty of women.

I did not notice for a long time that the faces around me had begun to twitch, that the women were shifting restlessly. When I suddenly became aware of the growing discomfort, I stopped. "Does someone have a question?" I asked.

The club secretary rose and drew me to the window.

"My dear," she said in a low voice, "it is history and culture they wish to hear about, not misfortunes." "But the truth is not misfortune; it is truth," I replied in a whisper, thoroughly confused. "Of course. But can't you leave out the bad parts? Talk about maharajas. And there are elephants and tigers, and you can even tell us about your beautiful sari, and show us how you put it on."

I looked down at the floor. There was an exquisite Persian carpet under my feet; I hadn't noticed. I remained by the window for a few minutes. The secretary had returned to her seat, and there were smiles and expectation on a few faces. "Ladies," I said, "my deepest apologies for meddling with your fantasies. Since I do not share them, and India is not a fairy tale or a novel by Rudyard Kipling, I must say goodby. Thank you."

Shallini Venturelli's experience reaches far beyond the effect of newsgathering. The making of stereotypes is a lifetime process, and one culture's knowledge of another can hardly be measured or defined. But any random sampling of foreigners—from Germany, Venezuela or Bhutan—will reveal that a great majority feel that Americans know little about the essence of their societies. And even if Americans cared, they could not easily bridge that gulf from what is reported in the United States.

"As part of a study program, I spent nine months reading nine [American] newspapers every day, along with the newsmagazines, and I watched network television news at least twice a day," said one respected Brazilian journalist late in 1977. "What I found about Brazil was almost nothing, and it was generally misleading." During that period, Brazil was covered more thoroughly in the large Eastern papers than most other stable nations. A Belgian journalist who spent two years in New York remarked, "The whole time, I saw two brief stories about Belgium. One was when some ministers disputed with the government. The other was about a kidnap in Antwerp." A Malaysian student at Harvard after the Vietnam war mused, "What do I learn from the papers about what is happening in Southeast Asia? Nothing."

This applies even to the most important industrial nations which Americans know best. In 1978, an American scholar strung together prime-time news film about France from the three networks over a ten-year period. The result, a 90-minute film, was shown to French and American journalists in Paris for comment. One eminent Frenchman observed, "This is extremely interesting, gentlemen, but it is not France." The television coverage, he said, had a tongue-in-cheek tone bordering on condescension. American journalists tended to agree. There was a distinct bias against Charles de Gaulle. References to him were often accompanied with flippant remarks or unspoken signals indicating anything from amusement to contempt. Although there were some excellent individual reports, the overall coverage focused more on stylish living and rich cheeses than on serious economic and political change.*

One French reporter invited to the showing had just spent twenty-four years as a correspondent in Washington. He was not surprised by the impression left by the film clips. "On the whole, including newspapers and newsmagazines, coverage is superficial," he said later. "When de Gaulle was around—that annoying old man—at least there was some reporting on France. It was the wrong side of the news, but it was news. Since then, there has been very little."

Even Mexicans and Canadians find their next-door neighbors are often ignorant about their respective countries. "They don't give a damn, that's all," commented a Mexican journalist in Texas. "Reporting is often shallow, and when they write about Mexico from here, it is often in derogatory terms. In Dallas, people tell me they think Mexicans are always having revolutions and killing their presidents. In Dallas, people say that. They are amazed when I tell them that Americans have killed more presidents than have Mexicans."

More reflective critics tend to consider the thin coverage of other countries as part of a general isolationist attitude. Thinkers from widely differing societies have expressed these thoughts in strikingly similar terms:

---

*It should be noted that the scholar also showed French reporting from the United States, and the Americans found it to be far off the mark, dwelling on dramatic rather than significant issues.

• The United States is an immense country of disparate regions, and the most footloose of Americans can wander a lifetime without crossing borders. It is protected by oceans, with only two contiguous neighbors, both very much in its shadow.

• As a result, Americans have an exaggerated idea of their own importance in the world, with a corresponding underestimation of their dependence on others.

• Also, few Americans appreciate the fundamental social forces behind political and economic change. Americans follow power blocs and surface changes, but they do not pay enough attention to background causes.

Proportionately, news organizations in a number of countries cover the world more thoroughly than the American media. In Japan, eight newspapers and two news agencies had 222 correspondents based on six continents in 1978; five broadcasting companies had another ninety correspondents. The largest newspapers keep fleets of private aircraft and well-equipped bureaus. More than a hundred reporters accredited by Japanese news organizations were based in six American cities during 1978. One Spanish daily newspaper with a circulation of around 150,000—the circulation of the Phoenix, Arizona, *Republic*—keeps staff correspondents in four world capitals and full-time stringers in another five. Australia, with a population of fourteen million, is extremely well informed. There were thirty-four Australian reporters in the United States alone during the late 1970s. (By comparison, there were two full-time correspondents covering Australia for American agencies, newspapers and networks, and both were Australian citizens.)

Obviously, there is a wide discrepancy over how American correspondents perform when they do turn their attention to a major story. A number of foreigners disagree with the American idea of what constitutes news, and they say U.S. reporters harp too strongly on the dramatic, the negative and the trivial. Among foreigners who believe in the Western concept of a free press, however, American correspondents are often highly regarded. Reporters from other countries frequently praise Americans for taking pains to pin down facts and to avoid unfounded speculation. Many are amazed at how U.S. correspondents—particularly television network crews—surround a major story from every angle, whatever the effort or cost. And Americans are widely respected for reporting frankly, no matter who they might embarrass.

American correspondents are hardly the only ones to hype a story from time to time or to stretch a point. When Biafra surrendered, and reporters rushed in to cover the aftermath, a Scandinavian television crew scattered coins in the dirt so they could film children scrambling for them. The accompanying narration said the famished youngsters were after food. And in the South Bronx, a Japanese television team hired a pair of derelicts to stage a mugging—and then convinced a carload of New York policemen to rush in for a mock arrest.

Large numbers of foreign journalists come to American universities for training, and there is considerable competition for intern jobs on American newspapers and at broadcast stations.

What most of these visiting foreigners find is that American journalists can do an excellent job when they decide to cover a story—or a country—thoroughly. But that situation, most foreigners seem to feel, does not occur very often.

13

Reporting Today's Wars

Early on the morning of January 28, 1973, reporters in camouflage shirts clustered around a car radio along Highway One west of Saigon listening to President Nixon tell the world the Vietnam war was over. It was eight o'clock sharp, the moment at which all sides had agreed to cease fire while they worked out a permanent accord. Nixon was saying, ". . . the beginning of an era of peace for all mankind," but the reporters could hardly hear him. South Vietnamese Skyraiders, which suddenly burst from the clouds to drop 500-pound bombs on North Vietnamese positions, were making too much noise.

For the correspondents, it was only mildly ironic that they had to scramble to avoid being the first casualties of peace in Vietnam. They understood all too well the nature of the war; that was why they were out watching the ceasefire on Highway One that morning. Every time someone back home talked about lights at the end of tunnels or a just and honest peace, they exchanged a few rude jokes and tossed flak jackets into their jeeps to head back up the road. Correspondents knew that the war that always seemed almost over to those far away was a deepening quagmire with no end in sight. That they had such trouble getting the message across to Americans was no surprise. No war, from the first clash of stone axes, has ever been faithfully depicted to those back home. No faraway reader or viewer—however plentiful his sources—can feel a war's full impact or truly understand its intricacies. And Vietnam was no exception.

The Vietnam war was covered more intensively than any in history, and reporters, for the first time, were able to use space-age tools and techniques. They had rare freedom to move around and to say what they saw. But the problems of covering a war are not necessarily physical, and they go beyond the general difficulty of transmitting reality. The new styles introduced in Vietnam had advantages, but they also had drawbacks. Depending on who you believe, television reporters and cameramen either brought the horror of the war into people's living rooms, or they desensitized it by capturing it in miniature in a small box with an off switch. Print correspondents either helped readers gain a new set of insights about war, or they numbed them to insensibility with a torrent of words. Political and social reporting gave wider dimensions to the conflict but also led many readers toward facile—and false—assumptions about the peoples involved.

Every modern conflict has demonstrated the same point: concerned citizens can be reasonably informed about a war only if they work hard at it. A reader and viewer must analyze every piece of information presented to him, and he must know who is presenting the information. Every battle account, political analysis and body count has to be seen in a larger context and fitted into an overall mosaic. Guesswork must be recognized as guesswork, however informed and confident the writer may seem. Declarations, promises, threats and revelations by the warring parties must be taken at no more or no less than face value. Keeping up with a war is a long process; there is no way to do it casually. Readers and viewers have to learn which reporters and news organizations to trust more than others, and that takes careful analysis of months of dispatches. They must add their own sense of history and context to each fragmented dispatch, since no medium has the space to repeat it all each time.

For those who really worked at following them, the events in Vietnam were not so confusing. As far back as 1947, the New York *Times*'s Bob Trumbull warned that the Vietnamese from the north appeared to be unbeatable, attacking by surprise at night, using sabotage and subterfuge, turning the enemy's strengths into weaknesses and fighting with extraordinary resolve. In the early 1960s, when the United States began to get involved in the war, young reporters for the New York *Times,* the AP, UPI, *Time* and other organizations produced firsthand evidence that officials were grossly underestimating the military threat. Even then correspondents in Saigon and in the war zones were writing about the political difficulties and the corruption of the governments which Washington supported.

As the war progressed, Americans who could not see it for themselves were given graphic vignettes of the battles and of the sociological effects of their nation at war. Writers spent weeks under fire and told about it in vivid first-person dispatches. Photographers caught a police chief shooting a prisoner through the head, a Buddhist monk immolating himself and children engulfed in napalm flames. In the thick of the war, Morley Safer of CBS turned a camera on a well-brushed young American marine, straight off a recruiting poster, as he ignored a weeping old woman pleading to keep her home. As the marine touched his Zippo lighter to the thatched roof, Safer delivered his message to Americans: This is the war in Vietnam.

But the reasoned, instructive reporting of a small group of professionals was very hard to follow. In the first years of the American involvement, the correspondents on the spot were overshadowed by Washington columnists and reporters on brief visits who accepted the American government's optimistic view of events. As the war escalated, a chorus of new voices obscured the picture. At one point, 600 newspeople of widely varying talents swarmed over Saigon and the scattered fronts. Instead of contributing to an overall portrait of the war, they contradicted one another and focused distracting attention on isolated incidents. Long-distance pundits wrote uninformed analysis. Some Washington reporters continued to echo the official line without checking it against reality. News agencies and newspapers often concentrated on headline-producing fragments: B-52 strikes, body counts, firebases won and lost.

In Vietnam, as in other conflicts, there were few good war correspondents, for one simple reason: it is extremely difficult work. These days there are almost no "war correspondents"; there are correspondents who cover news, including wars when they come up. Even the most seasoned veterans must start from scratch in every war. They must learn the tactics and fighting styles of the combatants and then plan out their own logistics. They have to develop accurate sources and study the historical bases—and immediate causes—of the war. They must figure out not only how to get to the most significant battles for a close look but also how to get back out alive. The job takes a staggering toll in mental anguish, emotional stress and sheer physical energy. A correspondent gambles not only with his life but also with his time. He must determine whether it is better to go up the road or to hang back for situation reports, briefings and intelligence estimates. And he must be confident enough to stay behind—if that is his decision—and not take unnecessary risks just to prove he is no coward.

The most difficult task for a war correspondent is mentally situating himself close enough to the story to report it but far enough away not to be involved in it. This is true in every aspect of reporting, but in covering war it is paramount. The immediate impact of death and suffering makes it next to impossible for a reporter to write at the same time with objectivity and passion. If he detaches himself enough to block out anguish, he is likely to provide little more than body counts and disjointed snatches of description. But if he lets himself feel the grief of an 18-year-old corporal holding the entrails of a platoon leader he must succeed, the reporter is hardly likely to see those little fuckers in the jungle with objective eyes. A minor skirmish can seem like D-Day to a reporter pinned down all afternoon by withering artillery. Few single actions determine the course of a war, but correspondents find it hard not to overestimate a microcosm incident if it affects them strongly.

Finding the right distance from the story also means putting away bias, as far as possible. Sometimes a correspondent's bias is direct and purposeful. "It depends on the war," says Homer Bigart, a veteran of thirty years of war. "In World War II, you were on the right side, and there was no question about it." He recalls one incident when German troops voluntarily held their fire to let an ambulance convoy pass. "I was surprised that they were capable of that," he said. "But I never wrote it. To my knowledge, no one did."

Even Korea was reported essentially as us-against-them. During the Vietnam war, reporters tried to cover both sides objectively, but they still occasionally referred to the Viet Cong as "the enemy." In the mid-1960s, one agency desk editor told a correspondent in Saigon not to keep writing about how tenacious and courageous the other side seemed to be. More often, bias is unconscious, and it creeps into copy in subtle ways. The good guys make driving advances and well-planned ambushes; the bad guys counter with brutal onslaughts and sneak attacks. One side questions villagers, while the other side terrorizes them. An unconsciously involved reporter is more apt to believe intelligence reports that say the other side has severe morale and supply problems than ones which say it is doing fine.

Bias comes in many forms. Even when there are no patriotic considerations, reporters often tend to lean to one side. This can be sympathy for the underdog or a desire to be on the winning side; there is no fixed pattern. But it is a natural tendency, influencing the best of correspondents. A reporter who travels with one army, sharing C-ration peanut butter and watching friends fall dead, finds it hard to separate himself from the men around him. Air raids threaten not only the army he is covering but also him personally. Particularly if he shares cultural values with "his side," he can understand why they are fighting. It is not so easy for him to see why the other side resists so unreasonably.

In general, when whites battle blacks, yellows, reds or browns, American reporting leans at least slightly in their favor. This is not so much for racial reasons as for simple practicalities. European armies—even white mercenaries—are usually more willing to accept reporters in their midsts to write with relative freedom. They are, in any case, usually easier to reach and are better supplied with field telephones, jeeps and medical evacuation facilities. The result is that more correspondents cover one side than the other, and this majority has better access to sources and communications.

The question of bias is particularly important, since readers and viewers tend to add their own distortions. Few people back home can accept the idea that anyone killing their sons and husbands is just one of the combatants in a multi-sided war. Logically, a person's attitude toward Jews, Arabs, black Africans or Cubans will affect how he interprets wars involving them. From far away, it is difficult to understand causes of hostilities and details of conflicts, even when they are reported with pristine objectivity. If elements of bias are added, serious misunderstanding is inevitable.

War reporting might be improved vastly if the same people could cover both sides, alternating back and forth. For obvious reasons, this is hardly practical. Military commanders are understandably chary about letting newsmen straddle front lines. And correspondents, unenticed by the prospect of being shot as spies, do not often press their luck. News organizations try to assign competent people to both sides of any important conflict. But circumstances rarely allow the net result to be evenhanded.

The Nigeria-Biafra war of the late 1960s showed how badly a conflict can be distorted. In Lagos, on the federal side, reporters had a relatively easy life, with communications and access to sources. But they could not really see the war. Trips to the front took weeks and months of cajolery, chicanery and risk. Occasional guided tours kept them well back from fighting. A few American correspondents were based there permanently, and a small number dropped in from time to time. Reporting was essentially dry, heavy on official claims and features on the effects of war on a large African nation.

On the Biafran side, war was all around in the shrinking secessionist state. Correspondents had to brave harrowing flights, stacked among dilapidated aircraft circling an unlit makeshift runway under constant threat of attack. Life was bracingly tough; the story was firsthand. Reporters wrote of hundreds of thousands of innocent babies starving, their bellies horribly distended. They described heroic efforts to distill gasoline in back-yard cookers and to feed families with boiled roots. Federal atrocities were recounted in grim detail, relieved by colorful portraits of Odumegwu Ojukwu, the saintlike Oxford-accented secessionist leader.

The picture that quickly emerged was one of an oppressed people fighting nobly for their ideals against imperialistic tyrants who forced their children to starve. As more Americans sympathized with the Biafrans' cause, there was a greater demand for copy to reinforce the image. What correspondents seldom wrote from Biafra was that profiteering by Biafran farmers and middlemen caused much of the food problem. Most ignored Ojukwu's personal enrichment and the enormous landing fees and red tape imposed on international organizations sending relief. Little was said about Biafran atrocities, including the slaughter of minority tribesmen in Rivers State. Reporters describing attacks on the airstrip did not seem to notice that little real damage was done by Nigeria's pilots. In fact, the mercenaries normally shot wide on purpose to avoid hitting their fellow pilots below, and the Egyptians on loan saw no reason to risk their necks in needless combat. And, from both sides, reporters missed most of the backstage machinations of diplomats, oil executives and financiers which kept the war going far longer than it might have lasted on its own.

Neither side was right or wrong. Biafran leaders wanted to secede, and the federal government wanted to keep the country intact. There were mixed feelings among both. On a few fronts, Nigerian and

Biafran soldiers played football together and assumed their battle positions only when officers came for inspection. On others, there was savage fighting. As in all wars, there was a complex mixture of atrocity, brotherliness, corruption, blame and suffering. But it did not come across that way.

The best correspondents can lessen some imbalances by careful interpretation. They can create images by attention to detail. Bias can be avoided, at least partially, with long quotes from those involved. John Burns of the New York *Times,* for example, joined blacks in the Rhodesian army on night guard duty and wrote a sensitive account of their feelings in their own words. But there is a limit to what they can do. The problems of sources, logistics, censorship and government pressure which bedevil correspondents in normal times expand greatly in war. After the 1973 Middle East war, Bernard D. Nossiter of the Washington *Post* put his feelings on paper:

> There is a singular frustration in covering a war in progress. Nothing and no one is worthy of much belief, and a reporter's own senses—sight, smell, and insight—are of remarkably limited use. Three weeks of reporting from the Israeli side left me more convinced than ever that journalism is much like firing a mortar. To get anywhere near the target, you must first overshoot, then undershoot and hopefully come close on the third round. There are two ways of doing the job: either sit in Tel Aviv to get the big picture or move out by press bus or rented car for a limited glimpse of a fighting front. Both were splendidly unsatisfactory.

On the Arab side, it was much worse. Reporters could not get the big picture in the capitals. And they were seldom allowed out for a limited glimpse of anything significant. Some Arab countries did not let correspondents in at all.

Today, with so many ramifications to every conflict, the way a war is reported is vitally important to those waging it. Governments can fall if enough citizens oppose the conduct of a war. Congressional appropriations and international support depend largely on what image correspondents convey. Even the most amateur military commands spend a great deal of time deciding what should be revealed, altered or covered up entirely. To get their point across—and to deal with correspondents seeking information—they rely on a class of people known as PIO's.

A PIO, for public information officer, must be a master of innuendo. Some of them lie baldly, but most are far too smooth for that. They give out bits of incomplete information, usually couched in military doubletalk, and answer direct questions as evasively as possible. In the Vietnam war, an American military spokesman once issued this communiqué:

ELEMENTS AMERICAL DIV. 11 LT INF BDE., MADE CONTACT WITH ENEMY FORCE UNKNOWN SIZE 9 KM NE QUANG NGAI. INF SUPPORTED BY USA HEL GUNSHIPS AND ARTY. SPORADIC CONTACT CONT UNTIL 1500H WHEN CONTACT LOST. 128 KIA/2 US KIA. 4 WIA (MEDEVACED) AND 6 WIA TREATED RETND TO DY.

It was only long afterward, when a freelance reporter, Seymour Hersh, criss-crossed the country on borrowed money and collected information by sneaking through an army camp and bullying soldiers that the communiqué was accurately translated: U.S. troops massacred several hundred men, women and children at My Lai.

Correspondents soon learn which PIO's they can trust, and the wiser spokesmen try hard to preserve their credibility. Since the PIO's depend on questionable situation reports from the front, sometimes they are inadvertently wrong. General Creighton W. Abrams, then commander in Vietnam, remarked in 1969, "When we get a piece of good news, we wait thirty-six hours and then, if we're really lucky, it turns out to be twenty-five per cent accurate." Officers at the Five O'Clock Follies, the daily Saigon briefing, were often late and incomplete with information, but they tried not to be too early and wrong. Setbacks were sometimes noted, but they were usually glossed over and buried on a page of other information.

Barry Zorthian, who directed information operations in Vietnam for years, said later that his staff learned the hard way that frankness is the best approach. Once, for example, spokesmen decided not to say anything about a project to test the use of noxious gas. But Peter Arnett and Horst Faas of the AP learned of it when they came upon a Vietnamese unit which had been accidentally doused with the CS4 gas. They took pictures of troops whose faces were affected and collected firsthand accounts. Before using it, they gave U.S. officials twenty-four hours to comment. At first the story was denied. But, with the evidence available, there were headlines all over the country about how the Americans were dabbling in gas warfare. "I'm sure that if we had just put out a little item noting that we were going to make tests with a type of tear gas, everyone would have read right over it and given it no particular attention. It was only a brief experiment and the whole project was scrapped anyway," Zorthian said.

Zorthian often said a smart PIO could capture headlines if he had "that fleeting quote"—that small detail or phrase—on which an editor could hang a front-page story. The real substance of the story was not so important as the brief catch phrase which made the point spokesmen wanted to make. The classic example was the body count. Until someone came up with the term, the casualty figures were just another element of the whole story. But suddenly editors all over America were aware of "body counts," and some followed the meaningless figures as closely as baseball standings. (Reporters use brief catch phrases as adeptly as PIO's. The battle of Hamburger Hill was just another skirmish until Dave Lamb of UPI arrived, several days after his competition had written about it in detail. He noticed a small sign calling the place Hamburger Hill, and he wrote his dispatch around that. The story was suddenly splashed across newspapers, and the battle became one of the most remembered fights of the war.)

Interviews with combat officers are almost always far more revealing than official briefings, and one job of the PIO is to keep officers from saying too much. A standing joke in Vietnam was about the PIO who would "interpret" remarks by combat officers when they spoke directly with reporters, breaking in periodically with "What the captain means to say . . ." A pilot, for example, would say, "Naw, we missed the bridge completely and just blew the shit out of the riverbank." The alter ego would pipe in, "What the captain means to say is that they failed to achieve their primary objective but they cratered the approaches." Sanitized PIO talk, which somehow lessens the impact of the war, can get by an overworked correspondent who fails to consider its meaning. When the "GIBS [guy in the back seat] expends ordnance," it means someone down on the ground is being blown to bits.

Some PIO's do not follow the Zorthian doctrine, and they lie through their teeth. Often, it is hard to double-check them. When the Nigerians finally defeated Biafra, briefers described how the remaining airstrip—a stretch of road—had been pulverized by systematic bombing. One reporter, who then wrote that the runway had been "pounded to rubble," felt slightly foolish when he later got to the area and sped along the widened surface without seeing a blemish on its surface. Much more significant lying was done by the Americans in Indochina. In Laos, during the late 1950s and early 1960s, they made up a war. Correspondents in Vientiane were briefed on how communist troops had destroyed villages in heavy fighting with loyalist troops. Each new reporter wrote about the war and left Laos. When several correspondents went to investigate, finally, they found there had been no fighting. A few years later, in Vietnam, the reverse happened. U.S. officials in Saigon swore there was no fighting in the Mekong Delta. Reporters who went to check found battalion-sized operations. And later, officials lied, distorted and withheld information about bombing and the CIA's use of mercenaries in Laos.

In foreign reporting, officials can sometimes get away with lies indefinitely. Often there are not enough correspondents concentrated long enough in a single place to uncover the truth. Many distorted official reports from Indochina went uncorrected until the war became, essentially, a domestic story, and newspeople began covering it as they would if it were being fought in Texas.

Reporting today's wars requires much more investigative digging than in the past. And correspondents now cover politics, economics and social situations as well as the military aspects. "In World War II," as Bigart put it, "reporters were there to cover the fighting—the natives were just part of the landscape, to be ignored." Still, non-military coverage remains thin in many instances. Most reporters in Vietnam who did go below the surface tended to get sidetracked with Saigon politics, giving too much importance to isolated infighting of people with no power base. Coconut monks and Sorbonne-trained national deputies are colorful, but they do not speak for the major political movements in the countryside where the war is being fought. Peter Braestrup, a reporter turned scholar who covered Vietnam for the Washington *Post* and, before, the New York *Times*, wrote later:

> The effects of lack of preparation, inexperience and the language gap showed most often in the coverage of political "crisis" or near crisis. We seldom got it right the first time. There was much talk of the importance of "Vietnamese politics" and "reporting what the Vietnamese think." Yet, in practice, most of us depended heavily on (a) a handful of experienced U.S. Old Vietnam Hands, most of them outside Saigon, (b) the embassy's political section, whose information was, at times, inadequate to

the occasion, (c) a Vietnamese politician or two, (d) our Vietnamese stringers. All too often, the stringers would meet over Coca-Cola at the Cafe Pagode at 7 P.M., trade rumors and gossip, and bear the informally syndicated composite version to rival American reporters. Naturally, every Vietnamese newsman had his own viewpoint . . . and his own personal friends and enemies in Saigon politics. Few had any contacts outside the capital. Fewer still had any professional training.

The Old Asia Hands did little better than the newcomers; they were hindered by their own experience. Many saw the war as an extension of earlier Asian wars, and they expected Ho Chi Minh to act as other communist leaders had. Because of this, they failed to see the vital peculiarities, even though they felt at east among the water buffalo and the street markets.

In every major war—and Vietnam was no exception—an enormous range of every sort of reporter flocks to the action. There is always a thin fringe of adventure seekers eager to pick up some dope money by stringing for whoever will have them. In Vietnam, anyone could get credentials with a letter from a hometown paper. Free loaders could live for a dollar a day in press centers. With fighting units, they could live for free. They could earn more than $100 a day just for relaying information to news organizations and for taping a few radio spots, if they were lucky enough to find action. A wider band of responsible freelancers also turns up, by custom, and most do well covering organizations with no staff correspondents on the spot. There is also the full gamut of regulars sent hurrying in by their editors. Of the lot, the best are most often energetic young correspondents with limited experience but large capacity to learn fast. They tend to have fewer biases and bad habits; they pick up the war and its requisites. The good ones shun gang reporting and slog out to see things for themselves.

Peter Arnett, the archetype of this category, said after the war, "The only way you could do it was to have a fresh mind and go look at the war up close. Every time I saw a story about a Viet Cong dying dramatically in the jungle or leaping up and shouting, 'Die G.I.,' I knew it was a phony. The guy was sitting back in Saigon imagining things. You never got close enough to the Viet Cong for that, and you didn't see them die in the jungles unless you happened to be passing low in a helicopter. That 'Die, G.I.' stuff is out of Japanese war films."

Age is not necessarily a factor, but energy is. My strongest memory of the Vietnam war was watching a colleague, Dick Blystone, in action near Hue. Blystone, doubled over with dysentery and worn out from weeks of non-stop work, dragged himself to a helicopter staging area where a Vietnamese unit was about to drop behind North Vietnamese lines. They were to go in shooting and then try to fight their way south to join their stalled front lines. If they made it at all, it would take a minimum of three days' hard march. Blystone, sick as he was, spent two hours trying to talk the commander into taking him along.

For many, Vietnam made instant reputations. Unknown television reporters were suddenly better known than movie stars. Agency reporters who came off the night shift in New York found their names on front pages day after day. Some became famous simply by exposure, like one television reporter who was hit by shell fragments on camera. But many others were able to demonstrate their judgment and courage by consistently producing good work.

The war also destroyed some reporters. A few veteran correspondents came to Vietnam after proving themselves on other stories, but they gradually started spending more time in opium parlors and bars than at the front. After the war, they just drifted off, headed nowhere. Others became too involved, and editors regarded them as unreliable. And some, because of bad luck or senses dulled by overwork or a single stupid mistake, were blown away.

War coverage takes some toll on everyone, but the casual observer would hardly believe it by watching correspondents at work. A visitor to the Danang Press Center might have thought himself surrounded by ghouls. Correspondents, with blood still on their boots, would gather nightly around gins and tonics and collapse in peals of raucous laughter. From their conversation, it seemed like the day's worst tragedy was not that dozens of men were killed but that old So-and-So had gone somewhere else and missed the battle. They rang Saigon and, in between jokes about venereal disease, dictated dispatches about death and anguish like local reporters calling in an account of a school board meeting. That is a facade—surface bravado which is almost essential as a shield against the pressure.

A truer picture emerged when the war finally ended, and the last ships slipped away into the South China Sea. Reporters stood on the decks in silent knots and stared at the disappearing coastline. If they talked at all, it was to reflect on what they had just survived. They remembered the helicopter pilots who had saved correspondents' lives by risking their own. They thought about men who were blown apart only moments after talking unconcernedly with reporters. One correspondent, who had spent years writing about the war with cool detachment, could not compose a line about the historic evacuation. His editors, who knew only that they had no story, sent sharply worded entreaties. He ignored them, checked into a Hong Kong hotel and saw no one. The experience left such an impact on a few reporters that they fell into a time warp, and years later hostesses were still striking them from guest lists for fear of having to relive Vietnam one more time.

Correspondents become so much a part of the wars they cover that important questions arise about where they fit in. In Vietnam, every correspondent had at least the equivalent rank of major, and they were allowed most privileges accorded to officers. They had priorities on aircraft and use of the military communications system. One recurrent debate was whether they should carry weapons. Most did not. They felt that as reporters, they were supposed to stay neutral, and the fact that they were traveling with one side or the other did not change that. In security terms, many felt their chances were better without a weapon. They could hardly claim to be considered noncombatants if they were armed. Some even threw away the card that identified them as noncombatants because it was marked "MAJ" in big letters under rank. There are, of course, divergent views. A former correspondent, Fred Sparks, once put it: "Suppose a gook suddenly jumps into my foxhole. What do I do then? Say to him, 'Chicago *Daily News*'?" Sparks was referring to an earlier war, but a few of today's reporters agree and pack at least a sidearm on risky patrols. Sometimes there is little choice. One correspondent, a former army officer, joined a mercenary commando unit assaulting a lake beach in the Congo. He took one quick look around, assessed his chances of getting out alive if he did not lend a hand, and he grabbed the nearest carbine.

Perhaps more important is whether a reporter should get involved in what he is reporting in order to save a life. In a speech after leaving Vietnam, Peter Arnett had this to say: "I stood one hot noon outside Saigon market and watched a Buddhist monk in brown robes climb from a taxi and squat on the pavement. He squirted gasoline over himself from a rubber bottle and flicked a cigarette lighter. Here was a political immolation a few feet in front of me. I felt horror and disgust as his body blackened and puffed out like a burnt pastry. I could have prevented that immolation by rushing at him and kicking the gasoline away. As a human being I wanted to. As a reporter I couldn't. This monk was one of many who committed suicide to dramatize the iniquities of the Diem regime in Saigon. If I had stopped him, the secret police who were watching from a distance would have immediately arrested him and carried him off to God knows where. If I had attempted to prevent them doing this I would have propelled myself directly into Vietnamese politics. My role as a reporter would have been destroyed along with my credibility. What did I do? I photographed him burning on the sidewalk. I beat off half a dozen secret police trying to grab my camera. I raced to the AP office, wrote the story and sent a radiophoto. It was on America's front pages the next morning. Three months later, mainly because of the monk immolations, the Vietnamese public unrest and the worsening war, the American government gave the signal to overthrow Diem."

The best correspondents define their role clearly and then stand coolly to the side and relate what is going on. Readers who follow their dispatches on a regular basis can form a reasonably complete picture of a distant war. But to find such solid reporting, readers must be prepared to hack their way through dense jungles of misleading wordage.

14

Economic Reporting

The *Sunday Times* of London reported on October 26, 1976, that the International Monetary Fund would withhold a badly needed loan to Britain until the pound dropped to a value of $1.50. Immediately, the pound plummeted from $1.65 to $1.59, one of its greatest one-day losses in history. Overnight, families with £10,000 life's savings lost $535 of it—in international terms—because of a newspaper article. For merchants dealing with the British and for tourists en route to London, it was a windfall. For large companies and governments with sterling holdings, it was a disaster.

The pound might have slipped anyway, but there was little question that the sharp slide was triggered by the *Sunday Times*'s report. The drop came immediately, before the IMF, officials of the Exchequer or the newspaper could debate the truth of the story. And it was a dramatic example of the importance of economic reporting. Although political writers might scare the hell out of people, lasting reaction usually comes only after the people involved have a chance to clarify the various positions. Economic reporters can cost people fortunes before they know what hit them.

Once the AP–Dow Jones financial wire reported a nickel find, and the mining company's stock shot up in price from $6.90 to $97.20 just on the strength of the dispatch. Fortunately, it was correct.

Another time, an agency issued an erroneous report from Belgium on African copper mining operations, and vast sums were won and lost in an afternoon.

Short of rumblings of war, no foreign news has a greater direct impact on Americans than a major economic story. And yet no category of news is reported with such obfuscation, convolution and esoteric jargon. But a failure to detect impending shortages, boycotts or currency collapse can leave millions unprepared for crises which affect their lives. Misinformation about economic terrorism—such as the poisoning of Israeli oranges for export in 1978—can cause needless panic or dangerous complacency. A distant devaluation alters the prices of countless items at the neighborhood shopping center. When President Carter went to London for his first economic summit meeting, in May 1977, Clyde Farnsworth of the New York *Times* noted in an article why Americans should be interested in the talks:

- One out of six manufacturing jobs in America produces goods for export.
- One out of three acres of American farmland was cultivated in export crops.
- Nearly one out of three dollars of American corporate profits came from multinational activities.
- American inflation was driven to double digits because of external forces.
- The United States depends on imports for more than a quarter of the 12 or 15 basic raw materials it needs for industry.

Reporting international economics is not only one of the most important functions of a foreign correspondent, it is also one of the hardest. Any general correspondent who has wrestled with snakes and floats on the Eurocurrency market or who has sweated to separate SDR's from LDC's knows that such stories require special skills. But in 1978 there were probably fewer than 20 solidly trained, effective reporters writing on international economics—at home and abroad— for the news agencies, the newspapers, the networks and the general newsmagazines. Specialized papers like the *Wall Street Journal* and the *Journal of Commerce* do a good job, but they cannot be everywhere, and they are accessible to a relative few.

"Would you believe it?" asked a New York *Times* executive, pondering over who to send to a major European bureau as an economic specialist. "Out of a newsroom of 387 reporters, we can't find a single person to write economics. Our first choice can't go for personal reasons, and we don't have anyone else we want to send."

The shortage is not surprising. A good economic reporter must, to begin with, be a good reporter. A misread balance sheet, a misplaced decimal point or a misunderstood phrase can be devastating. Prying information out of sources can be enormously difficult. Government officials and company executives who will prattle on for hours about political problems suddenly clam up when big money is involved. International negotiations, concessions, takeovers and trade deals depend heavily on secrecy and diversionary smoke screens. Communiqués at the end of important meetings are the tip of an ice floe, usually, and only careful canvassing of participants gives some idea of what really took place. With the basic facts in hand, the economic reporter must then become an economist. He has to know what else must go up when a finance minister says that something will come down. When loans and credits are announced, he must know what they will really cost and why they were really accorded. He has to know as much about Keynesian law and the concept of Mill as the officials who throw the terms around in an effort to mask their mistakes or slip in unpopular measures. And when he understands what is happening, he goes back to being a reporter to put it together in a brief, clear, lively account that will interest—and inform—the Bloomingdale's salesclerk who is reading the story while hanging from the subway strap.

The job requires waiting long hours around ornate hallways in Brussels for some delegation leader to walk out and raise his eyebrows meaningfully to give reporters a clue on which to peg their stories. It takes steady poring through soporific company reports and legal statements. And the rewarding moments of exhilaration are usually more cerebral than with other types of international reporting. The economic reporter, without high adventure and incoming shellfire, must be satisfied with the low howl of a red-faced industrialist caught with a swindle showing.

In the past few years, more young reporters have become interested in economics, and a few universities offer programs to turn the general reporters into specialists. But most economic and business reporting is left to garden-variety correspondents who do their best to keep up. Some do an excellent job, but readers would be well advised to cast a critical eye on all international economic reporting.

To begin with, all figures are at least slightly suspect, and they can mislead the most experienced specialists. Any smart statistician can juggle numbers to produce a favorable or unfavorable impression of just about everything to the casual observer. A finance minister who is hustling loans from international banks will emphasize different figures than those he might choose to cite when telling his nation how well the government is doing. Companies shuffle numbers for their own reasons. In the United States, directors generally try to show the highest possible earnings at the end of the year; it makes them look good and boosts the company's value on the stock exchange. In Western Europe, however, companies are loath to let union leaders, tax collectors and nationalization-minded politicians know what plums they really are.

Some governments don't bother to shuffle around statistics; they just lie. And often economic figures are totally unreliable even though no attempt is made to cook them. Sophisticated collection of information is a luxury for many poor countries, especially when large portions of their inhabitants live isolated in hinterlands. Because each government reports economic statistics differently, international comparisons are often meaningless. Two countries with exactly the same unemployment situation, for example, may differ five percentage points in their official unemployment rate.

The difference between statistics and reality can be preposterous, as in Argentina during the mid-1970s. A responsible government agency calculates official figures in Argentina, but during the last months of Peronist government its system fell apart. Inflation was determined by measuring price increases of a fixed list of staples. That was fine in theory, except that most of the items were available only at exorbitant black market rates—nowhere near the index prices. Some of the fastest rising items, like gasoline and transport, were not included in the formula at all. Official figures were broken down to the decimal, but in fact the actual inflation rates were up to three times as high. And even the government's statistics could be read in different ways. In March 1976, when Isabel Perón was overthrown, the consumer cost-of-living index put the annual inflation rate at about 650 per cent. But independent economists, extrapolating from the official wholesale price index for March, estimated that prices were actually rising at an annual rate of 45,000 per cent.

The easygoing approach toward numbers in many countries can make life miserable for serious correspondents. In Brazil, Bob Sullivan of UPI once spent an entire day trying to nail down a single figure for a one-line dispatch to his agency's special commodity service. He read in four major Brazilian papers that sugar prices in local markets would be raised 12 per cent to 5.50 cruzeiros a kilo by the following Monday. He started to write a brief story when he discovered he did not have the old price—and he had forgotten the formula for determining it mathematically. Obviously, he reasoned, 12 per cent of 5.50 was not the answer. He called a supermarket to ask the price and was told it was four cruzeiros. Sullivan, in Rio de Janeiro, called the economy ministry in Brasilia to ask the spokeswoman about the report. Ah, she replied, it was in the prestigious *Jornal do Brasil* and therefore had to be correct. When Sullivan explained that the difference between 5.50 and four was more than 12 per cent, she said she would call back. Later, as seldom happens, someone did call back. It was her boss, who said the report was correct. Sullivan asked him the old price, and he started out: "Let's see, twelve per cent of five-fifty . . ." After some discussion, the man said that in any case the ministry did not fix prices. Sullivan would have to call the special interministerial commission on consumer prices. He did, and a spokesman told him that of course the story was true. It was in all the papers, wasn't it?

At that point, Sullivan pleaded with the spokesman to check official announcements. When he called him back, he learned that the committee knew nothing about it. In fact, the spokesman said, it was funny, since only the commission sets the policy and it wouldn't be meeting for another month. Sullivan called the ministry again and went to one of the newspapers. From both sources, he found out the economy minister had mentioned a 12 per cent increase. But, calling still another man at the ministry, he discovered the new price was for refinery owners to be applied to wholesalers only. He then went to the economics desk of the *Jornal do Brasil* and, after a brief argument, got an admission that someone had indeed screwed up. He learned later that a group of local reporters had misinterpreted the minister's clear statement and, in gang fashion, worked out what the new price would be in retail outlets. Their math was bad. Just to make sure, Sullivan went to a local supermarket. He was told that if the price was increased, it could never be applied by Monday, since the old price was printed on the bags and it would take two weeks to a month for old stock to be sold out.

The next morning, Sullivan opened one popular paper which had not carried the erroneous report the day before. Its main headline read, "New Price Increase to Housewives for Sugar, 5.50 by Monday."

Correspondents in developing countries soon learn to deal with the bizarre numbers game, but their dispatches are sometimes rendered incomprehensible by the confused desk editors trying to help. One agency editor insisted on having all prices in dollars, since funny currencies only confounded American readers. He was at a loss when a correspondent, following his orders, reported that car prices rose by ten times in Argentina over a year—a small sedan went from $4,000 to $4,000. It was simple: an Argentine worker, who earns pesos and not dollars, had to pay ten times as many pesos. But the peso had been devalued against the dollar at a rate equal to inflation. The dollar figure remained the same. Each time gasoline rose, correspondents said the price went up 25 per cent—or whatever—and it was usually converted to about two dollars a gallon. But in constant terms, from the beginning of the Peronist economic crisis, the equivalent dollar prices rose to well over $20 a gallon.

Economic reporting from the industrialized countries with stable currencies can be just as confusing. Most editors insist that economic stories from Western European countries and Japan include wage and price figures, presumably so Americans can feel pleased or outraged by the comparison. But such numbers are only misleading without three or four paragraphs of explanation to adapt them to American terms. The simple statement that a French railway worker earns $500 a month means nothing. He might pay no taxes or medical expenses. His apartment might be heavily subsidized, and his social benefits and bonuses could be enormous. On the other hand, he might have to pay crushing indirect taxes and survive in one of the most expensive marketplaces in the world. If there are currency controls in force, most of his salary must be spent at home, since he may not be allowed enough foreign exchange to travel.

The question of prices is just as complex. If the Italian lira drops or rises against the dollar, the price of a good pasta meal—in American terms—will change abruptly. But an Italian earning lire still pays the same percentage of his salary for the dinner, and he feels no immediate effect. His imported tennis balls will cost more or less, but the whole concept of trade and currency fluctuation requires its explanation.

The reader cannot generally supply the missing information for himself, but he can look for comparisons that mean something. If he wants to know what a Swedish trucker earns, he should look for take-home pay, not the basic wage scale, and he should figure in the benefits of a socialized society. And if he wants to determine how far that really goes, he should look at the price of Volvos in Stockholm, not Chicago, and of food in local markets, not at rooftop restaurants in the big hotels.

Readers are sometimes cheated out of the basic details simply because they are extremely difficult to pin down. Sometimes reporters have no choice, and they get the details one way or another. When the French franc was devalued sharply against the dollar in 1969, the spokesman at Elysée Palace called newsmen down for a special briefing. He stood up and intoned, "The new value of the franc will be 160 milligrams of fine gold," and then he started to walk away. Correspondents almost fell on him, shouting questions. What does that mean? What was the old value? Why? The spokesman shrugged and said he had no idea, he was just given a piece of paper to read aloud to the press. Reporters dug out dusty reference books to find the old value of the franc in fine gold, and then telephoned business sources to make sure they understood what had happened. They eventually worked out the devaluation at 12.5 per cent. Hours after the briefing, Finance Minister Valery Giscard d'Estaing went on television to announce that the franc had been devalued 11 per cent. That threw correspondents into another frenzy until they realized both figures were correct—one referred to the franc's devaluation against the dollar and the other was the dollar's climb against the franc.

In less significant circumstances, the important background is sometimes dropped, particularly in broadcast reporting, when there is little time for details anyway. On a trip home, one correspondent heard a radio network report, "The Japanese yen dropped to 370 to the dollar today. In other news . . ." That is like saying, Here are the ball scores: 3–2, 2–0 and 4–1.

Artful economic reporting folds numbers and statistics carefully in with easily understood explanations of what they mean. Jonathan Kandell of the New York *Times* wrote what might have been a dry story on jobless immigrants in Europe. He started out by describing how street sweepers gathered around their union hiring hall early one morning waiting for work. American readers could identify with the problem and sympathize with the immigrants. Most of them knew about union halls. After luring the reader into the dispatch, Kandell used numbers to explain the extent of the problem.

Once when bauxite prices rose in the Caribbean, the *Christian*

Science Monitor wrote a straight account of the increase, and a readership survey showed almost no one noticed the story. When a similar
rise was announced later, the *Monitor*'s story began by relating it to
what housewives would pay for pots and pans. It was a simple device
—almost a cliché—but the survey showed the item attracted wide
interest.

Skillful economic writers use one or two numbers to make that
extra step toward the reader. An item about Ghanaian economic
troubles means nothing to an American unless he also knows he will
probably pay an extra nickel for hot chocolate.

Often the best economic reporting involves no numbers at all. In
mid-1977, industrial and developing nations met in Paris to sum up
a year and a half of crucial but frustrating talks over sharing the
world's wealth. The New York *Times* covered the final day fully, with
long paragraphs of statistics and quotes from joint reports. It gave the
impression the conference had great significance. But inside the paper
there was an analysis by Flora Lewis explaining what the confusing
"north-south talks" really meant. She wrote, " 'What it all proves,'
one north-south veteran said, expressing a widely held view, 'is that
international conferences just don't work anymore.' " Then she assessed the situation in a few paragraphs:

> The eight industrial countries [at the meeting]—called the rich
> although they all feel squeezed by inflation, unemployment and
> the threat of crisis ahead—were looking for a way to organize
> world trade with some assurance of oil and raw-material supplies
> at stable prices. They had come to see the developing countries
> as essential partners, and to accept their aspirations for some
> material advance as a desirable but difficult goal.
>
> The 19 developing countries—called the poor though some are
> starving and others are awash with fortuitous cash—were looking
> for a drastic reform of the trading systems and a rapid redistribu-
> tion of the wealth produced in the world. A new world economic
> order was their slogan, although it was never defined.
>
> The act of calling a conference and bringing the delegates of
> both sides to the negotiating tables created an illusion that the
> problems were soluble.

With economic news, the reader can seldom be guided by a dispatch's placement in the paper or the headline over it. The display of
stories on the north-south talks was classic: the hard news of what

actually happened was toward the front, with background analysis tucked away underneath or on the jump page where the front-page account is continued inside. But, unlike stories on Asian coups and deaths of opera stars, few editors have a clear idea about how to handle most economic items.

Economic reporting has come too far in too short a time for many editors to have decided what is fit to print—and where. In May 1977, an influential oil industry newsletter reported that eleven oil-producing countries would cancel a 5 per cent price increase which they had planned to levy above the Saudi Arabian price level. *Newsweek* editors, who had just enough time to slip the news into the magazine that week, decided the story had little meaning, since oil producers were not even getting their current price because of low demand. The New York *Times* carried the story halfway down its business page, followed by a quote from an American industry analyst who said the move was no surprise, as it would have been "virtually impossible" for the eleven countries to get a higher price. In fact, the story had little real meaning and was, in a way, misleading. But the Washington *Post* led the paper with the report, placing it in the top right-hand corner of page 1 under a large headline.

Because of erratic coverage, following important economic news can be a high art. Readers can sometimes find fair warning of rising coffee prices, for example, by reading the temperature tables for world cities. Tables often include along with major world capitals the Brazilian city of Curitiba. That otherwise undistinguished locale is in the heart of coffee country—if temperatures approach freezing, prices are likely to climb.

Economic reporting is better now than in earlier decades, of course, and there is growing emphasis on improvement among news organizations. Before World War II, few people knew that the United States was squeezing Japan's overseas markets and raw material supplies so tightly that there was almost no alternative to war. As a result, Pearl Harbor was a much greater surprise than it should have been. That is not likely to happen again. Even in minor African conflicts, news agency reporters inject phrases like "phosphate-rich Spanish Sahara" into their dispatches to indicate there are economic considerations involved.

But the failings are still enormous. Warnings of potential trouble seem somehow unreal, no matter how serious the threat. This is partly because readers, like correspondents and editors, have had little experience in evaluating economic reporting. And also it is because the system has habituated people not to pay much attention to a crisis story until it has been on the front pages a few days in a row.

It was partially because of this that the Arab oil boycott came as such a shock. Several reporters had written that oil might be used as a political weapon. And, months before the boycott was announced, the Washington *Post* ran a page 1 interview with Sheik Yamani of Saudi Arabia specifically warning that the boycott was likely. Ronald Koven, one of two *Post* reporters who spoke with the oil minister, said later, "It was there. We put it on the front page. If readers don't pay any attention, what can we do about it? I mean, you can't realistically run the same story over and over until people notice it."

That is one of the most important problems of journalism today. Few stories mean so much to readers as major economic developments. And almost no category is noticed less, understood less and believed less than economic reporting.

15

Reporting on Human Rights

Once I sat in a Buenos Aires restaurant with a news source who calmly explained how Argentine security agents dumped suspected guerrillas into the sea from helicopters. He said they preferred to drop them alive, because on impact they would breathe in water and sink like stones. In between bites of sirloin, he told me how interrogators liked to pour gasoline into prisoners' ears, causing such excruciating pain they would say anything in their delirium. If lucky, they would then be shot, my informant added.

Then he waved his fork at a nearby table and went on: "Funny how I found out about the case of those Uruguayan kids [two youngsters who had disappeared when their parents were mysteriously kidnapped and tortured to death]. I was eating right there with a guy from SIDE [the government's secret police], and he asked me if I wanted a kid. He said they had knocked off the parents and didn't know what to do with the children. So they were trying to give them away. When the newspapers started to make a fuss, they decided to leave them on a doorstep."

It was big news, but I could hardly rush for the telex.

At the time, just after the March 1976 coup d'état, no one had been able to link the military government or its police agencies to the "mysterious right-wing terrorist groups" which operated freely in Argentina. The government was still ostensibly moderate, and no clear evidence had been uncovered to link authorities directly to the hundreds of disappearances of left-leaning politicians, professionals, journalists, teachers and trade unionists. President Jorge Rafael Videla denounced torture and promised to protect human rights assiduously, but the abductions continued. It was obvious—and my lunchtime source confirmed it—that uncontrolled military and police units had been systematically eliminating leftists since well before the overthrow of Isabel Perón.

One well-known case involved four Uruguayans seized in predawn raids whose mutilated bodies were found riddled with bullets in a car parked in the center of Buenos Aires. One was a self-exiled political leader who had been invited to testify in U.S. congressional hearings on human rights in Uruguay. Another was the former speaker of Uruguay's lower house, which had been dissolved after a military takeover there. Neither was associated with terrorists or the extreme left; they were killed, my informant said, as a favor to Uruguayan security officers who watched over Argentine dissidents in Montevideo. The other two, the parents of the two small children, had been Tupamaro guerrillas. The Washington *Post*, *Time*, the news agencies and other organizations had written about the Uruguayans at length, focusing attention on the children as a peg to talk about human rights in Argentina. They told how police failed to respond during the abductions and how they refused to even lift fingerprints afterward. But none of us had been able to establish who was actually responsible. Now here were the missing pieces.

My source cleared up several other mysteries. The dozen bodies which had washed ashore in neighboring Uruguay, for example, were not Asians from some passing ship, as had been widely reported. They were Argentines who had been dumped too far to the north, before the helicopter pilots had correctly determined where to drop the bodies so they would be washed southward toward Antarctica.

I knew the man well, and I trusted him. His own sources were firsthand, and he was in a position to evaluate his information. He had no reason to lie or exaggerate. Still he was only one source, and he could not be identified even obliquely, much less named. By talking about the helicopter drop as though it was common knowledge, I got an air force contact at least to confirm that it was taking place. He could not be quoted either, however, and he revealed no new details. No one else would talk at all. With the same ruse, I learned more about the Uruguayans. But since everyone understood that talking for the record could mean a visit by the same death squads, I was not exactly deluged with Deep Throats.

I got most of my source's information onto the AP wire, in one way or another, but it had to be couched so carefully with qualifiers and with ritual government denials that only experienced readers could decipher its real impact. For example, ideally I would have sent something like "Suspected left-wing extremists—either still alive or dead from torture—are being dumped at sea from Argentine military helicopters at a rate of at least several dozen a week, [specific source named] said today." Instead, I could only write a general story which started out saying that security forces had cracked down harshly on suspected extremists. About the third paragraph, I could say, "Responsible sources who asked not to be identified in any way said military helicopters were being used to dispose of suspects—still alive or dead from torture—by dumping them out at sea. The sources said lower grade officers, acting without specific orders, were responsible. Official spokesmen deny any such activity."

Professional newspeople know that no serious correspondent would include an assertion like that unless he was personally convinced it was true. But to a casual reader such sidestepping vagueness is hardly convincing. My colleagues had their own sources, but they also faced the same problems. For long afterward, the Argentine military government retained its moderate image. Terrorism by the police and the military remained widely attributed to mysterious outsiders denounced by the government as an embarrassment to the country.

Human rights reporting is a new genre which evolved in the 1970s as more people in the world became concerned about widespread abuses. It can have an immediate effect on foreign governments. It can outrage U.S. public opinion and legislators, prompting action in Washington. And it is an important safeguard against official reporting which is oversympathetic to governments which abuse human rights. But it is extremely difficult for the correspondent to do and often misleading for the reader.

When reporters accuse officials of mass murder, torture or flagrant violation of their constitutions, it is not enough for them to be sure in their own minds. They must back up their assertions with specific attribution and supporting detail. But torturers and murderers operate secretly, and they are hardly willing to discuss their activities with reporters. Victims—if they survive—are of course good sources. But reporters cannot be certain that reliable-sounding testimony is not faked. Churchmen, diplomats and lawyers can be valuable sources, but they are always anonymous.

And it is not necessarily only a question of accurate sources. When Argentina's death squads first appeared, a New York *Times* correspondent decided to investigate them. He made two discreet preliminary inquiries on a Saturday, and the next day he received a polite anonymous telephone call: "Señor, we do not think it is wise for you to pursue the story." The message was clear. The reporter, not short on courage, informed his editors and said he would handle it any way they thought best. All agreed that if he wrote the story he would have to leave. So he waited until he was leaving anyway. Publish and be damned is an admirable credo for societies in which disputes are settled with libel suits and negotiations, but it is hardly practical in a country where letters to the editors are often in the form of car bombs and machine-gun bursts.

The main difficulty with human rights reporting is that there is no general agreement on what should be covered—and for what purpose. News organizations in the United States seem to be more concerned than those in most other countries with reporting on rights violations beyond national borders. But the extent of concern varies with each correspondent and executive. Some newspeople feel a human responsibility to draw attention to abuses, particularly in countries which receive American aid. Others, however, regard too much harping on rights as do-good meddling. They feel that harsh treatment is endemic in many countries, like bribery and inefficiency, and writing about it is belaboring the obvious.

Also, patterns of interest in human rights are totally illogical, and reporting of rights abuses is even more spotty than the coverage of general foreign news. Since the Soviet Union is regarded as a much bigger story than, say, Equatorial Guinea, the problem of a delayed exit visa in Moscow merits large headlines while the systematic execution of many thousands in the Equatorial Guinean capital is seldom mentioned. Although Soviet methods are hardly enlightened, they do not approach the brutality and arbitrariness of some of America's friends elsewhere. And yet many readers, if asked to rate human rights violators in order of depravity, would put the Soviet Union at the top of the list. A single Soviet dissident may be a cause célèbre, with daily stories and comment from Washington. Op-ed pages might carry the victim's writings, with letters of outrage from distinguished Americans. But scores and hundreds of nameless Nicaraguans can be murdered without a word appearing in any paper. These imbalances often occur with little logic or reason. Neighboring nations with similarly brutal policies might have totally different reputations.

Even the most conscientious news organization could not cover it all. The annual reports of human rights monitoring groups detail thousands of violations in scores of countries, including the United States.

Because of these problems, what is reported depends not so much on what is happening as on the level of interest, the availability of sources, the government's ability to manage news and the number, the skill and the courage of the reporters on hand. It also depends upon whether editors want to risk possible expulsions and whether they consider the story worth the space in competition with other news. The result is that few Americans have any real idea of how a particular government abuses human rights, or how widespread the violations are. And any comparative judgment—whether one regime is better or worse than another—is all but impossible.

What reporting there is has less impact than it might, because it is done with words, not news film or pictures. If a television crew could film sixty seconds of a brutal interrogation session, or even if a radio reporter could report a minute of the sounds from the next room, human rights might become a tremendously compelling issue. But since broadcast reporters are limited largely to interviewing political dissidents who are still in a position to talk on camera, they miss the worst depredations. Sometimes grim photographs are leaked to correspondents, but they seldom can be authenticated. One well-circulated photo from Uruguay showed a young man, naked except for a black hood covering his head, lashed astride a high saw horse in an obviously painful position. It was mailed to news agencies with a letter identifying the sender as a conscience-stricken military officer. There was no way to know if it was genuine or if it had been sent by extremists to make the government look bad. Some news organizations used it on the theory that even if that particular picture was a fake it represented what was happening. A few used it as the basis for line drawings to illustrate human rights articles. Others threw it away.

Part of the problem is terminology. Just the phrase "human rights" is hopelessly vague. At one academic seminar on human rights, one speaker decried with as much passion that Jews in Moscow could not always get matzohs on Passover as another did that people were tortured to death in Chile. It all fell under the same heading. Taken broadly enough, "human rights abuses" covers any violation of the weighty U.N. Universal Declaration of Human Rights, which includes such categories as the right to employment and freedom from hunger. But even if attention is narrowed to what one human rights expert calls "the big three"—torture, arbitrary arrest and summary execution—the terminology is still too vague.

The word "torture" means little by itself without some qualification. Nearly every police force in the world occasionally resorts to psychological hazing and rough treatment that might be stretched to fit under the rubric of torture. But a sharp elbow in the ribs hardly compares with the systematic use of dental drills on good teeth or alternately gang raping and electroshocking women prisoners chained to an iron bed frame. In some countries, an arrest is illegal if the suspect is not allowed to telephone his lawyer immediately or is not formally charged within a few hours. In others, it is perfectly legal for policemen with no warrant to break into homes and carry off suspects to detention centers where they may be kept indefinitely incommunicado. Trials might consist of a military officer with no legal training flipping through written briefs of defense attorneys, with no cross-examination or witnesses. In the shorthand of reporting, such distinctions are not always made—if an arrest is according to law, it is no violation of rights.

For readers, the constant use of such general words as "torture," "human rights abuses" and "arbitrary arrest" have a numbing effect. The best human rights reporting goes immediately to the specific, with graphic testimony and precise descriptions of individual cases. A well-phrased account of the persecution of a single family can have more impact than a general reference to the killing of thousands with nothing to help a reader form a mental image. Good reporting should establish some context at the same time by pinning down totals of prisoners and victims—or at least by explaining why such figures are impossible to calculate. But most dispatches tend to deal in well-worn catchwords and vague numbers.

The more clever despots can use these vagaries to mask their harshest methods. One popular defense is to admit that occasional excesses occur—because terrorists and bandits have subverted the judicial system and do not play by traditional rules—but to add that police are only doing what security forces do everywhere in similar situations. They create a fraternity of guilt which takes the heat off of everybody. If Americans protest, officials bring up CIA activities and U.S. methods in Vietnam. If the accusers are French or British, the counter arguments are Algeria and Northern Ireland. Leaders under attack can always point to other countries with similar policies which have not been singled out for censure. Since the U.S. approach has been to skirt human rights issues in countries where the United States has major interests, it is a compelling rejoinder.

In some cases, the strictures of our international reporting system help governments get away with murder. Again Argentina is a good example. Frequently, brief stories appeared in American papers beginning "Six anti-government guerrillas were killed in a clash today with security forces, authorities said." What they meant, often, was more like "Several suspected extremists died under torture or had to be eliminated and a raid was faked to provide a plausible cover." But even if the news agency reporter who sends the story is sure that the real meaning is closer to the second version, there is little he can do about it. Suppose that he receives a police communiqué announcing the alleged clash. He would probably be suspicious immediately, since Argentine police usually issue communiqués only when they are trying to sell something; more routinely, news seeps out through a special class of local police reporters.

But the agency reporter's options are limited. If he were in Denver, he would just put out the story, quoting police, confident that attorneys or witnesses would point out anything questionable about the official version. Since his agency applies the same style of conduct to Buenos Aires as it does to Denver, he must operate in the same way. He cannot say, "This sounds like obvious crap, readers," without firmly attributing the doubts to a source. The guerrillas have no press office. If there are witnesses, they are seldom crazy enough to talk. Diplomatic or intelligence sources might have an independent version but only if the incident is major, and rarely soon enough for daily newspaper deadlines. And it is always possible that the police report may be accurate. At best, he might include enough fishy-sounding details to warn the reader to be cautious. He might add, for instance, that although police said six guerrillas launched the surprise attack, in the ensuing battle all the guerrillas were killed and no policeman was hit.

In one actual case, police claimed that a prominent guerrilla leader was shot accidentally by his comrades when they ambushed a police car transferring him to a different prison. He was in the back seat surrounded by officers, but he was the only person hit.

Several days after a reported incident, the correspondent might get a call from a relative with proof that Roberto Fulano could not have attacked a police station on Tuesday because he was arrested Sunday night. But even if he saves that late information to be used as context in the next such story, it will probably be cut out for lack of space, or interest.

In human rights reporting, every detail must be absolutely accurate. If a correspondent or an editor makes any error at all, however slight, authorities can jump on it and dismiss the entire dispatch as "full of lies" and "tendentious." Reporters must beware of long lists of victims and abuses supplied by the most reliable of sources. Mistakes slip in, and if officials can produce someone who was reported dead—or if they can disprove just one allegation—they can impugn everything else written by the same organization for the next three years.

Since the mid-1970s, there has been more—and better—human rights reporting, and this has had a limited snowball effect. More editors, correspondents and readers are interested, so more space is devoted. Some congressmen and administration officials have become deeply involved in human rights, clearly a popular issue. The 1976 Helsinki Accords brought some loosening of communist controls over families seeking to emigrate and over correspondents seeking to ask them why. Some dissidents have found their plight improved with international publicity, and a greater number are willing to speak with reporters.

This increased reporting has had its drawbacks. Some Latin-American security forces drew a lesson from Chile: one reason for all the fuss was that torture victims had been allowed to live and were released to talk to reporters. As a result, there were more deaths. In the Soviet Union and Eastern Europe, authorities sometimes reacted hostilely to publicity, and dissidents found themselves worse off than ever. In general, however, a great deal of abuse has lessened because of light shone on it.

One positive step is that reporters and editors are now paying close attention to several energetic international organizations which monitor human rights conditions. Their reports are frequently cited in news stories. This attention has enhanced the groups' standing, allowing them to broaden their efforts to force or persuade governments to cease violations.

The largest human rights organization is Amnesty International, based in London with branches all over the world. Amnesty, which won the 1977 Nobel Peace Prize, likes to point out that it has been accused by the right of being communist and by the left of being fascist. Directors try to avoid politics, preserving their credibility by attacking abuses from all ideologies. Two other groups, the International Commission of Jurists in Geneva and the International League of Human Rights in New York, are also active, with solid reputations.

But these groups face similar problems as news organizations in reporting on human rights. Governments often refuse entry to commissions seeking to gather firsthand information. If investigators do get into a country, authorities often badger their witnesses and deny them access to detention centers and important records. For the bulk of their information, the human rights groups must rely on anonymous sources who sneak their reports out of the country or on whatever information is available from the outside. They cannot always be certain that their sources are well informed and reliable. Although they are seldom wrong on a general situation—if they speak of torture and summary execution, they can be believed—their facts might be off on individual cases. This allows governments to denounce all of their activities as untrustworthy.

Sometimes human rights groups and news organizations work together unwittingly to harden up reports. Say, for example, that an agency reporter learns that police are burning the bodies of tortured prisoners in Country X. He can't get solid sourcing, so he slips a heavily qualified mention into the body of a dispatch. An Amnesty researcher, seeing that, might add a line in his own report, saying, "It was reported that police were burning bodies of tortured prisoners." A different reporter for the same agency, having overlooked the original mention, might then see the Amnesty release and write, "Police in Country X are burning the bodies of tortured prisoners, Amnesty International said in a report issued today." This is an unintentional corruption of a system designed to ensure accuracy, but the effect is usually to highlight true information which might otherwise be ignored.

Since the end of the Ford administration—at the insistence of Congress and President Carter—the U.S. State Department has revealed more information about human rights abuses abroad. Embassies were ordered to pay close attention to the subject, and desk officers in Washington made new contacts with experts in the field. New laws required the State Department to issue reports on the condition of human rights in countries which were to receive military aid. Administration officials at times have been brutally forthright in criticizing abuses, giving reporters legitimate pegs to write at length on the subject.

Despite the increased interest, human rights reporting in the general press is still spotty, generalized and too heavily weighted toward the Soviet Union. Readers and viewers can expect no systematic coverage of the world situation on human rights; the best they can do is supplement the newspapers and magazines with information available elsewhere. Before going to other sources, however, they should look carefully for hidden clues folded into correspondents' dispatches. Even if these do not reveal much specific information, they at least point the reader in the right direction. Newspaper reports are a useful starting point because they are generally minimum statements. The situation is usually worse than a correspondent is able to say, and it is seldom better than he depicts it.

There are several alternative sources for interested Americans. State Department reports, like regular dispatches, are at least minimum accounts. They are often purposely vague, but they are long and detailed in many instances. Transcripts of congressional testimony and hearings often contain damning evidence. The human rights organizations produce regular reports on many countries. Amnesty's annual report has a region-by-region breakdown, with detailed entries on offending governments. Refugee and exile groups distribute literature on the regimes they oppose, although they frequently exaggerate their figures and sometimes falsify documents. With all sources, care should be taken not to read more into a report than the writer intended. Torture and murder are not always a widespread policy; they might be the work of a few uncontrolled officers.

Whatever elements a reader manages to assemble, his picture is not likely to be complete. No system can handle human rights reporting adequately.

16

Development
Journalism

The winds of change of the 1960s brought independence to dozens of former colonies and turned upside down the old world order. Newsmen, like many of the new leaders and new nations, were not ready for the abrupt shift. One afternoon a senior editor at an American agency, an aging veteran whose life was devoted to foreign news coverage, picked up a story from the United Nations correspondent about the Central African Republic (now the Central African Empire). He bellowed, "God damn it, don't just say 'central African republic.' Say *which* central African republic."

It was overwhelming for those who had to keep track of the changing world. Suddenly a flood of new names were competing for attention. Problems never before faced had to be explained with the old vocabularies. Different value systems and approaches to life had to be absorbed and understood. And at the same time, new trends in travel were bringing Americans and Europeans to places like India and Thailand and Peru, awakening new interest in ancient cultures which had been all but ignored.

As an obvious result, coverage from the developing world has tended to be ill-informed and superficial. The system leaves scant space for news about most countries of Asia, Africa and Latin America, much less the small ocean island states. The small amount presented has been laced heavily with turmoil, natural disasters and the more bizarre aspects of life. The most violent and chaotic nations captured headlines. Small peaceful ones went through birth and early years with scarcely a mention.

This inadequate reporting has been regarded as derisive by many leaders in developing countries, and it has brought a series of governmental actions. At first there were isolated retaliatory measures. Then, in the mid-1970s, disgruntled leaders began comparing notes and making collective complaints. The problem became a major international issue, studied by UNESCO, academic groups, intergovernmental committees and news organizations. Representatives from all sides have met repeatedly, in various types of conferences and seminars, to seek common ground. Although American reporting from the developing world has improved considerably, it is now being scrutinized more critically than ever.

Theoretically, if news organizations wrote at greater length and with more sensitivity about Third World affairs, there would be no difficulty. If Third World journalists and officials exchanged views with American and European newspeople, in theory, both sides would understand one another. But it doesn't work that way.

The conflict is not the result of misunderstanding. More cooperation could help ease the tension, but it would not solve the problem. There are deep philosophical differences over the role of the press and government in society. Whoever is right or wrong, few Third World leaders are prepared to accept the way Western correspondents feel they are obliged to report world news.

An Indonesian information official made no bones about his government's attitude when Lewis M. Simons of the Washington *Post* visited Jakarta in 1977: "These critical reports you've all been making lately hamper our speed of development. They draw the attention of the people away from development to other issues, which creates frustration . . . if correspondents employ the Western tradition of hitting issues face-on, they will not achieve their mission. They must follow the slower, more indirect Indonesian way, or else our government will ban foreign journalists and will ignore their reports."

The news organizations, on the other hand, say they cannot compromise fundamental points. They must report the news in the same way everywhere in the world, and they will do it whether or not they have access to certain countries.

At the very least, the confrontation has made editors aware of sensibilities many once ignored. Most now ask their correspondents to try to avoid cultural biases and to look at the development process through the eyes of the people on whom they are reporting. One news agency editor put it: "If a man writes about Somalia being backward in some respects, we want to be sure he also writes about the successful campaign against illiteracy. It is unfair to point out that the capital has only one stoplight unless we explain that it has no cars, either, and what that means to the society."

In the past, poverty and backwardness were often treated as though they were the fault of the government in power. General progress, efficiency and economic growth were measured by the standards of industrial nations. There was often a tongue-in-cheek tone, with an emphasis on strange-sounding names and ridiculing detail. Now more correspondents look at base causes—legacies of colonialism, demography, land quality, natural barriers to growth—in determining a country's success at development. They weave in historical and sociological background to explain why certain bizarre-sounding problems are deadly serious.

On the other side, Third World leaders are now sometimes reluctant to apply stern measures against Western correspondents for fear of international censure. At one time, news agency dispatches about soldiers beating a correspondent with rifle butts were tossed aside at most newspapers. Now they are likely to end up on the front page. Such items can do more to frighten private investors, foreign aid officials and lending institutions than critical dispatches.

Far-reaching solutions are particularly difficult because policymakers on both sides generalize widely, lumping disparate elements into large, meaningless categories.

In one corner there is the "Western press." This includes correspondents with advanced degrees in developmental economics and long experience living among the people they cover. It also includes callous young reporters who consider developing nations as little more than elaborate zoos for their particular amusement. Unfortunately, the common denominator is still low, largely because of distorted stereotypes in the United States about remote cultures. During the 1977 Uganda "crisis," when Americans were reported as hostages, wide attention was given to an order that they list their wealth, "including chickens, goats, pigs and other animals." One television correspondent at the United Nations was asked by his anchorman what this meant. He replied that it was only natural, since Africans used such livestock as legal tender. In Uganda and in parts of Africa, in fact, livestock is considered an important part of a person's holdings. That's why it was stipulated in the government order. But the clear impression was that Uganda was so backward it had no other currency, and the bank vaults had to be hosed down each night.

In the other corner, there is the Third World or "developing countries." The nations included are far less homogeneous than the various parts of the "Western press." Some of them had highly developed civilizations when Europeans were walking around barefoot in animal skins. Others are artificial entities carved out of bickering tribes and pushed out on their own by departing colonial powers. Each government responds to the rest of the world according to its own needs. No African colonel who seizes precarious power is going to consult international guidelines to determine how to deal with correspondents. Policies change radically even in the most stable of these countries. The press policies in India, for example, were totally different before and after the fall of Indira Gandhi.

There is another complication in finding solutions. A number of Third World leaders are not only concerned about what is written about them in the Western press, they are also worried about the news they receive from all other countries. Developing countries get almost all of their world news from AP, UPI, Reuters, Agence France-Presse or radio broadcasts from developed countries. Each of the four big agencies directs news wires to different regions in several languages. The more extreme critics of the system call this a Western cartel to dominate their minds. Others charge that such news is slanted—even if inadvertently—by cultural bias, and they say the emphasis is on the negative. And all say they don't get enough news.

In order to correct the various imbalances, a number of Third World countries have explored common stances they might take. The most popular of these is one known increasingly as "developmental journalism." The basic idea of this approach is much as the Indonesian information officer explained it to Lew Simons. All national resources—including the resource of information—must be directed toward development. If information is allowed to cause dissent or loss of international prestige, it detracts from the greater goal. By this reasoning, the control of news is not only a legitimate right but also a national necessity.

As a tool of developmental journalism, many countries have established or strengthened national news agencies. These agencies, routinely supported by government funds, collect and distribute news about the country. Almost always the reports of these agencies are available to Western correspondents. In some cases, authorities attempt to restrict correspondents to using these national agencies as their sole source of news. By 1978, virtually every non-aligned and Third World country had some form of national agency already set up or under study. They ranged from Yugoslavia's Tanjug, with forty-seven foreign correspondents and a vast domestic network, to tiny operations with a weekly mimeographed bulletin. Not every country with a national agency subscribed to the developmental journalism idea of managing news. But each at least got its viewpoint across via its agency.

And the process has gone a step further. A large group of countries support a "non-aligned pool," so that they can transmit and receive dispatches directly among themselves without passing through the big agencies. There are several pooling arrangements, but the largest operate through Tanjug under a system set up in January 1975. Editors in Belgrade receive about forty items daily from a handful of national agencies, and they redistribute them to pool members. In practice, technical difficulties have prevented the pool from expanding to any significant size. Many of the items offered are purely propaganda, and some of them are of no interest even to the most collective-minded editors in other developing nations.

At a summit meeting of the fifty-eight non-aligned nations which endorsed the pool idea in 1976, Indira Gandhi set the tone: "The media of the powerful countries want to depict the governments of their erstwhile colonies as inept and corrupt and their people as yearning for the good old days. Leaders who uphold their national interests and resist the blandishments of multinational corporations and agencies are denigrated and their images falsified in every conceivable way. . . . We want to hear Africans on events in Africa. You should similarly be able to get an Indian explanation of events in India."

Western news executives agreed with the idea in principle, because in international reporting it is always best to have the widest variety of sources possible. A regular source of officially sanctioned information would be an enormous help to any serious correspondent. Pero Ivacic, the director-general of Tanjug, assured in a UNESCO paper that the pool "in no way was viewed as a challenge to or competition with existing news reporting systems." Instead, he said, it was "to fill the previously existing vacuum in the international system." But the executives were deeply concerned at the number of pool members who embraced developmental journalism. They feared that strong national news agencies could be used as an excuse to ban independent correspondents, as is already happening in some countries. At one international conference, a Nigerian delegate emphasized the point in no uncertain terms: "The Nigerian news agency covers all the news. Why should foreign correspondents come to Nigeria? They should take the news from us."

By that sort of reasoning, pool members—and Western newspeople —who wanted details of the humiliating Israeli raid on Uganda to free hostages in 1976 would have gotten them from Idi Amin. The concerns are obvious. In 1976, when the Argentine army was slowly but steadily removing Isabel Perón from the presidency, the official agency, Telam, filled its news wire with sports scores from the provinces. After the Nigerian war, government spokesmen were in no rush to reveal that the Lagos docks were so jammed that a national fortune in cement was hardening in ships' holds and it was financial disaster for shippers to commit vessels to waiting months in the harbors. There are less serious but equally worrisome practical problems to any such system. A national agency, understandably, is hardly concerned with minor items affecting only foreigners. And any news agency in a developing country is likely to find it difficult to gather enough well-trained journalists. An item about an American arrested on a murder charge might come over the wire: "T. Tomson of America . . ." A correspondent has to know that he is really "Theodore D. Thompson, a 26-year-old candy maker from North Nowhere, California."

The whole subject is so clouded by rhetoric that few people realize there is already a great deal of common ground. At one international meeting, a veteran Asian editor, with a dramatic gesture, charged that "if any American correspondent wrote about something so boring as the Mekong Project in Thailand, he would be sacked . . . editors don't care about such quiet development." The next morning, by coincidence, the New York *Times* carried an entire column on the Mekong Project. Like that Asian editor, few critics know what Western reporters write about the Third World. A University of Hong Kong study in 1977 showed that more than 50 per cent of the items on the world wires of the four major news agencies were from or at least partially about developing countries. Less than 6 per cent of the stories dealt with violence, disasters or conflict. The majority were about foreign relations and economics. At the same time, some hard-line Western editors automatically equate any call for a different balance of news flow with a threat to freedom of the press. Few on either side realize that there is already a great deal of day-to-day cooperation among the big agencies and the smaller national agencies.

Those who criticize the monopoly of the big agencies seldom stop to think about how the "monopoly" really works. In practice, the four agencies compete intensely. Most news from developing nations is gathered and often written by locally hired nationals. By circumstance, the agencies are forced to present news objectively. All of them serve subscribers of widely varying ideologies—of all extremes—and they could not slant news even if they wanted to.

Often a story which seems naïve and superficial to Third World intellectuals is exactly what is needed to interest readers in industrial countries who know little of the background. A story starting out with statistics on a housing project would serve little purpose to anyone, because almost no one would stop to read it. A San Francisco editor put his finger on the problem in a conversation about such coverage: "Don't just tell me what happened on a street in Chad. First tell me what the street looks like."

When John Darnton of the New York *Times* covered elections in Gambia during 1977, he did not plunge immediately into complex politics and district returns. Instead, he wrote:

> During voting for consultative assemblies in the 1950s, a time of British colonial rule, it was noticed that when the paper ballots were retrieved from the ballot boxes they were in thick wads, folded together. This led to the not unreasonable suspicion that Gambians by the dozen were selling their franchise to election riggers who stuffed the boxes. An ingenious solution was hit upon.
>
> Today when a Gambian goes to the polls he is handed a marble. Inside the voting booth he finds two or three 50-gallon drums, each bearing the photograph of a candidate and the colors of his political party. The voter inserts the marble into a plastic tube leading to the drum of his choice, and as it passes through it strikes a loud bell. One clang, one vote.

Then he told what had happened when Gambians dropped their marbles.

Good correspondents use several different techniques to attract their readers' attention. John Burns, also of the *Times,* weaves substances into the bizarre. He wrote from Swaziland in 1977:

> In Africa, a continent with its share of improbable leaders, there have been few more unusual than King Sobhuza II, a septuagenarian who counts his wives by the score and rules autocratically through a cabinet composed mostly of his sons, sons-in-law and cousins.
>
> Yet the Lion of Swaziland, as he is known to his 500,000 people, is an anachronism only to those who look no farther than the sakabula feathers he sometimes wears in his hair. To most of his subjects, and to foreigners here who watch him closely, he has been a conspicuously successful ruler.

Lew Simons illustrated the general with the particular in a dispatch about corruption on his trip to Indonesia. It began:

> Shortly after daybreak one recent morning a herd of gnashing bulldozers rumbled into a quiet neighborhood on the edge of the city and began destroying the small, red-tile-roofed houses.
>
> The 20 families who lived in the settlement stood quietly by and watched their homes churned into the thick, brown mud. They had been told only the day before that although they held legal deeds to the property, the land had been taken over by a development company that has plans to build a golf course and a luxury housing project.
>
> The company, Metropolitan Kencana Ltd., is headed by a younger brother of Indonesia's President Suharto, Sudwikatmono. Other powerful businessmen and government figures own shares.
>
> For the small band of displaced neighbors, the bulldozers' arrival began a tragedy. They were shunted off into hastily thrown-up barracks. One man collapsed with a nervous breakdown and committed suicide. Another suffered a heart attack and is still hospitalized.
>
> A few lines about the incident appeared in one Jakarta newspaper, but no names of the company's officers were printed.
>
> This kind of incident and others of a far broader magnitude and with far graver consequences occur with regularity in Indonesia. "The people of this country expect their leaders to enrich them-

selves and members of their families," said a Western diplomat. Beneath the unruffled surface, frustration and bitterness are slowing mounting to a boil.

As Simons' dispatch showed, increased reporting from the developing world does not necessarily mean more favorable reporting. Correspondents are writing about hydroelectric projects and health programs, but they are also writing about problems which, by any standards, are serious.

The Los Angeles *Times,* for example, described the unreliability of African air travel in a story published in 1977. Once, it noted, long-distance Air Zaire flights were delayed two days because President Mobutu Sese Seko went off on a state visit with the only 747 and his wife had taken the DC-10. It said:

> In Africa, passengers are expected to take nothing for granted. While U.S. airlines are spending heavily to promote their on-time schedules and in-flight services, a new age of aviation has dawned on Africa—the age of creative timetables, no-frills flights and airport pandemonium. Nowhere in the world is air travel so expensive per passenger mile, and nowhere is it so unreliable.

Even in positive dispatches about development, correspondents sometimes dramatize a society's thinking by focusing on details which leaders may find embarrassing. From Singapore, Jay Mathews of the Washington *Post* wrote in 1978:

> In this city-state built by monumental risk-takers, children are no longer allowed to skateboard in the streets and Boy Scouts interested in night hikes must settle for walking blindfolded at 4 P.M.
> Industrious Singapore, once referred to as the "rugged society," seems to be going a bit soft.

An interested reader must search carefully for thoughtful and complete dispatches from developing countries; they are often hard to find. Because the reader can seldom supply his own framework for the material, such stories must run at length, with far more space devoted to context than in stories from the more familiar industrial nations. Even the biggest American newspapers can offer little more than a sampling of significant Third World news.

Television is rarely much help, since it pays scant attention to background reportage from developing countries. Ideally, television can do a superb job, showing the physical setting and the faces of the people. But unless there is careful narration, a film of backward-looking natives only reinforces stereotypes.

Often, valuable reporting can be found on op-ed pages or in special feature displays. These frequently allow non-traditional approaches—without the need for a misleading news peg—to explain long-range situations. The *Christian Science Monitor* did a two-page magazine-style spread on a Brazilian village, by Richard Critchfield, which started this way: "The greatest problems in the poor two-thirds of the world may no longer be finding enough food, jobs and shelter. Rather it could be a cultural breakdown. A generation of urban immigrants is finding that traditional village values have no place in anonymous, slum-ridden, industrial cities."

Critchfield touched on perhaps the most fundamental point of development journalism. All of us—correspondents, editors and readers—tend to forget how wide the gaps can be among different cultures. Physical appearances, customs and political systems are only the surface. John Nance, former Manila bureau chief for the AP, brought this home in an article on his encounters in 1972 with the Tasaday tribe in a remote Philippine jungle:

MANILA—How do you interview a man wearing only orchid leaves and earrings, who lived all his life in a forest and thought the greatest invention of all time was putting the handle on stone tools?

Slowly. And in somewhat of a daze.

Very slowly, in fact, with at least two translators—and the continual wonder of whether what is coming back to you can possibly be true.

Never seen the moon?

No word for fighting? Don't know about the wheel? Never been to a clearing before?

Incredible.

Ask them again, you tell the translator, who is fluent in English: "Do they really mean they had never seen the moon? Never?" . . .

The bearded translator, a leader of a lowland tribe, put the question in a different way this time to the chubby upland tribe woman who is best able to communicate with the shy folks in leafy G-strings.

It comes back: "Well, they say the light at night came into the forest and their ancestors had said it just came from the sky. But they never saw the body of the moon until they came to the clearing—the jungle was too thick. Amay [the most talkative of the 24 Tasaday] says that when they saw the moon the first night in the clearing they were very surprised. 'We didn't know that was stuck up there,' he says."

And so it went, for hours. . . .

Time presented special problems. So did distances.

Asked if they had other groups of people in their forest, they said yes, before, but those people had not been seen for a long time.

"How long?"

"Very long."

"How long is that?"

"Very, very long."

"Do they have any concept of weeks, or months or years?"

Blank stares all around.

17

Doing Better

There is a crowning irony in our reporting of the world. It seems clear that producers and consumers both want better coverage. And coverage could be improved, almost easily, at no added cost. To do better, we need not crowd out domestic news—or the juicy scandals and the comics which help sell papers. But since few of the producers appreciate the growing demand, and few consumers know how easy it is to make themselves heard, there is little change. That this seems simple is only part of the irony. It is simple.

A major reform is not realistic, but none is needed. Almost every news organization already has the resources to provide better coverage from abroad. All of us—correspondents, editors, executives, readers and viewers—can do better by degree within the existing system. Improvement is more a question of attitudes than of means. Having more correspondents and desk editors would certainly help, but there are enough now to do an adequate job if they are properly motivated and encouraged. Those who cannot break old habits and work more effectively can be reassigned to other staff positions. Good people cost little more than mediocre ones, and it is not difficult for a concerned executive to determine which are which. Newspapers and broadcast stations can make better use of the material they now buy from news agencies and syndicates. They would even save money by throwing away less and not hiring extra reporters to write secondary local stories. The agencies shape their coverage to what their subscribers say they want. If newspapers and stations demanded a different sort of report, they would get it. The newsmagazines and networks use only a fraction of what their own correspondents are capable of producing.

To put these resources to work, executives must be persuaded that it is worth the commitment. They have to see that there is a market for the news from abroad which their consciences urge them to print and to broadcast. And they must realize that there is no conflict between responsibility and profit. If solid foreign coverage does not necessarily increase audiences, it certainly does not diminish them. The most effective newspeople have found that there is no essential difference between local and foreign news. A properly presented dispatch from Tokyo can make the same impact as a story from the next town over. And a foreign story with no real meaning for Americans has no more place in the paper or on the air than a pointless local item. Even if a sharp distinction is made between foreign and domestic news, space is not the issue. With thoughtful trimming and selection, editors can provide far greater depth by using no more space than most are now devoting to sloppily handled dispatches.

Individual readers and viewers can play a large part in persuading executives and editors to improve foreign coverage. At most papers and stations, two or three people determine the balance of news content. These chief gatekeepers seldom hear directly from their audiences—and many take this silence as tacit approval of their judgments. They pay scant attention to routine "letters to the editor" or to casual remarks at cocktail parties or in barber shops. But most can be influenced by reasoned arguments and sincere presentations. Executives and editors will often take time to discuss their policies on the phone or in person with anyone who is seriously interested. Most of them accept invitations to meet with public service organizations or social clubs. Since most people think of "The Press" as unassailable, a surprisingly small number of readers and viewers ever try the personal approach.

To test a theory, I asked a sampling of key editors what the effect would be if only a half dozen readers rang them up during a single week to press for more foreign coverage. One typical reply came from the publisher of a large Southern daily: "Six people would certainly get my attention, particularly if they were a diverse mixture. Hell, we don't hear from anyone. We would like nothing better than to use more foreign copy. And it's cheaper. But we don't think our readers want very much. And we give them very little." Those readers who do not care about news from abroad seldom notice what is in the news columns anyway. As long as newspapers continue to run sports pages, school lunch menus and other regular features, there is not likely to be any adverse reaction from them to expanded international coverage.

Interest in foreign news has tended to run in cycles. After U.S. troops were withdrawn from Vietnam in 1973, and after the alarm over oil supplies subsided, Americans turned their attention inward to domestic problems. But during the late 1970s Americans grew increasingly concerned about world economic and social patterns which directly affected them. Well-attuned newspeople have seen this as an interest which is likely to continue. And they have developed new concepts—or built upon old ones—to relate foreign news more closely to their audiences.

The most compelling dispatches, for example, include what some correspondents call a "so what" paragraph. This is simply a sentence or two near the top which tells why it is worth someone's while to stop and read on. The reason may be direct: This revaluation of the Deutschmark means that everything German, from a bottle of Riesling to a Volkswagen, will cost you at least 14 per cent more. Or it might be more diffuse and long-term: Cubans in Africa not only stir up tension, they also restore Cold War confrontation, endangering détente with the Soviet Union and unsettling Western Hemisphere security. (Read, in more alarmist terms: It is risking holocaust.) Also, correspondents and editors might involve readers by adding different dimensions to a dispatch. This need not mean greater length. Instead of adding one more gory detail of a battle, a reporter might mention any immediate lesson for avoiding the next one. By forgoing a few misleading labels and extraneous facts, he can use the same wordage to say who the "right-wing Christians" and "left-wing Moslems" really are and what they each want.

Perhaps the most important of these new concepts is "people reporting." Rather than detailing one more Italian cabinet change, for instance, a correspondent might describe how an Italian worker deals with a shortage of Parmesan cheese, thus providing a framework for explaining politics and economics in a way that strikes responsive chords in the American reader. Reporters writing about tin strikes in Bolivia might focus on one miner's family, fitting global statistics into the story to show how the conflict touches families far to the north.

America's largest-circulation paper, the New York *Daily News,* has made a definite shift in that direction. Editor Michael O'Neill explains it: "All the colorful characters are walking off the stage and are being replaced by technocrats and economic issues which don't lend themselves to dramatic interest. I'm much more interested in finding out what's going on with people, what kind of fun they're having, what they are thinking, what games they are playing."

As early as 1968, Seymour Topping, then foreign editor of the New York *Times,* defined the dimensions of this style in a confidential memo to his correspondents:

> . . . We can be less preoccupied with the daily official rhetoric of the capitals. We should report more about how the people live, what they and their societies look like, how their institutions and systems operate. Our report should reflect more fully the social, cultural, intellectual, scientific and technological revolutions which, more than the political, are transforming the world society. And to comprehend, our readers must have more sophisticated interpretive writing.

Another approach to making foreign news more digestible is taking an overall view of a subject rather than reporting on separate fragments of it. A single dispatch explaining the broad lines and tactics of world terrorism might be far more effective than individual accounts of terrorist activities in Italy, Germany, Argentina and Mexico. One comprehensive piece on Latin-American inflation tells American readers more than disjointed stories from a handful of capitals. This style of reporting sometimes produces misleading generalizations and simplifications. But often it is the only way to keep track of important currents which cut across borders and continents. With the world's growing interdependence, it makes an essential contribution. AP foreign editor Nate Polowetzky, who probably has more direct influence than anyone on what Americans read and hear from abroad, tells his reporters, "We must strive for overlook copy—stories which cross borders and are part of a global concept, which wrap up events in a meaningful manner." These stories do not have to be rushed out competitively; they are about patterns which evolve slowly, with no defined dimensions or time elements.

One valuable new genre is called "comparative journalism." Many basic problems are common to all nations, and comparative journalism draws parallels and contrasts so that societies can learn from one another. Reporters explain, for example, how the Japanese handle gun control or how the Brazilians failed to solve their housing problem. Comparisons are made clearly with the United States so that readers can relate foreign experiences to their own lives. The approach can be extremely effective. If someone learns how to power automobiles on garbage, it is news in every industrialized and developing country. If the French find they can save fuel by empowering officials to burst into homes to check thermostats, it is fascinating reading.

The most formal application of comparative journalism is the International Writers Service, subsidized by the German Marshall Fund. It was established in 1975, based in Washington, to distribute articles to any paper willing to pay its token rates. The editor, Stanley Karnow, draws from eminent European and Asian journalists, assigning stories on everything from macroeconomics to waste disposal. But comparative journalism is now part of any good correspondent's repertoire. A UPI reporter in Israel might produce a story on irrigation which would be eagerly received by his agency's subscribers in Arizona and New Mexico. Comparative journalism stories from Third World countries are often welcome changes from dispatches about conflict. A number of developing countries have made progress in rural medicine, agriculture and education, which is as interesting to Western readers as to other Third World societies.

Many news organizations are now supplementing their regular foreign coverage with special background articles which explain a major story in detail and in depth. Sometimes these are simple chronologies, such as a minute-by-minute account of a complex hijack operation. They may take the form of questions and answers: a correspondent will list questions which readers might have about an important issue and then, one at a time, answer them. Occasionally correspondents will write historical articles which explain breaking news in terms of the distant past. Some newspapers run these background pieces on a daily basis; others put them together in a weekly section like the *International Herald Tribune*'s "Insight" page.

A few newspapers have their own staff specialists to interpret foreign events. The St. Petersburg (Fla.) *Times,* for example, hired former UPI foreign editor Wilbur G. Landry to analyze fast-developing stories from abroad. In a regular column, Landry takes three or four significant items and explains their impact on the world. Obviously, the success of this approach will depend entirely on the quality of the writer.

Along with these new approaches to coverage, editors are trying to make better use of their limited stables of correspondents. Some are assigning reporters to follow a single story from country to country, transcending traditional bureau boundary lines. This not only gives correspondents a wider perspective but it also prevents them from growing jaded at their home base and missing stories which no longer seem unusual to them. At the larger newspapers, foreign editors have had success with home-based international specialists who travel on carefully planned itineraries. These reporters can combine domestic and foreign aspects of the same story, bridging a serious gap in international coverage. They need not race off if a story breaks elsewhere. And, after they return home, they can contribute background stories and seek domestic reaction when crises erupt in areas they have covered. The Washington *Post* has instituted what it calls "Bureau X" —a non-bureau which is simply a fund to allow reporters to swing through groups of countries on specific themes, such as food supply or nuclear energy. Chicago *Tribune* teams have spent months at a time on special trips abroad. In 1978, two reporters and a photographer produced a series on South America which ran for 11 consecutive days. The material was later assembled into a booklet for schools and separate distribution. Later in the year, a six-man *Tribune* team, from the publisher to the economic news specialist, traveled for a month in eight Middle East countries to produce a special supplement. The *Christian Science Monitor* assigned its former foreign editor, Geoffrey Godsell, as a roving correspondent, based in Boston. The New York *Times,* among others, sends returned correspondents back out on special assignments. The Los Angeles *Times* has specialists on its foreign desk to add their own expertise to stories from different regions of the world.

The Washington *Post* is trying a new approach to sources, particularly in countries where reporters are banned. "There is nothing written in stone that says news has to come from a staff correspondent," says Philip Foisie. "We can get an eyewitness report any day of the week from Ulan Bator, and if we pick and choose we can find people of intelligence who can describe a situation as well or better than many journalists. We must be more imaginative and use these resources." Professors, economists, archeologists and businessmen have been asked to comment in news stories and on the op-ed page about countries and subjects which they know well. And Foisie is pursuing another concept in foreign news, what he calls a "distant early warning system" for crises. The idea is that non-breaking stories about possible trouble should be prominently displayed, and followed up, so that readers are warned beforehand. He noted that the *Post* did not sufficiently emphasize its own interview with Sheik Yamani, foreshadowing the oil boycott, because some editors did not take it seriously enough. He told his colleagues at a staff seminar, "We forget we live in an increasingly outlandish world, and we must learn to think more about the unthinkable."

The networks have also tried new ways to get across the essential economic and social stories they once ignored. Crews equipped with highly mobile equipment spend more time in Third World countries, and correspondents in Europe and Japan seek out visual means to report unemployment and currency chaos. Technical improvements mean faster relay of film and more direct coverage. And there is less emphasis on the traditional anchorman, to allow more flexible formats.

A few universities have sought ways to help improve reporting from abroad. Ohio University at Athens has a course in foreign reporting, one of the few available anywhere. Some institutions grant fellowships for correspondents to study and to renew their feel for the society to which they report.

Officials, too, have gotten involved to some extent. American legislators and UNESCO delegates have considered measures to protect correspondents at work. U.S. news organizations generally resist any form of government help, preferring to remain totally independent. But international accords against harassing correspondents—or U.S. State Department protests against arbitrary expulsions or arrests—could improve reporters' access to sources.

These different approaches and ideas have made an impact, but they barely keep up with the growing complexity of the world. In general, news organizations have a long way to go before they can report the world effectively for Americans. A 1976 sampling by the Indianapolis *News* gave an idea of the distance.

The *News*'s editors designed a poll to determine the significance which readers attach to world events. A big-city paper with a solid base among the small towns and farms of rural America, the *News* is an excellent bellwether. Most readers take it by subscription, so it need not compete for newsstand sales. As the *Wall Street Journal* once remarked, "If there is a proper, patriotic, church-going audience for a newspaper, then surely the News has it."

First, the editors put together their own annual list of what they considered to be the Top Ten stories of the year. Then they asked readers to vote on what they thought were the most important stories. To encourage serious response, the *News* awarded prizes to those whose lists most closely matched the results of the national poll conducted by the Associated Press among editors and news directors of member newspapers, radio and television stations.

The *News* editors voted this way:

1. The presidential campaign and election.
2. Revelations of illegal acts by the CIA and FBI.
3. Mao Tse-tung and Chou En-lai die; China changes.
4. Upheaval in Southern Africa, especially Angola, South Africa and Rhodesia.
5. Earthquakes in China, Italy, Guatemala, Central Asia, Indonesia and the Philippines.
6. Chowchilla, California, school bus kidnapping.
7. Washington sex scandals.
8. Legionnaires disease (which killed several in Philadelphia).
9. Civil war in Lebanon.
10. Two U.S. soldiers killed in Korean demilitarized zone.

The AP list—which included voting by television and radio news directors, who lean toward the more dramatic national stories—came out like this:

1. The presidential election.
2. Political change in China.
3. Bicentennial celebrations.
4. U.S. economy—recovery, unemployment, inflation.
5. Legionnaires disease.
6. Mars landing.
7. Washington sex scandals.
8. Patty Hearst trial.
9. Air France hijacking and Entebbe raid.
10. Chowchilla kidnapping.

But the readers' poll took an entirely different approach:

1. The presidential election.
2. Patty Hearst trial.
3. Washington sex scandals.
4. Legionnaires disease.
5. Bicentennial celebrations.
6. Swine flu (a threat that never developed).
7. Chowchilla kidnapping.
8. Death of Howard Hughes.
9. The Karen Ann Quinlan decision (the case of a young woman whose parents sought to disconnect her life-sustaining machine).
10. Mars landing.

The only story on the readers' list which might be considered a foreign story—the last one—involves a location which even the more intrepid correspondents would have trouble reaching.

One reading of the poll results is that news organizations are giving readers and viewers more substance than they want. The poll seemed to show that audiences, left to choose, would seek out more, not less, sensationalism and domestic news.

But the poll also showed something else: Editors—and correspondents—had not been able to get across the importance of foreign affairs to their audiences. Most newspeople, like those who assembled the poll's first table, believe that foreign news is important. But few think that their readers and viewers do. So, in the manner of shy people who mumble, they tend to present foreign dispatches almost apologetically, with far less care than they devote to other stories.

The sampling was designed to show not what readers thought was important but rather what they felt the nation's editors thought was important. If they believed that the death of Howard Hughes. was more significant than that of Mao Tse-tung, it was because no one had been able to convey to them what a shadow China might cast over their lives. American readers, like the cross-section who responded to the poll, have not been shown frequently or convincingly enough that their world does not stop at their borders.

There is cause for hope. As President Jimmy Carter told Congress on September 18, 1978, after the Camp David summit on Israel and

Egypt, "Our people have come to understand that unfamiliar names
—like Sinai, Sharm al Sheikh, Ras en Naqb, Gaza, the West Bank of
Jordan—can have a direct and immediate bearing on our well-being
as a nation and our hope for a peaceful world."

But Aleksandr Solzhenitsyn, the Nobel prize-winning Russian author, was less optimistic in a speech to Harvard's 1978 graduates.
Americans, he said, are unaware of world currents which threaten
their way of life—and their mass media, rather than alerting and
educating them, comfort them in their complacency.

Solzhenitsyn was right. Americans are reared in an insular society,
and their schools produce doctors and lawyers who, from first grade
to final degree, might not be told the difference between the Balkans
and the Balearics. In that sort of society, sex scandals in Washington
are bound to sell more papers than serious news from abroad. But that
is not the point. Whether or not there is change, there at least must
be balance. Whatever else is included, there must be room for carefully presented foreign coverage. Without it, Americans who do care
will be deprived of information they must have. And, perhaps worse,
Americans who should care will not know what they are squandering
away.

A democracy cannot function without an informed electorate, and
this applies no less to foreign affairs than to domestic matters. Foreign
policy cannot be left unchecked to a Washington elite, to specialists
or to interested lobby groups. World crises, if foreseen in time, sometimes can be avoided. But without reliable reporting from abroad,
citizens are vulnerable and weak. If many Americans do not realize
this, only reporters and editors—Knickerbocker's madmen—can
drive it home to them.

Index

225